A NATION
UNDER
LAWYERS

A NATION UNDER LAWYERS

*How the Crisis in the Legal Profession
Is Transforming American Society*

MARY ANN GLENDON

HARVARD UNIVERSITY PRESS
Cambridge, Massachusetts

First Harvard University Press paperback edition, 1996

Published by arrangement with Farrar, Straus and Giroux

A portion of chapter 8 first appeared in slightly different form, in *Commentary*. The passages from "Professionalism Revisited," by Steven Lubet, are reproduced with the permission of the *Emory Law Journal*. The punch line from Gary Larson's *The Far Side* is reproduced with the permission of Universal Press Syndicate. The passages from "A Come-All-Ye for Lawyers," from *The Common Law Tradition* by Karl N. Llewellyn, are reproduced with the permission of Little, Brown and Company. Copyright © 1960 by Karl N. Llewellyn. The passages from "Sad Strains of a Gay Waltz" and "The Idea of Order at Key West," by Wallace Stevens, are reproduced with the permission of Alfred A. Knopf & Co. Copyright © 1984 by Holly Stevens.

Library of Congress Cataloging-in-Publication Data
Glendon, Mary Ann.
A nation under lawyers : how the crisis in the legal profession
is transforming American society / Mary Ann Glendon.—1st ed.
p.   cm.
Includes index.
1. Lawyers—United States. 2. Practice of Law—United States.
I. Title
KF297.G58   1994   340'.023'73—dc20   94-13417   CIP
ISBN 0-674-60138-6 (pbk.)

For Edward R. Lev

CONTENTS

A NATION
UNDER
LAWYERS

INTRODUCTION

1

A Nation Under Lawyers

My friends, I'm here to tell you the lawyers won!

—Democratic Party chairman RON BROWN
to American Bar Association leadership
forum, November 1992[1]

Young Alexis de Tocqueville, journeying through the United States in 1831 and 1832, was struck by the pervasive, yet oblique influence of judges, practitioners, and legally trained officials. "I should like to get this matter clear," he wrote, "for it may be that lawyers are called on to play the leading part in the political society which is striving to be born."[2] A flourishing lawyer class, in his view, was just what the new republic needed. What other group was so well suited to keeping their fellow citizens aware of the eternal paradox that there can be no liberty without law? The legal profession would serve as a rudder for the democratic bark as she and her rowdy passengers set out on the perilous voyage of self-government.

What would a friendly observer like Tocqueville make, one wonders, of the diverse American legal profession of the 1990s? What are *we* to make of nearly 800,000 practitioners, judges, and teachers wielding more influence than ever, but rapidly shedding the habits and restraints that once made the bench and the bar pillars of the democratic experiment? What does it mean for our law-dependent polity that startling new attitudes about law and the roles of lawyers are emerging, not merely on the fringes of the profession but in traditional citadels like the Supreme Court, the American Bar Association, and the major law schools?

It was a sign of changing times when the late Grant Gilmore, a grand old man of law teaching, took the occasion of the legal academy's most prestigious lecture series in 1974 to scoff at the rule of law as a "meaningless slogan."[3] From the same platform where Benjamin Cardozo had once delivered classic lectures on the interplay of freedom and constraint in judging, Gilmore thumbed his nose, so to speak, at the words engraved on the portals of courtrooms and law schools across the nation: *Sub Deo et Lege*. "Ours is a government not of laws but of men," he declared. "It is only an occasional unreconstructed cold warrior who still proclaims the virtues of the rule of law." Gilmore was no rebel; nor did his views attract criticism from fellow academics. By 1974, legal educators from Cambridge to Palo Alto were preaching the rule of men, not law, with all the zeal of the boy prophet in Flannery O'Connor's *Wise Blood* proclaiming the Church of Truth without Jesus Christ Crucified.

If it were only in the legal academy that the rulemeisters had become restless, the political implications might be negligible. The 6,000 or so legal educators in the United States, after all, constitute less than 1 percent of the legal profession. But a new spirit is stirring among the country's 27,000-member judicial corps, too. That was plain in 1992, when three Supreme Court justices widely regarded as moderates claimed for the Court a more exalted role than any to which the original judicial activist, John Marshall, had aspired in his boldest moments. Chief Justice Marshall made history in 1803 by asserting judicial power to review legislative and executive action for conformity to the Constitution. But he never proposed, as did Justices Anthony Kennedy, Sandra O'Connor, and David Souter, that the Court's powers should include telling the country what its "constitutional ideals" ought to be.[4] Nor can one imagine Marshall proclaiming that the American people would be "tested by following" the Court's leadership.

Those extraordinary assertions were made in a case that was less notable for its result (substantially upholding a Pennsylvania abortion statute) than for the plurality's grandiose pretensions of judicial authority. Justice Kennedy, speaking to a reporter that day, seemed to be carried away: he twice compared himself to Caesar at the Rubicon.[5] Turning over in their graves must have been judges like Oliver Wendell Holmes, Benjamin Cardozo, and Learned Hand, forceful intellects and personalities who had striven mightily to avoid even the appearance of judicial aggrandizement.

But the open hubris displayed by the Court's least flamboyant members was very much of a piece with thirty years of decision making in which conservative and liberal justices alike had regularly made light of the principle that the basic course of our society is to be charted by the people acting through their elected representatives. The ill-concealed authoritarianism of recent high court decisions even got under the skin of a leading academic advocate of expanded judicial power to reshape old statutes. Yale Law School's normally diplomatic Dean Guido Calabresi wrote in *The New York Times*: "I despise the current Supreme Court and find its aggressive, willful, statist behavior disgusting—the very opposite of what a judicious moderate, or even conservative, judicial body should do."[6]

Over the past three decades, strange new currents have been flowing, too, among the hundreds of thousands of practitioners who make up the backbone of the legal profession. In the Law Day rhetoric of bar association officials, exhortations to uphold the rule of law increasingly have given way to self-serving portrayals of lawyers as vindicators of an ever-expanding array of claims and rights. In two successive revisions of its rules of ethics, the American Bar Association has removed almost all language of moral suasion, abandoning the effort to hold up an image of what a good lawyer ought to be in favor of a minimalist catalogue of things a lawyer must not do. Conduct once strictly forbidden is now not only permitted but widely practiced. Lawyers' advertising, to take a well-known example, has been pronounced legal by the courts and ethical by the bar. Not all of its forms are as blatant as the bulletin one group of Chicago lawyers sent to their clients: "We are pleased to announce that we obtained for our client THE LARGEST VERDICT EVER FOR AN ARM AMPUTATION—$7.8 MILLION."[7] But when old-line law firms began to hire marketing directors and public relations specialists, the rupture with former standards was even more dramatic. The ban on advertising, as we shall see, was but one strand in a great web of understandings that now hangs in shreds.

What does it mean when prominent law professors deride the rule of law, when judicial moderates openly disdain popular government, and when practitioners adapt ethical rules to fit changing behavior rather than orienting their behavior toward standards deliberately set high? These developments are instances of a far-reaching transformation of lawyers' beliefs and attitudes that has been quietly under way since the mid-1960s. Several radical propositions that were once but minor tributaries or countercurrents have achieved respectability and prominence, if not dominance, in mainstream legal culture: that we live under a rule of men, not law; that the Constitution is just an old text that means whatever the current crop of judges says it does; that all rules (including rules of professional ethics) are infinitely manipulable; that law is a business like any other; and that business is just the unrestrained pursuit of self-interest.

Lawyers themselves are confused by the enormous changes that have taken place in judging, practicing, and studying law over the past three decades. Those of us whose professional service spans that period know just how the hero in one of Louis Auchincloss's stories felt when "the basket in which for thirty years he had toted most of his legal eggs burst its bottom and dropped its cargo on the street."[8] The fact is that the unraveling of a familiar, elaborate network of institutions, habits, and attitudes caught the whole profession by surprise. As late as the early 1960s, no one seems to have envisioned any of it. The causes of the disarray, moreover, are so diverse, complex, and intertwined that our heads spun when we tried to make sense of what was happening. It was like unexpected turbulence in an ocean current; the sudden dispersion of a plume of smoke into a swirling cloud; Dionysus appearing at the gates of Thebes.

Caught up in the tumult, most lawyers regard the transformation of the profession with mingled excitement, apprehension, and bewilderment. Nearly every one of them welcomes the profession's increasing concern with social justice, its growing diversity, and the livelier atmosphere in law schools. In fact, what makes it all so perplexing is that most of the developments now stirring anxiety seem to be by-products or outgrowths of genuine advances. Judicial adventurousness did not seem objectionable when official segregation barred access to ordinary politics. Few who struggled to open the legal profession to women, Jews, and racial minorities dreamed that their ideals could harden into dogmas of political correctness. The tough-talking realism of Gilmore's generation was a refreshing change from the tendency of many of his predecessors to ignore the political and economic context of legal issues. It makes eminent good sense to treat law as, in certain respects, a business. (Abe Lincoln was not ashamed to admit it, why should we be?) Yet the fresh air that is now blowing through courtrooms, classrooms, and law offices seems to be carrying something intoxicating, even unhealthy.

It has not escaped popular attention that all is not well in the world of lawyers. The fact that lawyers figured prominently in the Watergate affair of the 1970s and in the savings and loan scandals of the 1980s threw a harsh spotlight on legal ethics. The no-holds-barred judicial confirmation battles over Robert Bork and Clarence Thomas touched off strident debates on the power and politicization of the judiciary. Critics have sounded alarms about hair-trigger litigiousness. The competitive frenzy that seized the profession in the takeover decade made it plainer than ever that the practice of law is subject to the same maladies that can afflict other profit-making activities.

Less noted by the public or lawyers themselves are the tectonic shifts that have taken place in lawyers' opinions and attitudes over the past thirty years. In that relatively short period, a significant reordering has been taking place in what lawyers believe, or profess to believe, about law and their own roles in the legal system. A major struggle is under way among competing ideas of what constitutes excellence in a judge, a practitioner, a teacher or scholar of law. There has been a quiet revolution in how various types of legal work are valued and rewarded. This reshuffling of values is about the only thing the legal profession does not advertise. Yet, being systemic, it has far more serious implications for our law-dependent polity than any number of flagrant instances of misconduct by individual lawyers.

Changes in legal culture are widening the gap between what lawyers believe about law and government and what their fellow citizens believe. Only a few months before Grant Gilmore scornfully dismissed the rule of law as an empty formula, the nation had been embroiled in a grave constitutional crisis. On October 19, 1973, one man, armed only with the rule-of-law idea, had rejected a direct order from the President of the United States to cease using the courts to obtain tape recordings of White House conversations about the burglary of Democratic Party headquarters during the 1972 presidential campaign. As we now know, the firing of Watergate special prosecutor Archibald Cox was the turning point in the crisis of the Nixon presidency. When notified of his removal, Cox had issued a terse one-line statement: "Whether we shall continue to be a government of laws and not of men is now for Congress and the people to decide."[9]

A meaningless slogan? Hardly. On that occasion, as well as when he argued to Judge John Sirica that "happily, ours is a system of government in which no man is above the law,"[10] Cox tapped into deeply felt popular sentiments. Our legalistic traditions, in fact, made all the difference in the Watergate drama. In many other liberal democracies, the outcome would surely have been different. The foreign press was bemused at the fuss Americans made over the incident. But incorrigibly legalistic Americans were not prepared to be so blasé about the idea of government under law. More than the break-in at Democratic headquarters, more than the subsequent cover-up, it was the spectacle of a White House openly flouting the law that citizens found unsettling and alarming.

Cox's defiance of a lawless President excited widespread

Watergate Special Prosecutor Archibald Cox: "Whether we shall continue to be a government of laws and not of men is now for Congress and the people to decide." *(Photograph courtesy Harvard Law Art Collection)*

admiration. He was a steady, reassuring presence as affairs of state spiraled alarmingly out of control. Americans honor Cox for the same reason that generations of Englishmen have paid tribute to Lord Edward Coke, who instructed James I that even the sovereign must bow before law. A modern-day Coke in a button-down collar, Cox stood firm against the most powerful man on earth. When the lawyer President and his men (many of them lawyers) acceded, the nation breathed a sigh of relief. Cox had upheld, indeed personified, a cherished principle in the midst of moral turbulence.

But if Cox reflected the general mood of the country, it was Gilmore who more exactly mirrored the legal academy to which both he and Cox belonged. Many of the same professors who had applauded the downfall of Nixon exchanged knowing smiles when the "rule of law" was invoked. Like Gilmore, they fancied themselves tough-minded men and women who could live without naive "illusions."

There is a good case to be made, however, that Cox was more realistic than Gilmore. Surely no American adult needs to be told that we live under a rule of men in the sense that laws are made, interpreted, and administered by real men and women. Nor are Americans unaware that those men and women are subject to a tantalizing variety of temptations. Everyone realizes that attorneys may chisel and that judges may be unfair, in the same way they know that a preacher may lie or covet his neighbor's wife. But just as awareness of the frailties of clergymen has not significantly dampened Americans' persistent religiosity, their unsentimental appraisal of judges and lawyers has not, thus far, destroyed their attachment to the idea of a nation under law. The grass-roots legalism to which Cox had appealed was clear-eyed, hard-nosed, and stubborn.

In *From Here to Eternity*, James Jones captured that attitude perfectly. Private Robert E. Lee Prewitt of Harlan County, Kentucky, is trying to make Mess Sergeant Maylon Stark of Sweetwater, Texas, understand why he won't give in to pressure from higher-ups to join the regimental boxing squad. Prew says:

"Every man's supposed to have certain rights."

"Certain inalienable rights," Stark said, "to liberty, equality, and the pursuit of happiness. I learnt it in school, as a kid."

"Not that," Prew said. "That's the Constitution. Nobody believes that any more."

"Sure they do," Stark said. "They all believe it. They just don't do it. But they believe it."

"Sure," Prew said. "That's what I mean."

"But at least in this country they believe it," Stark said, "even if they don't do it. Other countries they don't even believe it."[11]

The conversation is pure Americana, right down to Prewitt's confusion of the Declaration of Independence with the Constitution, and Stark's naive jingoism.

How closely a country approaches the target of a rule of law, as Sergeant Stark might have told Professor Gilmore, depends on whether those who administer the laws "believe it" and on the degree to which they discipline themselves to "do it." The rule of law is no empty formula; it's a set of institutionalized, time-tested principles that are nothing if not realistic about human nature.[12] Toward the end of minimizing official arbitrariness and securing reasonably stable conditions for social and political life, it proclaims: that law is preferable to the use of private force as a means of resolving disputes; that executives, legislators, and judges are all subject to the law and are to be held accountable if they violate it; that official decisions must be grounded in preestablished principles of general application; and that no citizen can be deprived of freedom or goods except in accordance with due procedural safeguards.

Americans use the rule-of-law idea as a tuning fork to test not only the performance of their officials but also the quality of their society. So far, our nation's response to failures by those who administer the laws has been to change the officials, not to lower the standards. We are rightly fearful of dispensing with measures that have proved their worth in concrete historical circumstances. Most citizens understand that being oriented toward an ideal like the rule of law does not guarantee conformity to it. But people also understand that, in the clutch, ideals reinforced by friends, teachers, colleagues, supervisors, and respected role models will often carry the day. In the end, Cox was the true realist, because, strange to say, legal ideals are an important component of American reality.

It is precisely because of the unique role of law and lawyers in American life that a significant advance of arrogance, unruliness, greed, and cynicism in the legal profession is of more concern than similar developments in, say, banking or dentistry. As Tocqueville noticed long ago: "In the United States the lawyers constitute a power which is little dreaded and hardly noticed; it has no banner of its own; it adapts itself flexibly to the exigencies of the moment and lets itself be carried along unresistingly by every movement of the body social; but it enwraps the whole of society, penetrating each component class and constantly working in secret upon its unconscious patient, till in the end it has molded it to its desire."[13] A breakdown in self-discipline among lawyers, then, cannot be without consequences for the wider society.

The legal presence that made such an impression on our nineteenth-century visitor is magnified many times today. With the expansion of commerce and the rise of big government, American lawyers wield influence in ways, and on a scale, that Tocqueville could scarcely have imagined. Twenty-three of our forty-one Presidents have been lawyers. At present, the majority of U.S. senators and nearly half the members of the House of Representatives have law degrees. Of the eighteen-member cabinet appointed by lawyer President Bill Clinton in 1993, thirteen were lawyers. For the first time, the President's wife is a lawyer, more visible than her predecessors in shaping policy. Lawyer-dominated legislatures and bureaucracies now extend their reach into every corner of contemporary American life—taxing, subsidizing, licensing, attaching conditions, granting dispensations, mandating or encouraging this and forbidding or discouraging that. The positions that lawyers occupy throughout the corporate, financial, and commercial worlds are no less strategic. Judges increasingly seem to have the last word on the most divisive and hotly contested questions of the times.

It cannot be a matter of indifference, therefore, that so many judges, practitioners, educators, and scholars, like sorcerer's apprentices, have slipped off the restraints that their greatest predecessors wore with pride. The ensuing transformation of legal culture, while by no means complete, inevitably affects performance of the roles that Americans, more than ever, expect lawyers to play in our society. In a country like the United States, small changes in legal culture send out ripples. Major changes produce waves that can rock the ship of state.

The upheaval in the profession has been substantial enough to raise troubling questions:

To what extent will future Americans be able to count on practitioners to subordinate self-interest to client representation and public service? On judges to resist the temptation to be wiser and fairer than the laws enacted by their fellow citizens? On legal educators to promote those upright habits and attitudes along with an array of useful problem-solving skills?

What influence do the new ways of lawyers have on the ideas, habits, and manners of their fellow citizens? Is the adversarial culture of real and fictional litigators even now "working in secret" to transform the "body social"?

Are lawyers, in the aggregate, currently promoting or undermining the orderly pursuit of dignified living in these latter-day law-saturated United States? With so many of them clambering toward the helm, or cavorting on deck, what happened to the steady hand on the rudder of the democratic vessel?

Tocqueville was right that it's important to get such matters clear. This book is an effort to do so. In attempting to make sense of this turbulent period in the life of the American legal profession, I have not aimed to write a primer on legal pathology. My effort has been twofold: to portray an evolving tradition in the process of coping with momentous internal and external challenges and to signal the broader political implications of that process. To those ends, I have focused less on eruptions at the volatile margins than on motions in the normally placid middle of the profession. In treating the great innovators who have crossed the legal stage in the present century, I have been more attentive to those who labored to develop creative approaches to governmental complexity, economic change, and social pluralism than to those who simply exposed the moral and technical inadequacy of existing arrangements. In the spirit of the great French friend of the American version of democracy, I have tried to look not just for what may be amiss but for what is sound, healthy, and capable of development.

Let us begin, then, with the world of practice, where counselors, planners, and litigators ply their arts in the nation's law firms, government offices, and corporate legal departments. What do these busy men and women believe about law and their own roles in the legal system? How do their views compare with what most Americans think they believe? As we observe their activities and listen to what they say, we cannot help but notice something perplexing. American lawyers, wealthier and more powerful than their counterparts anywhere else in the world, are in the grip of a great sadness.

PART I

PROFESSIONALISM AND ITS DISCONTENTS

Lawyers have never wielded more political and economic power than they do today; yet they report a declining sense of control over their own lives.

American lawyers are the wealthiest in the world; yet in all branches of the profession lawyers reported that their levels of satisfaction with their work plummeted by 20 percent in the six years between 1984 and 1990.

Women now enjoy unprecedented opportunities in the law; yet they are twice as dissatisfied as their male counterparts.

College graduates still flock to the nation's law schools; yet nearly one lawyer in four says he would not become an attorney if he had it to do over again.

In influence, affluence, and prestige, practicing lawyers surpass most other occupational groups; yet there is a high incidence among them of clinical depression, and conservative estimates say one lawyer in six is a problem drinker.

Why are so many lawyers so sad?

2

When Just Being a Good Lawyer Isn't Enough

The term [profession] refers to a group of men pursuing a learned art as a common calling in the spirit of a public service—no less a public service because it may incidentally be a means of livelihood.

—ROSCOE POUND[1]

The problem with applying Roscoe Pound's high-sounding formulation to the legal profession, Karl Llewellyn informed the members of the Class of '61 at the University of Chicago Law School, is not that it's untrue, but that every aspiration it expresses is potentially at war with all the others. In the tent-meeting voice he used when he wanted to implant something permanently in our gray matter, he told us: "The lawyer is a man of many conflicts. More than anyone else in our society, he must contend with competing claims on his time and loyalty. You must represent your client to the best of your ability, and yet never lose sight of the fact that you are an officer of the court with a special responsibility for the integrity of the legal system. You will often find, brethren and sistern, that those professional duties do not sit easily with one another. You will discover, too, that they get in the way of your other obligations—to your conscience, your God, your family, your partners, your country, and all the other perfectly good claims on your energies and hearts. You will be pulled and tugged in a dozen directions at once. You must learn to handle those conflicts."

We had already heard a good deal about situations where

our duty to a client might be in tension with our obligations as "officers of the court." But Llewellyn now told us that that was only the kindergarten lesson. Did we imagine that our professional lives would be devoted to the genteel pursuit of a "learned art"? Think about what happens to care and craftsmanship under constant pressure from deadlines and economic exigency. A "common calling"? Yes, but we would regularly be at odds with other lawyers, even sometimes with our own partners and colleagues. Nor would it ever be easy to reconcile the need to make a "livelihood" with "the spirit of public service." The choices we would have to make would hardly ever be clear-cut. Sometimes they would involve competing goods; sometimes the lesser of evils. Many of our decisions would be fraught with moral ambiguity, and followed by haunting doubts. Our lives, he warned us, would be as complicated as a three-dimensional chess game. "But don't ever think it's a game," he thundered. "You're responsible for other people!"

"Have any of you heard of the 'handwriting on the wall' in the Book of Daniel?" he demanded one day. We studiously examined the spiral bindings of our notebooks. This was no time to risk eye contact.

"What exactly was written on that wall?" Silence, eyes down.

"Mene, Mene, Tekel, Upharsin!" he roared. Nervous laughter.

"What that means, brethren and sistern, is: 'You have been weighed in the balance and found wanting.' How will *you* measure up at the end of your legal career? When you die (as you will, you know), will you have left the law better or worse than you found it?"

None of our other teachers talked to us that way. Student opinion was divided about Llewellyn. Some thought he was a buffoon; others thought he was a genius; still others thought he was a bit of both. On certain days, though, all of us felt that we were in the presence of a tremendous moral and intellectual force. One thing about Llewellyn was especially baffling to us twenty-somethings: he passionately loved "the law." What was one to make of this weird infatuation? As the leading member of the "Legal Realist" school, he knew the flaws of the legal system better than anyone. But he thought "the law" was beautiful! Not content to keep this embarrassing passion to himself, he wanted us to love what he loved. Even on graduation day, he wouldn't give up. There he was again, insisting that we repeat an "oath" he had written. Ridiculous, we thought. Yet I still occasionally take out that yellowing piece of paper dated June 1961, and think about the writing on the wall. Here is what he made us say:

> In accepting the honor and responsibility of life in the profession of the law, I engage, as best I can,
> —to work always with care and with a whole heart and with good faith;
> —to weigh my conflicting loyalties and guide my work with an eye to the good less of myself than of justice and the people; and
> —to be at all times, even at personal sacrifice, a champion of fairness and due process, in court or out, and for all, whether the powerful or envied or my neighbors or the helpless or the hated or the oppressed.

As far as the four women in that class of 112 were concerned, the most worrisome conflict of all was one that Llewellyn had touched only in passing. Nancy McDermid, the best student in our tiny band, was already juggling the demands of law school with the need to care for her baby daughter and her commitment to the nascent civil rights movement. When her grades earned her an invitation to join the Law Review, she amazed her envious classmates by declining. But, in her circumstances, work on the Review was simply too time-consuming. After law school, Nancy went into university administration, where she has had a distinguished career. Roberta George and Lois Adelman found ways to combine law practice with child raising by associating themselves with small firms—Roberta with her father; and Lois with her husband, Art Solomon, another classmate. I was the only one of our group to choose large-firm practice. Within five years, shortly after my first daughter was born, I shifted into law teaching. "Don't lecture *us* on conflicts," we were already thinking in 1961, "we've got the patent on them."

None of us—not Llewellyn, not the women students trying to figure out how to combine career and family without wrecking both, not the young men who expected to give themselves more fully to practice—had any inkling that the conflicts of which Llewellyn spoke were about to intensify. How could we have known we were in the last days of what legal sociologists now call the "golden age" of the big law firm? This is how that era now looks to Marc Galanter and Thomas Palay:

> We locate this golden age in the period of the late 1950s and the early 1960s . . . when big firms were prosperous, stable, and untroubled. . . . It was a time of stable relations with clients, of steady but manageable growth, of comfortable assurance that an equally bright future lay ahead.[2]

Partners in large firms enjoyed a confident sense of control over their working conditions and their destinies.[3] Graduates of the better law schools, groomed for business practice, were as secure in our prospects as young lawyers have ever been.

Yet, within a few years, almost all of us would experience the sinking feeling that came over the lawyer in the Auchincloss story when the bottom fell out of his legal egg basket. Many of the best and brightest of our generation came to grief when the rules of the game changed in large law firms, sending shock waves across the entire profession. Those who were most shocked were the upwardly mobile men and women who had entered the legal profession on the assumption that talent and hard work were all they needed to prosper in their chosen careers. For smart, ambitious law students who possessed neither family connections nor business-getting skills, the big firm was the ideal destination. The firms' clients were like the hats of Beacon Hill matrons: one didn't *get* them, one *had* them. The work was important and interesting. No one dreamed that the day was fast approaching when it would no longer be enough to be merely a good lawyer.

The basis of our sense of security was the knowledge that most large firms made their hiring decisions with the expectation that associates whose work was of high quality would in due course become partners.[4] We knew that there would be a weeding-out process, but were comfortable with the system that gave us what seemed a fair chance. Those who didn't make it would be eased into other jobs. Partnership itself, like marriage in those days, was understood as a permanent commitment. Sometimes the firm solidarity built on those understandings even shielded associates from layoff when firms experienced economic setbacks. In the depths of the Depression, when Thomas Nelson Perkins of Boston's Ropes, Gray, Boyden & Perkins was told the firm would lose money unless it trimmed the payroll, he is supposed to have said, "No young man is to be let go. The senior partners will take zero compensation." And so, the story goes, they did.[5] Few firms claim to have gone to such lengths, but many made adjustments to keep all hands on board while storms were weathered.

Even when the partners erred in hiring someone, they tended to live with the mistake until the person in question could depart with dignity. I recall the particular gentleness with which my old firm, Mayer, Friedlich, Spiess, Tierney, Brown & Platt (now Mayer, Brown & Platt), handled the situation of a young associate suffering from a strange malady which causes its victims to erupt in periodic outbursts of obscenities. A senior partner who happened to be on the board of the Menninger psychiatric foundation made sure that everyone knew that the associate's startling and unpredictable displays were the result of illness. The associate was given "back room" research work for a couple of years until hopes of a cure faded and another position could be found.

Those associates who failed to make partner were protected by a widely shared understanding "that it was not nice to fire a lawyer."[6] In New York, some major firms had a rigorous "up or out" system, but most large firms went to some lengths to help a disappointing junior save face. They would keep the associate on for the time necessary to find an alternative placement and would actively help in the process. Nearly every firm had a few "permanent associates." In the 1970s, that relatively comfortable situation began to change. Like distant thunderclaps, reports of bloodletting at big firms here and there began to circulate. The numbers of associates involved were small, but the shift in understandings represented by the layoffs was immense. The news struck fear into the hearts of associates everywhere. If Boston's Bingham, Dana & Gould would send a whole cohort of associates packing, who was safe? By the end of the 1980s, layoffs of highly paid associates in their second to fifth year of practice were commonplace. Firms that had thrived on corporate finance, tax, real estate, bond, and merger work were tightening their belts as the takeover era came to an end. A 1991 survey of 105 of the country's largest firms found that 93.4 percent had dismissed associates in the preceding eighteen months and that 86 percent expected to make similar layoffs within the next year and a half.[7] In 1993, almost half of the 250 largest firms reported that they had "downsized."[8]

Economic concerns were real. Law firm revenues, after rising about 12 percent a year from 1977 to 1989, began to decline. Not only did the upstart megafirm Finley, Kumble go belly-up in the 1980s but so did the venerable Boston firms of Gaston, Snow and Herrick, Smith. Most lawyers found it unsettling to see those fixtures vanish from the legal landscape, sending partners and associates alike scrambling for new jobs. At the demise of the Boston firms, pundits shook their heads knowingly. They said that the longer a firm postponed the inevitable changes and the harder it tried to do right by its youngsters and oldsters, the more surely it sealed its own doom.

For a while, partners in prosperous firms, at least, thought they were secure. As new executive committees looked into every nook and cranny of their firms with the searchlight of cost-effectiveness, however, many senior lawyers had a devastating experience similar to that of displaced homemakers.

They had joined their firms at a time when partnership was understood to be a lifelong relationship. Settled understandings about role division and profit sharing recognized the mutual dependence of client-getting lawyers and the expert office lawyers to whom rainmakers turned over much of the actual work. The division of labor among specialties had operated as a risk-pooling arrangement; if one field went dry (say, through sudden deregulation), partners in the hotter areas would carry the redundant lawyers until they retooled. Firm esprit and solidarity were often remarkably strong.

Imagine, then, the dismay of Ingrid Beall in the mid-1980s when top management tried to squeeze her out of the giant Chicago-based firm of Baker, McKenzie shortly after her colleagues had paid her the honor of nominating her, in an advisory at-large election, for the firm's executive committee. Beall, a respected international tax expert, was puzzled when she learned that several members of the group that had come to power after the retirement of the founding partner were blocking her appointment to the committee. Twenty years earlier, she had been a key member of the team that built the medium-sized Chicago firm into an international powerhouse with over 1,600 lawyers in several countries. (I well remember meeting her once in those years at the firm's Brussels office—an intelligent, well-spoken, elegant woman, radiating competence and confidence.) Shortly after management rejected her for the executive committee, they stopped routing new business her way. Beall's annual draw decreased by nearly two-thirds between 1988 and 1991.[9] In 1991, Beall, who had always been a team player, took the extraordinary step of filing suit against the firm, alleging sex and age discrimination.

Antidiscrimination statutes offer no remedy, however, for Beall's fundamental grievance—Baker, McKenzie had changed one of the most basic rules of the game. Whatever a court decides about the role played by her gender and age, Beall was a casualty of the decision of most large firms to abandon their longstanding "lockstep" (seniority-based) compensation systems, which had promoted risk sharing when dividing the partnership pie.[10] The lockstep system was never so rigid as the term implies, but it operated roughly like a form of self-insurance. Its replacement with a productivity-based system for dividing profits provided more incentives and rewards for business-getters, but was a disaster for people like Beall who had established themselves mainly by being excellent lawyers, relying on colleagues with different sorts of talents to bring in the clients. The common term for the new system—"eat what you kill"—speaks volumes. Beall's complaint that the firm was no longer sending business to her cut no ice with a Chicago lawyer of the new breed who commented: "When you're a partner at a major firm, you're not supposed to get work, you're supposed to generate work."[11]

Between 1961, when Beall became Baker, McKenzie's first woman partner, and 1988, when the door of the inner sanctum was slammed in her face, an entire network of professional understandings had fallen apart. The firm solidarity promoted by its courtly founder, Russell Baker, had been eroded by increased lateral movement of partners and associates, by the firm's enormous growth, and by the rise in Baker, McKenzie, as elsewhere, of the "star system" that rewarded rainmakers more handsomely than ever. Needless to say, the greatest power and prestige in law firms have always belonged to the well-connected and highly competent partners who are able not only to service clients but to attract them. Still, when Ingrid Beall began practicing law, career prospects were excellent for lawyers who were simply very good at practicing law. In fact, the talented office lawyers who kept the clients satisfied as a rule had greater prestige among their peers than the litigators—or the genial scions of wealthy families whose contributions consisted mainly in business-getting. A survey of the Chicago bar in the 1970s showed that the lawyers who commanded the most esteem were those (like Beall) who were engaged in tax and securities work for large corporations.[12]

Even New York's aggressive Cravath, Swaine & Moore paid lip service to the understandings on which Ingrid Beall and so many others had relied. Robert Swaine had written in the firm history: "[B]usiness-getting ability is not a factor in the advancement of a man within the office at any level, except in so far as that ability arises out of competence in doing law work."[13] Once gender and color bars were relaxed, that sentiment was music to the ears of the women and minorities who integrated the large firms. For a brief interlude, we could flourish professionally without having to surmount business-getting hurdles as well.

The tune changed in the 1980s. In some firms, rainmaking became everything. In the years when Skadden, Arps was riding high on merger and acquisition work, the managing committee rewarded the top partners in that field with seven-figure bonuses.[14] The festering resentment created among the other partners (who referred to the bonus fund as the "Pig Pool") predictably contributed to a bitter power struggle when takeover work fell off. The era when firms could assume that the steady stream of business from a stable roster of clients would flow on forever was drawing to a close. Corporate managers discovered that much of a company's routine legal business could be done more cheaply by salaried lawyers in expanded "in-house" legal departments. Then house counsel began to question the customary practice of awarding nearly all of a corporation's legal business to a single firm. Why not shop around for expertise and a good price? By the mid-1980s, no firm could take the loyalty of its clients for granted. Business-getting lawyers were once again at a premium—as they had been in the rough-and-ready gilded age when the large firms were founded.

Women and minorities were among the first to feel the change in atmosphere. But they had plenty of company. When the bell tolled for Ingrid Beall, it tolled for every big-firm lawyer who had counted on intelligence and professional skill to see him through. Beall's experience was replicated across the country as the powerful partners who controlled business cut back shares of longtime colleagues, relegating them to something like the status of employees. For many senior lawyers even greater shocks were in store: 59 percent of 105 large firms surveyed in 1991 had terminated partners in the preceding eighteen months, and 53 percent expected to do so in the near future.[15]

With hindsight, it's easy to see that partners' security in big firms had rested on something beyond individual talent and hard work. That something else was the set of relationships that develops in collegial environments where everyone knows and interacts regularly with everyone else. "Partnership" was not just a legal form. As the name implies, it involved a set of close personal relations.[16]

When I joined Mayer, Friedlich (now Mayer, Brown) in 1963, it was the second-largest firm in Chicago. Despite its size, there was an extraordinary sense of fellowship among the seventy or so partners and associates. The firm was proud of its "ecumenical" Protestant-Jewish-Catholic composition, as well as of its intellectual and open-minded atmosphere. It was one of the first big firms to hire women and minorities, and did well at making them feel welcome. Not only did Mayer, Friedlich's lawyers interact closely in the office; we saw one another frequently in a variety of social contexts. By the time I left in 1968, however, the signs of change were in the air. The firm had close to a hundred lawyers; a professional administrator had taken over many of the duties of the managing partner; senior partners were beginning to give up on learning the names of new associates. Bureaucracy had arrived, bringing a more impersonal attitude toward performance, merit, and reward. Mayer, Brown today is on its way to megafirm status, with nearly 600 lawyers.

Those sorts of changes in firms prompted the restructuring of several partnerships and made it easier to sever longtime relationships. Increasingly, "nothing personal" was involved when a lawyer left or was eased out. In 1960, fewer than a dozen firms had over a hundred lawyers. By 1986, more than 250 had passed the hundred mark.[17] Many firms created new categories of employee-lawyers, including various types of "non-equity" partners who were somewhere between associates and full partners.[18] Firms began to merge with other firms, and even to raid partners from one another. The recruitment of lawyers from another firm, once unthinkable behavior, became a common practice. Talented partners began to keep an eye out for greener pastures. But the same survey that documents the attenuation of relationships within firms also shows how strong the old understandings of lifetime association had been: over 80 percent of the firms had never developed any procedures or policies to follow for termination. As a spokesman for Hildebrandt, Inc., the consulting firm that conducted the study, remarked in 1992, "Basically, we're dealing with a new phenomenon."[19]

Another sign of changing times involved associates' training. Because many legal skills must be acquired on the job rather than in the classroom, the centuries-old system of legal apprenticeship has never completely died. John W. Davis, who learned his trade by working alongside his father in West Virginia, long had a custom of inviting each new associate at the Wall Street firm of Davis Polk to work with him on at least one case.[20] Many large firms devoted so much time to training novices that, even in the days of low starting salaries, they did not show much profit on a young lawyer's work until the second or third year.

Today, many senior lawyers still pride themselves on teaching new associates how to deal with clients and opposing counsel, tutoring them on the fine points of drafting and negotiation. In the process, the mentors honor the memory of the other lawyers who once supported their own efforts, praised their achievements, corrected their errors, and consoled them on setbacks. But tutelage consumes valuable time of partners, as well as associates, that cannot be billed to clients. Thus it is hardly surprising that one-on-one sessions became shorter and formal continuing education programs were established in firms as competition for clients intensified in the 1980s. The mentoring system received another blow when starting salaries shot upward in 1986 as top firms competed for the top law graduates. No one wanted to spoon-feed a twenty-four-year-old making $85,000 a year.

In 1992, *The National Jurist*, a magazine for law students, posed a question to the hiring partners of several firms: "What qualities are large firms seeking in new associates?" Samuel Hoar, of Boston's Goodwin, Proctor & Hoar, replied that job applicants ought to have demonstrated their ability to "hit the ground running." He explained, "There simply is not enough time nowadays to wait several months until someone matures enough to be a decent lawyer."[21] Those views were seconded by a former chairperson of the ABA's Law Practice Management Section: "Hourly billing quotas are the rage in many law firms and are imposed equally on senior partners and new associates. As a result, senior lawyers no longer have time to mentor new lawyers or to leverage the firm's store of information and experience."[22] ABA Litigation Section Chair Louise LaMothe ruefully observed, "The decline [in mentoring] has occurred just as women and minority lawyers began entering the profession in ever-increasing numbers."[23]

Some firms, especially in New York, had a reputation for hardball dealings with associates even before the competitive 1980s. Lawrence Lederman's description of his apprenticeship in the late 1960s to two of Cravath, Swaine & Moore's leading dealmakers conveys the best and the worst of large-firm practice at that time. The work was exciting, and in his one-on-one relations with gifted mentors Lederman developed discipline, judgment, and an appreciation of the joy of craftsmanship.[24] Yet he received many signals that prospects for partnership in that firm were not particularly good for associates who had neither the right schools nor the right social connections. My own interview at Cravath, Swaine in the early 1960s was consistent with Lederman's impressions. It was no use hiring me, a senior partner bluntly explained, because "I couldn't bring a girl in to meet Tom Watson [of IBM] any more than I could bring a Jew." The "golden age" was a time of shameless exclusionary practices.

The new emphasis on profitability brought more opportunities to some of the previously excluded. At the same time, however, it radically changed the nature of a career in law.

The ideal of the well-rounded generalist, the lawyer sought after for judgment as well as technical skill, became increasingly elusive. Until the 1980s, many firms had fostered the development of experience-based judgment by rotating new associates from one department to another, exposing them to a wide range of skills and specialties. Now, leading corporate lawyers advise law students to specialize early, despite the risk that any given niche may decline or even disappear with the vagaries of politics and the business cycle. Mayer, Brown's Leo Herzel adds another reason for specialization that did not play a major role in a young lawyer's calculations in the early 1960s: "Specialists find it much easier to change jobs or professions."[25] Generalist lawyers in the 1990s, according to Herzel, will be found mainly among "older lawyers who are senior partners in large corporate firms or general counsels of large companies." In other words, they are a vanishing species.

Before the "billable hour" concept became standard, corporate firms had a more flexible approach. Simon Rifkind's recollections capture the attitudes that prevailed in the elite legal world he knew in the 1930s. "The only cases in which we kept time records were those for which the fee was established by the court. How did we bill? Billing was a fine art. We asked ourselves the question: 'What have we accomplished for the client?' When we were successful, we were very well paid."[26]

Metering lawyers' time and hourly rates for billing became standard in the 1950s, but these practices did not immediately dominate the lives of lawyers.[27] Commenting on the "tremendous pressure" to generate revenues reported by lawyers today, Judge Harry Edwards recalls, "When I practiced law at a large firm [in the early 1970s], I felt no such pressure, nor did my colleagues. We enjoyed our work, because we felt the work was valuable—valuable to society, and to ourselves. The billing of clients was not the single, overriding goal that it has now become."[28]

By the 1980s, however, the billable hour had evolved from a sensible tool of office management to a frenetic way of life. Some say the change was forced upon the profession by corporate clients. Others, like Timothy May, the managing partner of a Washington firm, are of the view that "the change was driven by greed."[29] According to May: "We started reading stories about other law firms, about other lawyers making millions of dollars. The bidding war for associates drove up the costs of doing business. And once the costs went up, we had to run the firm like a business." The income of profit-sharing partners, moreover, correlates directly with the amount of time billed by salaried associates. Whatever the reason, most lawyers today, in large and small firms alike, log at least 1,800 billable hours a year.[30] The well-paid associates in many top firms are expected to bill a whopping 2,200 hours a year (7 hours a day, 6 days a week, 52 weeks a year). Keep in mind that billable time does not (or is not supposed to) include time spent eating, chatting, taking a break, answering personal phone calls and correspondence, attending firm or bar association meetings—or developing new business. It doesn't include the 50 hours of pro bono work that the ABA exhorts all lawyers to perform each year or the 15 hours that the average large-firm lawyer actually does devote to pro bono activities.[31] Nor the extra hours that beginning lawyers fail to report for fear of appearing slow or inefficient. For harried lawyers, it often takes 9 to 12 hours in the office to yield 7 hours of billable time.

A scene in Barry Reed's novel *The Choice* conveys something of the frenzied atmosphere in high-pressure firms.

"That kid's a doer. He'll be a shaker before long." Sturdevant tweaked the wisp of his white mustache. "Billed twenty-seven hours in *one* day to Comp-Tech Computer in their takeover by Delaware East. Can you believe it?" He gave the *Journal* a resounding whack on the bannister.

"In one day?" . . .

"Damn right!" Sturdevant broke into one of his rare smiles. "Worked right around the clock here in Boston, then took a plane to L.A. and logged three additional hours. Wait until Comp-Tech gets the bill. Hell, Galvin, I'll bet no one will ever top this!"[32]

Preposterous? Perhaps. But it was a case of art imitating life. Eben Moglen, now a Columbia law professor, actually did bill 27 hours for Cravath, Swaine in just that way in 1984.[33]

Some attorneys have found less strenuous ways to deal with the pressure to log long hours. A 1991 study found that about 60 percent of the private practitioners surveyed admitted to personal knowledge of bill padding.[34]

In the new specialized firms that began to handle proxy wars and hostile takeovers in the 1970s, lawyers began to see hourly rates as an impediment rather than an aid to high profits. They wanted more of the client's action. In his entertaining tales from the takeover era, Lawrence Lederman describes how hotshot dealmaking lawyers began to wonder why architects of immensely profitable transactions should be compensated at the same level as office drones or even litigators. "We discovered that a small expert group could command premiums for expertise and premiums for favorable outcome. We began to bill like investment bankers, on the basis of the size and complexity of the matter."[35] In the high-flying 1980s, the annual take of many lawyers shot up to a million dollars and more. Money was no longer just a means of livelihood, even of a very good livelihood; it was a way of keeping score. Established firms, which had remained aloof from takeover work just long enough to create a niche for the new specialized firms, overcame their scruples and leapt into the game.

The new scorekeeping mentality is both reflected and promoted by another recent phenomenon—breezy trade publications that report on lawyers' earnings and profile highly successful lawyers. *The American Lawyer*'s annual ranking of the 100 highest-grossing firms startled the legal world when it first appeared in 1985. Law firms traditionally had been extremely secretive about compensation. Most lawyers used to have only a sketchy idea of how their own earnings compared with those of their counterparts in other firms. *The American Lawyer* does not pretend to complete accuracy, but the results of its investigations are eagerly and nervously awaited each year. Its listing is widely credited with fostering an open market in legal services—and blamed for fueling lawyer discontents.[36]

By the 1990s, the billable hour had become just one of many alternative billing arrangements—some preferred by lawyers themselves, others adopted under pressure from powerful and cost-conscious clients. But the billable-time mentality left its mark on the legal culture. "Let's get back to billable time" became a standard way of bringing a coffee break to a close. Most significant of all, it has become acceptable for prominent lawyers to admit interest in making money—a lot of money. Explaining why large firms pay special attention to the summer work experiences and part-time jobs of prospective associates, Goodwin, Proctor's Samuel Hoar told *The National Jurist* with disarming candor: "That indicates that they are greedy and eager."[37]

It is difficult to imagine a hiring partner of the 1960s uttering such a sentence in public, so strong was the taboo against associating the practice of law with ordinary business. Partners who harbored gender bias or ethnic prejudice might express themselves freely, but an innocent interest in money had to be kept to oneself. My law school classmates and I used to watch with fascination as interviewers from a certain firm (with a reputation for being more businesslike than was generally thought nice) unerringly singled out for offers the students who (at least in the judgment of their peers) were the most rapacious.

How, we wondered, were these perfect matches achieved on the basis of a half-hour interview? What made it seem mysterious was the fact that it would have been a dreadful gaffe for a student interviewee to exhibit anything more than the most casual interest in the financial aspects of the job. Salaries were not discussed at all, except in the form of vague references to the "going rate." In the interviews of the 1990s, by contrast, money is up front. My students tell me it is not uncommon for interviewers to produce copies of firm balance sheets or for a candidate to ask to see one.

Lawyers' ideals of independence, always shaky, also have come under special stress in recent years. Those ideals once meant turning away business under certain circumstances and telling existing clients things they did not want to hear. Nearly every firm bragged of lawyers like John G. Johnson of Philadelphia, who would not sit on a client's board of directors and who, when J. P. Morgan sent a special train to Philadelphia to take him to an important conference, is supposed to have refused the summons, saying, "I'm busy."[38] Justice Potter Stewart once recalled that the senior partner of the Cincinnati firm where he had practiced "felt so strongly about not only the reality but the appearance of professional objectivity and independence that he would not leave his office to see a business client."[39]

That such anecdotes bore some relation to reality is indicated by Jerome Carlin's study of the New York bar in the 1960s and by Galanter and Palay's 1991 study of the transformation of large firms. Carlin showed that lawyers in large firms, with their diverse mixes of affluent clients, not only enjoyed substantial independence in the 1960s but were insulated from many pressures to violate ethical norms.[40] As one commentator has summed up what we now understand as the anomalous situation that prevailed from the 1920s to the 1960s: "Free to conduct their affairs as they saw fit, the established practices could all but ignore such boorish concerns as efficiency, productivity, marketing, and competition."[41]

Elite lawyers could afford to brush aside temptations that were often overwhelming to hungrier low-status lawyers. As a beginning litigator, I frequently had to attend routine motion call in the Cook County Court. I would arrive promptly at 9 a.m., check with the clerk to find my place on the docket, and wait for my case to be called. Often I spent the whole morning awaiting my turn, fuming as other lawyers, who could not afford to sit around, openly slipped the clerk a bribe to move their cases up on the list.

It is, of course, easy to denounce the sins that we ourselves are not tempted to commit. The main pressures on the ethics of large-firm lawyers always came from powerful corporate clients who were not interested in being lectured on the public interest or the good of the legal system. The typical large firm's relative independence from any one client permitted it to resist the commoner sorts of pressures for questionable practices. When serious competition for clients set in, though, elite attitudes began to change. The much-despised contingent fee, for example, began to appear in a new light when valued clients asked for special pricing arrangements. Respectable firms have begun to depart from hourly billing in many instances—offering discounts, piecework prices, and, yes, even taking a percentage of recovery as part of the fee.

Now that corporate clients handle much routine work in their own legal departments, the nature of the tasks performed in big law firms is changing. No longer securely ensconced in long-term arrangements to supply almost all of a business's legal needs, large-firm lawyers are being retained on an "as needed" basis for particularly difficult tasks.[42] The familiar day-to-day relationship that used to exist between corporate managers and valued counselors in firms has given way to regular consultation with house counsel. Corporate clients now seek the assistance of high-priced outside specialists mainly when faced with a major lawsuit, a large public offering of securities, or some other extremely complex problem or transaction that requires special skill and experience. What companies now want most from outside lawyers is what low-status clients have always desired in highly charged, one-shot situations: zealous representation, rather than co-deliberation.

Large law firms found it increasingly hard to take the high ground as the balance of power in the lawyer-client relationship shifted. Savvy corporate counsel (often former partners in law firms) began to monitor billing practices, to raise questions about "overlawyering," and to engage in comparison shopping for lawyers. House counsel consolidated their own power by parceling out legal business, rather than continuing their companies' traditional ties with a single firm. As clients exercised their newfound clout, one staid firm after another, with new policy committees in place, began cutting corners. Archibald Cox lamented, in a speech to the ABA, that few lawyers in the 1980s seemed to be willing to say to clients, "Yes, the law lets you do that, but don't do it. It is a rotten thing to do."[43] Certainly many lawyers for Charles Keating (of savings and loan fame) bit their tongues as he played round-robin with seventy-seven law firms, threatening to replace them if they didn't go along with his wishes.[44]

The transformation of large-firm practice that began in the 1960s has affected lawyers' imaginations as well as their behavior. With increasing competition and bureaucratization, ideas of what being a lawyer is all about are changing. Some practitioners have taken to the new environment like ducks to water; others feel like the main ingredient in duck soup. Most feel torn between two worlds: their mental picture of what a lawyer is supposed to be doesn't match what they see and do every day.

With hindsight, what seems remarkable about the American legal profession from the 1920s to the 1960s is not that lawyers often failed to live up to the ideals their leaders publicly professed, but that lawyers were so widely oriented for so long to a common set of ideals. Even more remarkable is the evidence that lawyers' ideals had important effects on their habits and practices—effects that could and sometimes did override a variety of personal and economic considerations.[45]

The new big-firm ethos does not bode well for the preventive lawyering and independent counseling on which lawyers have traditionally prided themselves. The old "wise counselor" ideals were part of the idea of professionalism articulated by bar leaders in the earlier part of this century and summed up by Roscoe Pound in the epigraph to this chapter.[46] They held that lawyers can often serve their clients best by discouraging litigation, or by deliberating with them about a proposed course of action, rather than by unquestioningly carrying out the client's desires.[47] They assumed that most clients value the opportunity to explore all the angles of a problem with a knowledgeable adviser, one who is apt to come up with new insights, ideas, and perspectives. Law was supposed to be a learned and liberal profession, an art as well as a proud craft. The practice of law was a means of gaining a livelihood, but was to be pursued "in the spirit of public service." Its practitioners were to be independent both of clients and of government. Their relations with one another were to be civil and courteous as befits members of a common calling. A lawyer's advice to a client would be unaffected by possible benefits or detriments to the lawyer himself or his firm.

As critics of the profession never tire of pointing out, those ideals were often honored in the breach. But it would be a mistake to dismiss them as mere empty talk or camouflage. The lawyers who gained ascendancy in the profession from the 1920s onward were more skilled and better educated than American lawyers, as a group, had ever been. They were university-trained, genteel, and eager to distinguish themselves from the buccaneer lawyers of the gilded age. As described by legal historian Robert W. Gordon, they were a socially diverse group, united in their desire to improve the ethical tone of the profession:

> [B]oth patricians (for example, Henry Stimson, Grenville Clark, Francis Biddle, Dean Acheson) and middle-class WASPS (for example, Elihu Root, John J. McCloy, David Lilienthal Jr., A. A. Berle Jr., W. O. Douglas) have embraced the ideal of independent lawyering. The ideal has also found some of its greatest exponents among Jewish lawyers (for example, Louis Brandeis, Louis Marshall, Felix Frankfurter, Jerome Frank) who, excluded from the inner circles of the WASP elite, had the vantage point of marginality from which to scold that elite for selling out its public service traditions to business clients.[48]

Many prominent specialists in commercial law, tax, banking, corporation and securities law, trusts, and estates gave substantial time and effort to rehabilitating the profession's tarnished ideals and to framing ethical norms suited to novel modern dilemmas. They seemed concerned not only to distinguish themselves from the lawyer sidekicks of robber barons but also to make clear they were no mere tools of their own clients. "About half the practice of a decent lawyer," lawyer-statesman Elihu Root is supposed to have said, "consists in telling would-be clients that they are damned fools and should stop."[49] Indeed, it was once considered to be a lawyer's duty to persuade the client to attend to the spirit as well as the letter of the law.

The concepts of professionalism promoted by bar leaders were remarkably stable and consistent from the 1920s to the mid-1960s. Rayman Solomon, after studying hundreds of speeches and articles from that period, concluded that for several decades "the bar's understanding of the meaning and responsibilities of being a legal professional remained relatively unchanged."[50] Forty years is a relatively short interval in legal history, but it was long enough to create the illusion of certain dependable verities in the world of corporate practice: associates who did good work would ordinarily progress to partnership; others would be let down gently; partnership with its role divisions was a reasonably secure status; independence from clients could and should be asserted when the occasion required; economic considerations would be subordinated, if need arose, to firm solidarity or to ideals of right conduct.

Today's lawyers are wandering amidst the ruins of those understandings. A learned profession? Early specialization and relentless time pressure mock the aspiration to be more than a technocrat. A common calling? Ask the associates and partners who were laid off by the same people who talked up "firm spirit" in job interviews. Independent professionals? When house counsel began switching business from one firm to another, how many lawyers told erring clients they were "damned fools"? Public service? Sure, just as soon as they've billed their 1,800 hours. Law "incidentally" a livelihood? Only in the dreams of Roscoe Pound.

Lawyers' cherished image of themselves as independent

professionals is threatened from two directions: the increase in clients' bargaining power and the growing numbers of lawyers who are technocrat employees in state or federal government offices and private industry. Those types of employment are highly satisfying to many people, especially those for whom the potential rewards of private practice do not outweigh its pressures and risks. But they are hard to square with the image of an independent professional.[51]

The traditional ideal of lawyers that has flourished most in the new atmosphere is client loyalty with its concomitant duty of zealous representation. The friend-of-the-client ideal is easy to espouse under current conditions, a real crowd pleaser. According to a recent survey, the trait of lawyers that the public most admires is "putting clients' interests first."[52] A lawyer who regularly gives priority to client loyalty not only can simplify an otherwise complicated life but can generally look good while following the course of least resistance. His or her other aspirations—to be an artisan of order, a peacemaker, a public-spirited court officer, or a lawyer for the situation—don't have to be completely abandoned, just subordinated.[53] The client-centered approach not only makes it easier to deal with competing obligations; it seductively promises to reconstruct a more pragmatic sort of professionalism. The lawyer is relieved from the agonizing struggle to give each of his loyalties its due and becomes a virtuoso of single-mindedness—like a professional soldier, or the surgeon who drapes all but the affected part of the patient under a sheet.

A decided emphasis on client loyalty has, of course, long been the hallmark of litigators' ideals, especially of litigators engaged in criminal defense work. In fact, it's a good guess that public appreciation for that quality owes a lot to the portrayal of the courtroom lawyer's single-minded devotion in films and television series. (In a 1993 poll, one real criminal defender, F. Lee Bailey, and one fictional one, Perry Mason, topped the "most admired lawyer" list.[54]) If we are currently observing a certain drift among lawyers to a particular version of litigators' ideals, it seems worthwhile to inquire into what has been happening in the world of those specialists who have most wholeheartedly embraced the ethic of zealous client representation.

Over the past three decades the conflicts that Karl Llewellyn taught his students to expect have proliferated. There is the conflict all lawyers experience as they are pulled and tugged by competing claims on their loyalties. There is the conflict within the profession as a whole, and within the soul of each individual lawyer, between rival visions of excellence. And there are the social conflicts that lawyers are called upon to mediate and prosecute on behalf of others. When disputes between citizen and citizen, or citizen and state, fail to yield to ordinary methods of settlement, the most colorful members of the legal profession appear on the scene: the men and women who may be called the connoisseurs of conflict.

3

Connoisseurs of Conflict

[A]n advocate, in the discharge of his duty, knows but one person in all the world, and that person is his client. To save that client by all means and expedients, and at all hazards and costs to other persons, and, among them, to himself, is his first and only duty; and in performing this duty he must not regard the alarm, the torments, the destruction which he may bring upon others. —LORD BROUGHAM[1]

Lawyers know that Lord Brougham's celebrated description of the advocate is vastly oversimplified. But the image of a single-minded champion has strong popular appeal. Indeed, nearly all of America's legendary lawyer heroes have been litigators. When we hear their stories, we think: "That's the kind of person I'd like to have by my side if I were in deep trouble." Even if John Adams had not been a revolutionary leader and President, he would have gained a place in legal history for his brave and successful defense of the British soldier accused of firing the first shot in the Boston Massacre. Adams, as one commentator has pointed out, "perfectly illustrated what would become the archetypal positive image of the virtuous lawyer in the United States—a protector who stands with his or her client against all the world no matter what the odds; indeed, no matter what the attorney's personal political views or estimate of the client's 'guilt' or 'innocence,' a matter left to judge and jury."[2] We admire Clarence Darrow and other colorful champions of unpopular clients and noble causes not only for their courage but for their single-minded devotion to their clients. They are the closest thing America has to the Knights of the Round Table.

Though other lawyers perform the bulk of the nation's legal

work,[3] it is litigators, especially criminal prosecutors and defenders, who fascinate the public. The prestige of litigation *within* the profession, however, has varied. It declined considerably around the turn of the present century, concomitant with the rising status of corporate counselors. In recent years, it has risen again as corporations have abandoned their traditional reluctance to sue one another. Until the late nineteenth century, the profession was not so rigidly divided between office and courtroom lawyers as it is now. Most attorneys offered a full range of services, including the conduct of trials and appeals when other methods of resolving disputes broke down. Unlike their counterparts in England or on the Continent, where a stricter division of labor has long existed between transactional lawyers and litigators, lawyers in early America had to be jacks-of-all-trades. They were generalists by necessity. They learned their craft through apprenticeship and served a wide variety of clients.

By the early twentieth century, however, the era of the generalist country lawyer was basically over. With the rise of large corporations, the practice of law became increasingly specialized, as to both clientele and subject matter. Lawyers responded to demands of corporate clients for particular kinds of highly skilled services by forming larger partnerships where they developed the sorts of expertise that big businesses required. Those corporate law firms, in turn, transformed the practice of law. They not only promoted a separation between the cultures of counselors and advocates; they also accentuated the distinctions between elite and low-status lawyers.

The division of labor within firms devoted to business clients led to the creation of separate litigation departments. But these departments were initially regarded as a necessary evil, and kept small. At the turn of the century, according to the historian of Cravath, Swaine & Moore, "the great corporate lawyers of the day drew their reputations more from their abilities in the conference room and facility in drafting documents than from their persuasiveness before the courts."[4] An aspiring courtroom lawyer seeking association with the predecessor of the Cravath firm was told by a senior partner: "New York is not a very good field for one who desires to make a specialty of court practice or litigated work. The business connected with corporations and general office practice is much more profitable and satisfactory and you will find that the better class of men at our Bar prefer work in that line."[5]

Recalling his days in a leading Boston firm in the 1930s, Judge Charles Wyzanski wrote,

> I do not think most people realized how cut off Ropes and Gray was . . . from the judicial system. Surely, we were not as much involved with judges and with courts as is the present Harvard faculty with its peripatetic professors, lining their pockets with fees which would never fit within the small pocket of the barrister's gown.[6]

As Galanter and Palay put it: "Disdain of litigation reflected the prevailing attitude among the corporate establishment that it was not quite nice to sue."[7]

The distaste of the "better class" of lawyers for litigation, coupled with the large firms' lack of interest in plaintiffs' personal injury, criminal, and domestic relations work, left niches for others. This created opportunities that were especially welcome to the Irish, Italian, and Eastern European Jewish lawyers who appeared on the scene in the wake of the great wave of immigration between 1891 and 1920.[8] The barrister ethos in the United States even today retains some flavor of the cultures of ghetto Catholics and Jews who were long excluded from elite firms. Litigation is now a respected specialty within high-status firms, but the habits and attitudes of litigators remain somewhat different from those of the transactional lawyers down the hall.

Although few of the leading partners of prestigious firms earlier in the century were litigators, there were some notable exceptions. In 1921, when former Solicitor General John W. Davis joined what is now known as Davis Polk & Wardwell, that firm immediately became a magnet for clients seeking his services and for young lawyers who hoped to learn the arts of advocacy from an acknowledged master. Davis's specialty was appellate work, the more cerebral branch of litigation.

Davis was the consummate appellate advocate of the first half of the twentieth century. While the founders of other Wall Street firms were helping their clients destroy competitors and bust unions, he was learning his trade in a small law office in Clarksburg, West Virginia.[9] In those years, he and his father handled the affairs of individual clients and small businessmen, as well as the new corporate enterprises, moving back and forth from office to courthouse. Davis always maintained that a lawyer should try to prevent strife whenever possible. A wise legal counselor, he claimed, had "as many opportunities to do good as a clergyman." But when strife was inevitable, he did not flinch. He gained early local notoriety for representing a group of striking coal miners charged with violating one of the injunctions commonly used in those days to harass workers' associations. During his West Virginia years, Davis acquired a reputation for effective courtroom work, as well as all-around craftsmanship. A colleague later recalled: "His bearing was uniformly serious and dignified, his manner courteous, his arguments logical, his diction exact, almost to perfection, and he scrupulously never violated his unvaried duty to the court and the respect due adversary counsel."

In 1910, the young Clarksburg attorney successfully ran for Congress, where his speaking and drafting abilities earned him a reputation as the ablest lawyer in the House of Representatives. That renown, in turn, led to his appointment as Solicitor General of the United States. As the government's lawyer from 1913 to 1918, Davis grappled with the legal aspects of the major social and economic issues of the times. He appeared in antitrust prosecutions of corporations charged with monopolistic or restrictive trade practices, and in a host of cases where he defended the constitutionality of federal and state health and safety regulations, including a federal ban on interstate sale of goods made by child labor. Though he lost the latter case, *Hammer* v. *Dagenhart*, he had the satisfaction of seeing his reasoning adopted in Oliver Wendell Holmes's stinging dissent from that now discredited decision. In two early civil rights cases, Davis successfully attacked a literacy law that effectively barred many African Americans from voting, and convinced the Court that Alabama was running its prison system in violation of the Thirteenth Amendment's ban on slavery.[10]

Davis had private doubts about the wisdom of some of the positions he was obliged to defend. But the government was his client and he believed that the merits of the legislation in question were not the concern of the Solicitor General.[11] Holmes regarded Davis as the best advocate he had ever heard. "Of all the persons who appeared before the Court in my time, there was never anybody more elegant, more clear, more concise or more logical than John W. Davis," Holmes said.[12]

After serving as Solicitor General, Davis was appointed Ambassador to the Court of St. James's. Thus when he began his career as a Wall Street lawyer in 1921, he was nearing the age of fifty and had been away from private practice for eleven years. In a letter to his daughter, Davis confessed anxiety: "How far, I wonder, has my hand lost its cunning?"[13]

The answer was plain a year later when he persuaded the Supreme Court that a Pennsylvania mining regulation was unconstitutional. The statute sought to remedy the situation created when mine owners sold surface rights to land, retaining ownership of the underlying minerals. Later, when the companies began to take out the coal, the soil in many places subsided, threatening the dwellings of the surface owners. The Pennsylvania legislature's solution was to require the mining companies to leave enough coal in place to support the surface. That regulation, Davis argued, would have been constitutionally permissible if the state had engaged to compensate the companies for the unminable coal. But to flatly forbid the coal companies to remove what was theirs was a "taking" of private property without "just compensation"—just as if the state had carted off the coal and burned it in the furnaces of public buildings. Justice Holmes, though ordinarily disposed to defer to legislative action, agreed. Here, he was dealing, not with vague language like "due process," but with an explicit constitutional provision protecting private property from uncompensated taking. Any regulation which went "too far" in depriving an owner of the benefit of his property, Holmes ruled, was equivalent to a taking. Holmes's opinion in *Pennsylvania Coal Co.* v. *Mahon* became the leading authority for decades on the limits of governmental power to regulate private property.[14]

Two years later, in 1924, Davis again interrupted his legal career, this time to run as the Democratic Party's candidate for President. The American people chose Calvin Coolidge, however, and sent Davis back to the practice of law. Over the next three decades, by all accounts, Davis was even more polished and persuasive than he had been as Solicitor General. His strengths resided in the way he could win over his listeners merely by stating the facts of the case, in his ability to identify and explain the essential points in a complex matter, and in his skillful resort to the reasons behind and policy consequences of the rules on which he relied.[15] Even Felix Frankfurter and Learned Hand, both of whom questioned his intellectual depth, found it hard to resist the spell of his advocacy.[16] When Davis rose to speak, Frankfurter recalled, "throughout the courtroom murmurs would cease and the court would sit back in anticipation of a superb performance."[17] Hand confided to Joseph Proskauer, "I do not like to have John W. Davis come into my courtroom. I am so fascinated by his eloquence and charm that I always fear that I am going to decide in his favor irrespective of the merits of the case."[18]

Davis in his Wall Street period often found himself (as in *Pennsylvania Coal*) arguing positions opposed to those he had taken as Solicitor General. The same lawyer who had once championed the progressive legislation of the Wilson era was now challenging the constitutionality of such New Deal statutes as the National Labor Relations Act. This use of his talents, plus Davis's impressive portfolio of corporate clients, drew disapproving comment from progressives and New Dealers. Felix Frankfurter was sharply critical of him for putting his gifts in the service of business, even implying that Davis cared more for money than for the public interest.[19]

That was hardly fair to Davis, whose love of the law was no less than Frankfurter's, but whose commitments and concepts of public service were different. From his corner office at Davis Polk, the senior partner was a one-man legal aid society for fellow West Virginians, to whom he felt united by tradition and sentiment. He wrote several opinion letters a year to men and women from his home state in all walks of life. Frequently, too, he came to the aid of West Virginians who ran afoul of the law in the bewildering streets of New York. The receptionists at Davis Polk had instructions to admit anyone who claimed acquaintance with the senior partner.[20]

Davis also provided pro bono representation in several high-profile cases. The best known of these was theologian Douglas C. McIntosh's challenge to an interpretation of the naturalization laws that barred from citizenship individuals who were conscientiously opposed to bearing arms. Though Davis lost that case in the Supreme Court, he once again had the satisfaction of provoking a dissent joined by the most distinguished members of the Court, including Holmes.[21] Years later, that dissent, authored by Chief Justice Hughes, became the basis of the majority ruling in a case where Davis and the ACLU filed a friend-of-the-court brief urging the Court to reconsider its interpretation of the naturalization laws.[22] In the cold war era, Davis lent his assistance to J. Robert Oppenheimer's efforts to regain his security clearance and appeared twice as a character witness for Alger Hiss. Morris Ernst recalled, "There was no difficulty in getting John W. Davis to take unpopular cases."[23]

What really galled Frankfurter seems not so much Davis's mid-career move to Wall Street as his conservative social and economic views. But just as Frankfurter strove with considerable success to put his progressive views aside while judging, Davis seems to have been able to keep his conservative convictions from interfering with his advocacy until, as we shall see, the fateful last argument of his career. Overall, something like the classical English barrister's view of advocacy seems to have been Davis's polestar: "The advocate lends his exertions to all, himself to none."[24]

Davis's crowning achievement as an advocate came in May 1952 when, at the age of seventy-nine, he convinced a Supreme Court majority that the President of the United States had exceeded his authority by "seizing" the nation's steel industry. Harry Truman, in order to avert a steelworkers' strike during the Korean War, had issued an executive order putting the Secretary of Commerce in charge of running the mills. That action was enormously controversial. It brought the President and the Court into uncharted constitutional territory that American public officials have generally avoided. Seldom does a President test the outer limits of his powers. Rarely does the Supreme Court issue an order to the chief executive. To constitutional scholar Paul Freund, Davis's historic victory in *Youngstown Sheet & Tube* v. *Sawyer* echoed "the ancient voices of Bracton and Coke proclaiming that not even the King is above the law."[25] The decision was an important precedent years later in the next great confrontation between the Court and a President, *United States* v. *Nixon*.[26]

In the view of many of his admirers, Davis should have chosen to rest on his laurels after the steel case. But almost immediately, against the advice of friends, partners, and his daughter, he agreed to appear before the Supreme Court one last time. The case involved the question of whether South Carolina's segregated public elementary and high school system could withstand scrutiny under the Equal Protection Clause of the Fourteenth Amendment to the Constitution. The legal argument centered on an 1896 precedent, *Plessy* v. *Ferguson*, upholding a state statute mandating separate but equal accommodations (on passenger trains).[27] The South Carolina litigation, consolidated with a number of related cases from other states, reached the Supreme Court under the name of the Kansas case, *Brown* v. *Board of Education*.[28]

Brown was the culmination of a strategy worked out over a period of many years by NAACP leaders Charles Hamilton Houston and William Hastie, with the assistance of their general counsel, Thurgood Marshall. As a law student at Howard University in the early 1930s, Marshall had often cut classes to watch Davis argue cases. Marshall later recalled that, on those occasions, "I'd ask myself, 'Will I ever, ever . . . ?' and every time I had to answer, 'No, never.' " Davis was then at the top of his form. He was Marshall's "beau ideal" of a lawyer.[29]

Marshall, in his mid-forties at the time of *Brown*, was at the height of his own powers, having argued and won cases attacking the constitutionality of white democratic primaries, segregation on interstate buses, racially restrictive covenants, and the exclusion of blacks from public institutions of higher education. An admiring eulogist would later describe him as "a legal strategist, farseeing to the point of genius," who had carried out a "battle plan worthy of Clausewitz."[30] The first step in the NAACP's strategy was to convince a white judiciary to mandate equal treatment to a small and sympathetic class of black plaintiffs—well-qualified young men and women who had been denied admission on grounds of race (as Marshall himself had been) to graduate and professional schools in state universities. Those precedents then became the basis for further attacks on the system of segregation, building up to the historic assault on the citadel of segregated public lower schools. Judge Constance Baker Motley, a member of the NAACP legal staff in those days, recalled that Marshall used to tell the lawyers over and over: "Our Constitution is color-blind." That quotation (from the first Justice Harlan), she said, "became our basic legal creed."[31] Along the way, Marshall set exacting standards for himself and his associates, determined that no one should ever charge the NAACP with filing sloppy pleadings or briefs.[32]

When Marshall heard that John W. Davis would be his opponent in the South Carolina school desegregation case, he assumed that Davis was animated primarily by his long-standing concern for states' rights.[33] But Davis was as emotionally engaged in the historic contest as Marshall. Born eight years after the end of the Civil War, Davis was a man of the old South. He believed, according to his biographer William Harbaugh, not only that segregation was constitutional but that it

John W. Davis and Thurgood Marshall chatting on the day of their first fateful encounter in the school desegregation cases, December 2, 1952 *(AP/Wide World Photos)*

was part of a morally acceptable way of life. He regarded blacks, in the aggregate, as inherently inferior to whites.[34] He took the case without a retainer and wrote much of the brief himself.

In December 1952 and again in reargument a year later, the two giants faced each other in the most celebrated Supreme Court litigation of the twentieth century. Both Marshall and Davis, it is said, were at their best in their first encounter. By December 1953, however, Davis was showing his age. At eighty, he still looked majestic in his morning coat. But his memory, sadly, had begun to fade; at one point he lost his train of thought and stumbled.[35] Marshall (whose motto had long been "Lose your head, lose your case") was calm, at ease, conversational, laying out his argument in a clear and rational manner.

When Marshall sat down, Davis's daughter Julia congratulated Marshall's wife on his performance. "So you are the daughter of John Davis," said Mrs. Marshall. "My husband admires him so much."[36]

In strictly legal terms, Davis had made the best possible case for his clients. But a new era was dawning. Between the first and second arguments in *Brown*, a fateful event had occurred, prompting Felix Frankfurter to remark to a clerk that "this is the first indication I have ever had that there is a God."[37] On September 8, 1953, Chief Justice Fred Vinson suddenly died of a heart attack at the age of sixty-three. On September 30, President Eisenhower named Earl Warren to replace him. The decision in favor of the school desegregation plaintiffs came down on May 17, 1954.

Marshall had been a gracious opponent, forbidding his younger associates to make snide remarks about Davis. Davis, for his part, was noble in defeat. Though "shattered" by the Court's ruling, he called Marshall that afternoon to congratulate him, and later wrote to an old friend that it was good for the country that the decision had been unanimous.[38]

Marshall's civil rights victories, which culminated in the school desegregation decision, would by themselves have earned him a place with Davis in the pantheon of appellate advocates, but other distinctions lay ahead of him. In 1961, he was appointed by President Kennedy to the Second Circuit Court of Appeals. At President Johnson's request, he left the bench to become Solicitor General. Then, in 1967, Johnson named Thurgood Marshall the country's first African-American Supreme Court justice.

At first glance, Davis and Marshall would appear to have been as different from each other as two lawyers could be. Marshall was devoted to a single cause from beginning to end, while Davis, until his involvement in the school case, kept a certain aloofness from his clients and their varied concerns. Most of Marshall's career was devoted to eradicating the way of life and worldview that Davis had been unable to fully transcend. As advocates, however, they had much in common.

Davis and Marshall represented ideals of advocacy that soon would be rivaled by radically different visions. Just how much the two lawyers shared is plain when one contrasts them with the new breed of litigators who took center stage from the late 1960s onward.

Both Davis and Marshall refrained from thrusting their individual personalities to the fore. There was no question in either man's case that the client's interest came before his own. In contrast to their many media-conscious successors, both were remarkably self-effacing. "I never saw [Davis] steal the spotlight," said Burton Pine, the U.S. District Court judge in the highly publicized steel seizure case.[39] Upon learning that the stenographic transcript of his winning argument in that case was hopelessly garbled, Davis merely shrugged and remarked, "So my oral argument vanishes, as most oral deliverances should, into the limbo of the past."[40] Thurgood Marshall, though more of a showman, always kept his clients and their causes in the foreground while he relentlessly persevered in the long-term strategy to eliminate Jim Crow.

Neither Davis nor Marshall was recognizably related to what has come to be known as a Rambo litigator. That now familiar creature, as former American Bar Association president John J. Curtin, Jr., has put it, is a lawyer who treats litigation as a variant of scorched-earth warfare. Curtin took the occasion of a presidential column in the *ABA Journal* to sound an alarm about the spread of unprofessional tactics. He deplored the use of military terminology to describe legal maneuvers; the manipulation and misstatement of facts and law; the abuse of motions and discovery for harassment; the lawyers who put themselves, rather than the client, at center stage; and the rising incidence of incivility.[41] (A new low under that last heading may have been reached recently by the Chicago lawyer who wrote his opponent that if she would not stipulate to a continuance he would "send someone over to perform a clitoridectomy" on her.[42])

Both Davis and Marshall belonged to a legal world in which their specialty, litigation, was still generally regarded as a necessary evil, the last resort after all other methods for resolving disputes had proved futile. Like the country lawyer he once was, Davis regarded preventive advice as one of a lawyer's primary responsibilities, and would turn a client away rather than invent ingenious devices to circumvent the law.[43] It was a litigator's duty, he often said, to discourage litigation whenever possible. Thurgood Marshall and his colleagues, as we often forget today, originally turned to litigation because all other avenues were tightly closed to those they represented.

Over Davis's and Marshall's lifetimes, litigation steadily rose in prestige. In some respectable firms, like Boston's Hale & Dorr or Chicago's Jenner & Block, trial work as well as appeals became leading specialties. Courtly litigators like Joseph N. Welch and Albert Jenner were widely respected. The twinkly-eyed but sharp-tongued Welch became something of a folk hero for besting Senator Joseph McCarthy in several televised exchanges during the Army-McCarthy hearings. Jenner, a policeman's son who rose to head a major Chicago firm after working his way through school as a boxer, was a legend in midwestern legal circles. His reputation for skill and integrity earned him appointments to the Warren Commission investigating the Kennedy assassination and to the national commission on violence appointed by President Johnson. He showed his independence when, as minority counsel to the House Watergate investigation, he concluded (to the dismay of many fellow Republicans) that President Nixon should be impeached.

By the mid-1970s, however, a new breed of litigator was coming into prominence. Old-school lawyers, encountering new tactics, began to play rougher. The country was in the midst of what has come to be called the "litigation explosion." That term was much bandied about in the 1992 presidential campaign, when President Bush and Vice President Quayle charged that costly and excessive litigation was wrecking the court system, undermining our country's competitive position, contributing to the rising cost of consumer goods and insurance, and benefiting no one so much as lawyers. The organized bar was quick to dispute the effect on competition and to retort that our litigation system is second to none in protecting the poor, compensating for injuries, redressing injustice, and assuring corporate accountability. What, actually, is the litigation explosion, and how bad is it?

All parties to the debate seem to agree that the term "explosion" refers to a dramatic increase in the use of federal courts, where filings tripled between 1960 and 1990. State courts, though severely overcrowded, have witnessed a much less steep rise in use. The largest single category of lawsuits filed in federal courts, according to a 1993 study, consists of contract disputes between large corporations, reflecting the increased propensity of businesses to sue one another.[44] The rest of the leap in federal filings is attributable mainly to the following types of cases: new civil rights claims, personal injury suits (often related to mass injuries such as those in connection with asbestos or new technologies); prisoner petitions; social security cases; and government suits for recovery of overpayments.[45]

Legal sociologist Marc Galanter belongs to the school of thought that pooh-poohs alarmist rhetoric about litigiousness. A rise in litigation is only to be expected, he argues, as people try to work out their problems in a complex, technologically advanced, populous regulatory state where fewer and fewer social mechanisms for dispute resolution are available.[46]

According to Walter Olson, who takes the opposite view, America's high litigation rates afford cause for serious concern. The marked erosion, he contends, of the formal barriers and informal understandings that once made it difficult to haul someone into court without first laying out a plausible basis for suit is itself a major problem.[47] That change, he argues, is partly due to the work of a generation of activist judges. The escalating legal uncertainty and unpredictability, adds critic L. Gordon Crovitz, "makes U.S. law the subject of endless fascination and horror, especially to foreigners. Silly lawsuits are reported overseas the way we might chuckle at British toad crossings or Japanese commutes."[48]

A customary practice that long separated big-firm litigators from their small-firm counterparts was the refusal of the former to enter into "contingent fee" arrangements. In most other nations, lawyers are forbidden to bring lawsuits with the understanding that their fee will take the form of a percentage of the recovery, if any. The reason for the ban is that such arrangements are thought to promote harassing litigation designed to extort settlements, as well as to tempt lawyers to put their own interests ahead of the client's.[49] But the countries that have outlawed contingent fees generally address their citizens' legal needs by regulating legal fees, or by providing broad-based legal assistance, comprehensive social insurance, or some combination thereof.[50] Under American circumstances, where such measures are absent, the contingent fee provides many people with their only practical chance of access to the courts. What is new and noteworthy in the United States is that, as business clients have flexed their muscles and demanded competitive pricing arrangements, large firms have managed to overcome their scruples against contingent fees.

Until the 1980s, elite lawyers also professed to abhor the idea of advertising, which was banned by the professional canons of ethics. Advertising, they said, smacked of soliciting business and even of stirring up litigation, two things that no respectable lawyer was supposed to do. Chief Justice Warren Burger once told an American Bar Association group that if he were in private practice he would rather dig ditches than advertise for clients. A well-earned reputation for competence and integrity was the best advertisement, bar leaders solemnly maintained. Once again, however, this was a case of condemning activities that corporate law firms were hardly ever tempted to engage in anyway.

Opponents of the advertising and solicitation bans had always pointed out that those rules made it difficult for poor, uneducated persons to obtain information about lawyers who might help them vindicate their rights and obtain redress for their injuries. In 1977, the Supreme Court agreed, holding that blanket bans on lawyer advertising violated the right to free speech. The Court said they "served to burden access to legal services, particularly for the not-quite-poor and the unknowledgeable."[51] Subsequent judicial decisions relaxed the traditional ban on solicitation. Within a decade, many of the nation's largest law firms decided that a little self-promotion might not be such a bad thing after all. Still looking down their noses at TV ads and lawyers who flock to the scene of mass disasters, many firms engaged public relations agencies to promote their images. A growing number hired full-time, in-house marketing directors.

Litigators in elite law firms, moreover, are routinely resorting to tactics that would have scandalized John W. Davis.[52] All lawyers know that often the best thing a litigator can do for a client is to discourage the bringing of a lawsuit or to arrange its early settlement. No one has ever put it better than Abraham Lincoln:

> Persuade your neighbors to compromise whenever you can. Point out to them how the nominal winner is often a real loser—in fees, expenses, and waste of time. As a peacemaker the lawyer has a superior opportunity of being a good man. There will still be business enough.[53]

Contemporary lawyers, to the contrary, are apt to see negotiation and settlement, not as peacemaking activity, but as war by other means, an effort to gain victory by intimidating, outspending, or otherwise grinding down one's opponent. Big-firm litigators are sought out as often for their ingenuity in wearing out their adversaries through expensive delaying tactics as for their courtroom skills. Indeed, many an associate who eagerly joined a litigation department has never been in court.

That state of affairs was brought about in part by the realization many years ago that certain procedural reforms designed to promote settlement and streamline trials could be deployed to harass opponents. That abuse was not foreseen by those who designed pretrial "discovery" rules permitting each party in a lawsuit to pose written questions to the other (interrogatories), to inspect documents in the other's possession, and to take formal statements under oath (depositions) from parties and potential witnesses. The basic idea that all parties would benefit from advance disclosure of testimony was a sound one. But attorneys representing economically powerful clients now regularly use these devices to outwait and outspend their opponents as well as to obtain pertinent information. A financially weaker party can often be brought to his knees under barrages of interrogatories spewed out by word processors, lengthy and intrusive depositions, and voluminous demands for production of documents.

The Diaghilev of discovery seems to have been the late Bruce Bromley, a leading partner at Cravath, Swaine & Moore. Bromley once boasted to an audience of Stanford law students, "I was born, I think, to be a protractor. . . . I could take the simplest antitrust case and protract for the defense almost to infinity. . . . [One case] lasted 14 years. . . . Despite 50,000 pages of testimony, there really wasn't any dispute about the facts. . . . We won that case, and, as you know, my firm's meter was running all the time—every month for 14 years."[54] Mr. Bromley's grateful partners endowed a chair in his memory at the Harvard Law School, from which Arthur Miller, the Bruce Bromley Professor, has declaimed against an out-of-control discovery system:

> This pre-trial structure permits artful attorneys to hide the ball and keep alive hopeless claims, as well as defenses, for a much longer time than [formerly]. In many ways, contemporary federal litigation is analogous to the dance marathon contests of yesteryear. The object of the exercise is to . . . hang on to one's client, and then drift aimlessly and endlessly to the litigation music for as long as possible, hoping that everyone else will collapse from exhaustion.[55]

The discovery system has proved difficult to reform, not for want of constructive ideas, but because plaintiffs' and defendants' lawyers have joined forces to resist measures designed to limit abuses.

In recent years, American advocates have begun to take on

an eerie resemblance to their counterparts of late Roman times. That "splendid and popular class," according to Gibbon, "are described for the most part as ignorant and rapacious guides, who conducted their clients through a maze of expense, of delay, and of disappointment; from whence, after a tedious series of years, they were at length dismissed, when their patience and fortune were almost exhausted."[56] One busy practitioner told me that he has seen contemporary versions of those Roman rascals appraise one-shot clients and remark, "There's more meat left on that turkey."

Just as clients' increased bargaining power and firms' furious competition for business wreaked havoc with counselors' ideals, the same developments plus the litigation explosion seem to have left advocates' ideals in a shambles as well. The political and financial scandals involving lawyers in the 1970s and 1980s led to much outcry and hand-wringing about the decline of legal ethics. "How in God's name could so many lawyers get involved in something like this?" asked John Dean, voicing the question on many minds when the Watergate saga unfolded. And as the events leading up to the Lincoln Savings & Loan debacle came to light, Judge Stanley Sporkin asked where the attorneys had been: "Why didn't any of them speak up or disassociate themselves from the[se] transactions?"[57]

Still, if one's benchmark for corporate firms is the palmy days at the turn of the century when lawyers were using every tactic in the book (and many that were not) to help clients bust unions, consolidate monopolies, drive competitors out of business, and obtain favorable treatment from judges and legislators, it would be hard to demonstrate a marked ethical decline. Many among the founders of today's grand Wall Street firms were no strangers to the kind of behavior that again became rampant in the 1980s. Men whose portraits now adorn the walls of paneled law libraries were often up to their sideburns in Tammany Hall–style corruption. Many collaborated with and covered up dealings of railroad builders, oil pioneers, and utility magnates that included bribery and violence.[58]

If, on the other hand, we take as our base for comparison

the 1950s and the early 1960s, there have been striking changes in the habits and attitudes of legal elites and opinion leaders. Legal ethicists still insist that the essence of a lawyer's role is "to provide independent, professional judgment" in counseling and litigation alike.[59] But lawyers' independence, always a shaky concept, has been rendered even more precarious in recent years, according to Robert Nelson, who began studying large-firm culture in 1979. Forced to compete aggressively for business, firms find it nearly impossible to maintain a discreet distance from their clients. "They cannot take the posture of neutral experts seeking to achieve a just resolution of conflicting positions; they must present themselves as zealous advocates."[60]

Thus the professional ideal of independence has begun to recede while the client loyalty ideal advances. Heightened competition has put much less strain on lawyers' ethical obligations to their clients than on their duties to court and community. Giving highest priority to zealous client service preserves the aura of professionalism even when other traditional ideals become more difficult to realize in practice. It enables the lawyer to look good while doing what clients want him to do. But that superficially appealing solution to the conflicts that attend a lawyer's role sweeps serious problems under the carpet. The popular image of the lawyer as the client's champion against a hostile world is drawn from criminal defense work—in which the case for full-bore partisanship of the type described by Lord Brougham is strongest. Yet even in the criminal context, traditional ideals of litigator conduct once encompassed independence and a duty to the legal system along with client loyalty. No-holds-barred advocacy is deeply problematic when the client is a powerful corporation in a civil case, or one of the many groups that style themselves as serving the "public interest," or a prosecutorial or inquisitorial arm of the state.

Client loyalty, moreover, no less than lawyer independence, can be a fig leaf covering the naked self-interest of lawyers. The drift at present seems to be toward a situation in which the first priority of many advocates and counselors alike is neither client nor court but the lawyer's own concerns. Critics seize on the increasingly open pursuit of narrow self-interest by lawyers as proof that law has become just another business. But that critique, as we shall see, rests on a faulty understanding of commerce. What actually happened as the profession adapted to new conditions by adopting a skimpy version of litigators' ideals was more complicated—and more tragic.

4

When Ethical Worlds Collide

A lawyer is a representative of clients, an officer of the legal system and a public citizen having special responsibility for the quality of justice.[1]

The prevailing notion among lawyers seems to be that the lawyer's duty of loyalty to the client is the first, the foremost, and, on occasion, the only duty of the lawyer.[2]

Chicago's financial district and the seat of its city government are only a few blocks apart, yet they belong to two different worlds. I learned this in my first few months of law practice when, as low person on the totem pole, I had to handle routine motions in both state and federal courts. There was scarcely any difference in atmosphere between my firm's sedate quarters in the Continental Bank building and the austere federal courthouse just around the corner from the bank. An aura of solemnity surrounded the federal judges in their courtrooms, as it did our senior partners in their spacious but simply furnished offices. Lawyers exchanged pleasantries and conversed genially in the hallways of both places.

To walk from lower La Salle Street to the municipal and county courts on Washington between Clark and Dearborn, however, was to pass through a culture warp. From the outside, Chicago's new Civic Center on its massive plaza was no less imposing than the federal building. Within its crowded corridors and elevators, however, the hubbub was a marvel to behold. The Civic Center was filled with everything that made Chicago such an exhilarating and alarming city—jostling, shouting, joking, cajoling, backslapping, backstabbing, bargaining, dealing, favors granted, grudges paid with interest, intimidation, bribery, conciliation, grand gestures, obscene remarks, and the occasional spontaneous act of generosity.

Inside the courtrooms, protocol was more or less observed, but the strain was too much for some lawyers and judges. Lapses from decorum were frequent. One young litigator from my firm never forgot his first appearance in municipal court. Full of himself, he stepped up when his case was called, and began, as we were taught to do in law school: "May it please the court, my name is Edward R. Lev of Mayer, Friedlich, Spiess, Tierney, Brown & Platt and I represent the Continental Illinois National Bank and Trust Company of Chicago." The judge glared down at the unfortunate newcomer and remarked (to the delight of seasoned onlookers): "Well, bully for you!"

Another of my colleagues reported hearing the following exchange in open court one day while waiting for his own case to be heard:

"Counsel, the court believes it smells alcohol on counsel's breath."

"Is that so, your honor? Well, counsel believes he smells garlic on the court's breath."

In my own case, there was only one common thread between my experiences in the federal and state courts. The first time I appeared before Judge Julius Hoffman ("Julius the Just" of Chicago Seven fame) in the U.S. District Court, he interrupted my opening remarks to inquire: "Are you a lawyer, little lady?" Shortly after that incident, I was appointed to represent an indigent prisoner charged with murder, a man with the unusual first name of Coylee. When I sat down between the client and my co-counsel, Jim Brandvik, the Cook County Criminal Court judge asked me if I was the person accused of killing the taxi driver.

The separate spheres of Chicago's legal universe generally kept to their own orbits. Attorneys from large firms had relatively few dealings with small-time lawyers, and their business seldom took them to the county or municipal courts. As for the criminal courts, out by the jail at 26th and California, they might as well have been on Mars. They were the preserve of state prosecutors, public defenders, and the private criminal defense bar. In the mid-1960s, when I served on a Chicago Bar Association committee that provided trial attorneys to persons unable to afford a lawyer, we "downtown" types were tolerated as daft do-gooders by members of that tight-knit community. But we always knew we were on somebody else's turf. Our clients, accused felons who had exercised their right to have a volunteer from the bar association rather than a public defender, gambled that we outsiders would make up in legal ingenuity what we lacked in street smarts. One ex-con facing an armed robbery charge, however, tried to revoke his choice when I showed up to represent him. He wanted a real lawyer, not some girl who was obviously just out of law school. He was very annoyed when the judge refused his request, and disappointed again when Brandvik and I declined his invitation to represent him further after securing a not guilty verdict for him.

A former Chicago legal services attorney has recorded a rare occasion when the separate worlds of La Salle Street and the Civic Center intersected in a dramatic way. The courtrooms Steven Lubet frequented in the 1970s hadn't changed at all since I had visited them a decade earlier.

> The judges were nasty and peremptory. They rushed through the cases without allowing the defendants to talk, and they ridiculed defendants for attempting to say a few words in their own behalves. The clerks and bailiffs were worse, refusing to answer questions or give explanations. . . . Every courtroom on the eleventh floor seemed to operate in continual bedlam. The plaintiffs' attorneys were always huddled and talking to each other. The clerks were always shouting orders to the ill-fated defendants. The judges were always barking out their judgments—seven days to move, thirty days to pay, add on the attorney's fees, and do not ask any questions.[3]

One day, Lubet was sitting in one of the most disorderly courtrooms in the city. To his amazement, when the clerk bawled out the name of the next case, a well-dressed lawyer approached the bench and said, "Your honor, I would like to present Mr. Albert Jenner." Lubet tells what happened then:

> Once Mr. Jenner's presence was announced, the entire courtroom suddenly metamorphosed. The muttering plaintiffs' bar fell silent. Clerks began answering inquiries from unrepresented defendants. The judge actually asked questions about the facts and the law. . . . Furthermore, this effect lasted for the entire day, long after Mr. Jenner left.[4]

The appearance of Chicago's best-known litigator (apparently as a favor to a friend) was like a visitation from royalty. Long afterward, Lubet recounts, the regulars would mention the time when "Bert Jenner handled a case in our courtroom."[5]

Traders and Raiders

Why do corporate lawyers and lawyers for "people" move past each other in the legal system like bishops of different colors on a chessboard? To many, the answer might seem obvious: "It's social class, stupid!"[6] But the most recent work of Jane Jacobs reveals that there is more to the story. Jacobs maintains that human beings have had basically only two ways of making a living from prehistoric times to the present. One way of life is concerned with acquiring and protecting territories, the other with trading and producing for trade.[7] By a process resembling natural selection, humankind has developed its approaches to the ethics of making a living around two (and only two) matrices. Each system of economic ethics is perfectly calibrated to promote success and survival in the way of life it grounds.[8] Though the two survival strategies are strikingly different from each other, they are symbiotic in modern societies—for we need traders to invent, produce, and market goods and services and we also require raider-guardians like soldiers and policemen to maintain conditions of order and stability. Raiders and traders are almost inevitably uncomprehending or disdainful of one another. But Jacobs points out that from a global point of view each system is valid; and each in its own way is indispensable to the general welfare.

Today's guardians are descended, so to speak, from the hunters, gatherers, and warriors that once subsisted through sorties into unknown or hostile territories, picking up or forcibly taking what they needed. Modern soldiers, police officers, and politicians are usually more concerned with defending or administering territories than with acquiring or exploiting them. But like their forerunners, they flourish when certain qualities are in good supply among their members: cunning, prowess, display of strength, obedience and discipline, ostentation, largesse, readiness to take vengeance, respect for hierarchy, and, above all, loyalty. The loyalty that is the bedrock of their relationships not only promotes their common objectives but keeps these dangerous people from harming one another. They are rightly suspicious of trading, for raiders' loyalty to each other and to their task must not be for sale.

In the societies that emerged when human beings began producing, selling, and figuring out ways to improve crops and goods, the central value is honesty, for the good reason that commerce and science cannot prosper without a good deal of trust. Traders set great store by habits and policies that reinforce trust and honesty: shunning violence; reaching voluntary agreements; respecting contracts; thriftiness and lack of ostentation; willingness to compromise; tolerance; and courtesy. Unlike the clannish raiders, traders collaborate easily with strangers. They are justly wary of force and deception, despite the tempting short-term benefits of such tactics, for traders' prosperity in the long run depends on reliable understandings and relationships.

To Jacobs, lawyers were a puzzle. They are associated with

both guardian and commercial ethics, often switching from one role to another depending on the task. In some contexts, an honesty-based ethic seems to prevail; in others, loyalty seems to be the highest value. Their official canons of ethics are an ambiguous blend of court officer and client service ideals. In the best scientific tradition, Jacobs treated this strange profession that did not fit her theory as an invitation to further investigation and possible discovery.

She noted with interest that the culture of English barristers, historically at least, had a strong raider cast. (The English legal profession is formally divided between solicitors, who deal directly with clients on legal and business matters, and the much smaller corps of barristers, who are engaged by solicitors for special tasks, the most important of which is advocacy in the higher courts.) Endowed with a virtual monopoly on lawyers' most raiderlike activity—the planning and conduct of courtroom battles—barristers went to great lengths to shun trading. They did not discuss payment for their services (their clerks did it) and would not sue to collect their fee. On the back of the barrister's gown there is still a little pocket that in former times enabled him to be paid without actually seeing or handling money. Unlike solicitors, barristers chiefly belonged to social circles that looked down on persons "in trade."

American conditions, however, were different from the beginning. Lawyers often had to be barristers and solicitors rolled into one. Many of them even sat as justices of the peace, or filled in, on occasion, for an absent judge. Abraham Lincoln's legal career, to take one famous example, involved him in all of those roles.[9] Nor is there any reason to think Lincoln was unique in his ability to perform as a peacemaker among neighbors one day, a zealous advocate for the Illinois Central Railroad on another, and an impartial magistrate on the next. After all, a powerful set of informal community sanctions was in place: lawyers in his day were apt to be under close scrutiny not only from their fellow professionals but also from their friends and neighbors.

Legal education in the United States today still purports to provide a foundation for all types of legal work. Unlike many other countries, we have a one-track system for business lawyers, family counselors, and litigators. The fact that most legal work has both raider and trader aspects, together with lawyers' apparent versatility in juggling their complex roles, suggested to Jacobs that members of the legal profession might have mastered a knack that deserved wider study. For, in her view, a great problem in modern societies is how to maintain a workable symbiosis between the culture of enterprising, inventive traders, on the one hand, and that of vigilant, protective guardians, on the other. Under modern conditions, segregation is not an option. But since raiders and traders cannot simply go their separate symbiotic ways, misunderstandings or worse are bound to be common. Thus, folks who can recognize and adapt to the different systems ought to be handy to have around. Lawyers, more than any other occupational group, seemed to Jacobs to have discovered how to be flexible enough to adapt to either set of values as need be and knowledgeable enough to know when to do so. Though an anomaly for her theory, the legal profession might be a carrier of an important new survival trait.

Jacobs thus is one of the few people since Louis Brandeis to propose that lawyers actually have something to teach other occupational groups about ethics. That notion is so endearingly contrarian that one hates to express reservations about it. It must be said, nevertheless, that generalist lawyers, for whom the case is strongest, have become increasingly hard to find. Long ago, two momentous changes transformed the legal world that Abraham Lincoln knew: the increased specialization that has affected all modern occupations; and a large influx of lawyers from relatively unassimilated ethnic groups.[10] Nearly a century ago, more of a separation began to develop between legal raiding and trading functions, but not along neat English lines. The American profession was striated rather than split, reflecting the different legal worlds of small-town and urban lawyers, the growing social stratification of the bar, the increasing division of labor between litigators and office lawyers, and the development of various specialized fields of practice.

Once the dust settled on the era of the robber barons, trader values gained ascendancy among the establishment lawyers who dominated the professional organizations that promulgated codes of ethics. This was only to be expected, since they and their corporate clients avoided courtroom confrontation as much as possible and concentrated primarily on what Jacobs would classify as trading activities. To be sure, some of the old versatility survived. Corporate litigators knew how to confine their raider skills to the formal arena of combat. Transactional lawyers knew how to switch hats when involved in adversarial negotiations. But elite legal culture up to the close of the "golden age" had a definite trader cast. Certain other segments of the practice were trader strongholds as well: small-town counselors, specialized areas like conveyancing, estate planning, and much of business law.

In some areas of practice, however, raider qualities were more conducive to success and survival. Litigation was a specialty of many small firms and urban solo practitioners. Certain low-status fields—plaintiffs' personal injury, debt collection, domestic relations, and criminal defense—revolved around raider fortresses: police stations, city halls staffed with patronage employees, and local courts. Clients caught up in such difficulties, and litigation clients generally, were apt to regard the lawyer (and he was apt to see himself) as a champion, a special friend in need. Ethnic lawyers, even when engaged in traderlike activities, tended to regard themselves, and to be perceived by corporate lawyers, as outsiders.[11] Whether fighting for their clients or struggling for their own economic survival, they often had to operate in strange or hostile territory. They were at home in a milieu where favors were an important currency; where (as Thomas Shaffer puts it) clients were friends, and friends were clients.[12]

To low-status lawyers, the elite legal world looked like a fortress of hypocrisy and snobbery. Karl Llewellyn, who devoted much of his professional life to studying traders, long ago explained why this is so. That "elusive figment, 'The Market,' " he wrote, is composed of two commonly recurring and very different situations.[13] In one, the participants are strangers to one another, the buyer is often an outsider, a one-shot customer, "whose money is more wanted than his trade." In the other, buyers and sellers are in repeat relationships. Merchants in the first situation are often slower in coming to the realization that trust and courtesy are the basis of prosperity. That distinction led Llewellyn, far ahead of his time, to the conclusion that laws developed by and for merchants were inappropriate for relations between merchants and unsophisticated consumers.[14] (In the 1960s, that point of view led to the enactment of consumer protection laws.) The distinction also helps to explain why the gentlemen's milieu didn't look very genteel to those outside the charmed circle of relationships among establishment lawyers and their clients. Very probably, many elite lawyers were not as punctilious with outsiders as they were with one another.

To establishment lawyers, such a double standard would be easy to rationalize, for the legal world outside the financial district looked to them like a hotbed of sharp practice, hustling, ambulance chasing, and generally deplorable ethical standards. Interviews and research by a father-daughter team of legal ethicists, however, convincingly demonstrate that many ethnic lawyers were oriented to a coherent ethical system that was simply not recognized as such by the legal establishment.[15] Thomas and Mary Shaffer discovered two quite different ethical systems operating side by side in the profession: the "old WASP" or "gentlemen's" values prevalent among small-town and establishment lawyers and an "old world" ethic prevalent among lawyers from the communities formed by immigrants from Ireland, Italy, Poland, and Eastern Europe.[16] The old world ethic tended to place more emphasis on the lawyer's role as friend of the client, while the old WASP ethic stressed the lawyer's independence and his role as officer of the court. As one legal historian has nicely put it, one professional ideal "stresses loyalty to the client, even at the cost of some warping of the legal framework. The other emphasizes fidelity to the framework and its improvement, even at the cost of sometimes having to resist the pressures of clients."[17]

The Shaffers' old world and old WASP ethics correspond at many points to Jacobs's loyalty-based and honesty-based systems. But their research also suggests an interesting connection between the ethics of making a living and differing concepts of personal virtue. The old WASP ethics were rooted in Protestant rectitude and a well-understood gentlemen's code. The ethical systems that once prevailed among old world Jews and Catholics reflected a worldview that placed clients ahead of institutions and treated relationships as more important than rules.[18] From the old world vantage point, the gentlemen's way often seemed harsh, flinty-hearted, even inhuman. To establishment lawyers, the immigrants' irreverence toward the law and its minions looked more like rascality or cynicism than a way of keeping the things of the world in their proper place. Human nature being what it is, ample support could be found in either camp for the most negative interpretations. Putting the insights of Jacobs and the Shaffers together, one can easily see how raider tactics came to be deployed by some lawyers to avenge the slights of class, as well as to advance a client's cause. And how trader courtesy often did not extend to persons who were not perceived as gentlemen. Still, both ethical systems reflected a vision of the virtuous life. And both contained the seeds of corruption.

The Faces of Corruption

Ask any lawyer who complains about a decline in the ethical tone of the profession to name the beast, and the answer is apt to be "commercialization." If there is one dogma to which high-minded lawyers cling more tenaciously than to any other it is that the legal profession should be above the "morals of the marketplace."[19] It should give one pause, however, to reflect that Abraham Lincoln was quite comfortable with the idea that law is a business, and seemed to think that virtue in a lawyer was not much different from common decency in any other calling.[20] The idea that law is not a business, or only "incidentally" so, was a conceit seized upon by elite attorneys in the early years of the present century to distance themselves from their buccaneer predecessors and from "hustling" immigrant lawyers, as well as to assert their independence from their own clients. Typical of the genre is an often-quoted speech by Louis D. Brandeis in which he deplores the commercialization of the legal profession and suggests that lawyers should try to raise the level of business by "professionalizing" it.[21]

Many old-school lawyers still chant the refrain. The "most serious threat to the legal profession" at the present time is "commercialism," according to former Solicitor General and Harvard dean Erwin Griswold.[22] Albert Jenner, in his final public appearance, told a gathering of Chicago lawyers, "We need to reorient our way of thinking about the law away from the concept of the legal marketplace and law firms as profit centers and revenue producers, and law as a business."[23]

That careless use of "commercial" as an epithet is mischievous. It is true that lawyers assume higher responsibilities toward those they represent than businesspersons do toward customers, and that lawyers understand themselves as having special public obligations. But lawyers' stubborn refusal to recognize their affinities with other highly skilled, well-educated sellers of services seems to rest either on the arrogant assumption that businesspeople have no ethics or on the dubious proposition that businesspeople invariably place short-term profits ahead of all other considerations. Those cramped concepts of business ethics, however, are widely recognized in the business world as evidence of economic and moral pathology.[24] Unfortunately, lawyers' disdain for commerce is no mere harmless affectation. As lawyers increasingly admit that law is, among other things, a profit-making business,[25] all too many seem to believe that ethical bets are off.

If Jane Jacobs is right, the lawyers who look down on the morals of the marketplace have it exactly backward. The English barrister's raider disdain for commerce was always ill suited to the American legal world, where most lawyers, most of the time, regardless of specialty or social standing, do not engage in courtroom work. But somewhere along the line American lawyers lost the intelligent flexibility about roles that many lawyers must have possessed in Lincoln's time. That paved the way for the loss of a sense of appropriate business ethics and the spread of raider values to trader settings.

That seemingly innocuous confusion of values appropriate to different ways of making a living sets the stage, on Jacobs's analysis, for trouble. Jacobs's original contribution to the understanding of the sources of ethical corruption is her theory that one cause is, tragically, inadvertent. With a series of arresting examples, she shows how the introduction of trader values in a guardian system, or vice versa, can often change things just enough to shatter the old system, to "literally demoralize" it. The affected group loses its ability to discipline its members. Virtues convert to vices—as traders indulge extreme proclivities to acquisitiveness, and raider destructiveness runs amok. What Jacobs calls "systemic corruption" affects the entire moral ecology of a community.

Thus, in one of Jacobs's illustrations, it was disastrous for the hunter-gatherer Ik tribe of southern Uganda when its members were forcibly resettled from hunting into farming. The Ik had no difficulty learning how to grow crops, but they were unable to make the mental adjustments necessary to sustain a trading way of life. Clinging to their old ways while adopting the new manner of making a living, they turned to raiding each other. Another museum of raider corruption described by Jacobs is the Sicilian Mafia, a "monstrous hybrid" created when mutual-defense societies on that oft-invaded island applied their force and cunning to trading.

Closer to home, we can observe more familiar forms of guardian corruption when police officers and public officials trade in what should not be for sale. Chicago, in the years I practiced there, was governed by one of the great raiders of all time, Richard J. Daley. Chicagoans still argue over the personal probity of the late mayor. (He did not leave a large estate.) But the party machine and the city government he headed were theme parks of corrupt raider culture. A federal investigation in the 1980s confirmed what every Chicago lawyer already knew or suspected: it was not only clerks but certain judges who were on the take. "Operation Greylord" made clear that the disorder was deep and systemic.

When an entire system is corrupt, the individual lawyer often finds herself in a pickle. A client of my law firm once had an urgent need for some tools and dies that belonged to the client, but were stored on the premises of another company that was shut down by a strike and surrounded by angry picketers. Our solution was to bring a friendly lawsuit against the strikebound company to "repossess" the client's property. Under Illinois law, the plaintiff in such an action, upon posting a bond, could have his property removed by the sheriff as soon as the action was filed. The sheriff's police, we were fairly sure, would be permitted to pass through the picket line. Everything went smoothly until I took the replevin order to the Cook County Sheriff's Office.

There I found a roomful of deputies having what appeared to be a jolly midmorning coffee klatch. It crossed my mind that it would be fun to sit down and joke around with them. After I explained my business to the burly man who ambled over to the counter, he flipped through my court papers as though he were looking for something. Then he told me that he and his colleagues were extremely busy. He really didn't know when they would have the time for this job—unless, of course, I was prepared to make it worth his while. Taken aback, I stammered that I would have to consult with my superiors and walked back to the firm, assuming that the senior litigator with whom I was working would know what to do about this unexpected snag. That gentleman, however, reacted impatiently when I reported my difficulty. "Tell the cretin that Mayer, Friedlich does not pay public servants for doing jobs they are already paid by the taxpayers to do. And get those tools and dies out by tomorrow afternoon."

I walked back to the Sheriff's Office in a cold sweat. I envisioned my exile from litigation to something like trust accounting. I imagined how I would explain my demotion to my parents. ("I've always liked working with numbers.") I considered renting a truck and repossessing the damned stuff myself. I wondered whether the deputy, despite his tough exterior, could be moved by the sight of a woman in tears. When I arrived, the county employees were still yakking it up, but I no longer felt like joining in. My man came right over when he saw me at the counter. In my desperation, I was all set to begin weeping and begging, when suddenly I had an inspired thought. Looking at him as though he were Sydney Greenstreet and I were Peter Lorre, I said in a low conspiratorial voice: "I am authorized to say that if you do this job immediately, my principals and I will be *very* grateful." "I'm on my way," he said.

A few hours later, the phone rang. "All done," my pal reported. "Thank you," I replied. "Thank you very, very much." I still shudder when I think of what must have happened to the next associate from Mayer, Friedlich who showed up in the Cook County Sheriff's Office.

As Jacobs makes clear, systemic corruption can wear pinstripes as well as polyester. Her prime example of what happens when a trader society takes up raiding is American investment banking in the takeover era. The experience of legal trader strongholds in the same period provides an equally telling case study. Into the risk-averse worlds of corporate lawyers and bankers in the 1970s came a new generation of raiders, a mogul horde the likes of which had not been seen since Jay Gould and other grandees of greed held sway. The takeover artists' business was turned away at first by established firms. This was due partly to fear of offending and losing important existing clients; partly to a feeling that tactics such as using lawsuits for pure harassment were unsavory. As a partner in Shearman & Sterling recalls, the view then was that "gentlemen didn't do takeovers."[26] That opened a legal niche to be quickly filled by younger, more aggressive firms (formed by Catholics, Jews, and graduates of second- or third-rank schools—many of whom had been snubbed by the old-line firms).

The established firms soon found themselves forced to defend their clients against hostile takeovers. Eventually, most began to represent raiders as well. Louis Auchincloss, who retired from a Manhattan firm in 1987 to devote himself to fiction, observed sadly, "There was a time when you brought a suit only to right a wrong or collect an obligation. That all the finest firms [now bring takeover suits] is the single most corrosive factor in the ethics of the bar."[27] Office lawyers and litigators joined forces in the exciting new work. They jointly hunted enterprises ripe for capture. Together they plotted acquisitions and lawsuits. The workaholic Rambo was born.

Listen to how Lawrence Lederman, who began his career in the Cravath firm, describes what drew him from ordinary corporate law to takeover work: "Besides agility, attempting a takeover requires craft and the willingness to take risks."[28] "Given a choice I preferred representing raiders. Besides enjoying the planning, as an outsider I was attracted to the entrepreneurial clients, interesting men with a sense of themselves who were trying to make their mark and didn't mind challenging and dismantling rigid corporate empires."[29] "[L]ittle else in business galvanized people and brought them together as cohesively as organizing an attack that would require speed, surprise, and precision timing." "I found that all the mystery and excitement of sex, of breaking down resistance, of scoring and conquest, were associated with a takeover. Manliness was at stake, and measured." "[T]he takeover told of cunning and daring and the power to take what you wanted."[30]

No sooner had the takeover frenzy begun to subside than the professional world was rocked by the savings and loan debacle. When federal agents in 1986 began their investigation of Lincoln Savings & Loan, the regulatory audit quickly escalated into a no-holds-barred adversarial battle. Lincoln's lawyers in the New York firm of Kaye, Scholer, Fierman, Hays & Handler fought the government's requests for information every step of the way. Government lawyers struck back in kind, filing a suit that charged Kaye, Scholer attorneys with lying to regulators, obstructing the investigation, and remaining passive while Charles Keating provided false information. The government's hardball tactics included an administrative order freezing the partnership's assets, a move that brought Kaye, Scholer quickly to its knees. The firm paid $41 million for a no-fault settlement of the charges. The following year, Jones, Day, Reavis & Pogue paid a record $51 million in a similar Lincoln Federal–related settlement.

Shaken by those unprecedented suits and settlements, lawyers began to debate such questions as whether Kaye, Scholer attorneys had simply been helping their client in time-honored fashion to do what it wanted to do within the limits of the law. Was a hostile regulatory audit the equivalent of litigation for ethical purposes? Do lawyers for publicly regulated clients have a special duty to the public?[31] What ethical constraints should government attorneys observe? Should an administrative agency be allowed to freeze a firm's assets without showing any reason other than to force a settlement?[32]

One question that was seldom in the foreground was: What had become of the old counselors' dictum that "about half the practice of a decent lawyer consists in telling would-be clients that they are damned fools and should stop"? The author of a study of Wall Street firms in the 1950s had concluded that corporate lawyers then possessed enough independence to permit them to serve not only as advisers but also, at least "sometimes," as "conscience" to big business.[33] The picture that emerged from a similar study published in 1988 was very different. If corporate firms had ever served as checks on the narrow self-interests of their clients, Robert Nelson contended, their increased dependence on clients had deprived them of much of that autonomy.[34] Three out of four large-firm lawyers in Nelson's study could not recollect a single instance in which they had ever even disagreed with a client.[35] The motto of the day seemed to be another old saying attributed to Elihu Root: "The client never wants to be told he can't do what he wants to do; he wants to be told how to do it, and it is the lawyer's business to tell him how."[36]

The takeover phenomenon and the savings and loan affair were only the most notorious in a series of developments that have drawn elite law firms out of the trader mode and away from "gentlemen's" ethics. Standard explanations in the legal community blame the heightened competition among law firms for a decline in independence and reduced emphasis on the lawyer's role as an officer of the legal system. A key part of the picture, however, is the fact that corporate clients themselves were undergoing fundamental changes. Just as the robber barons of old found willing accomplices in the legal profession, so did the new breed of corporate managers. Many lawyers wanted to be joint venturers with their clients, rather than mere advisers and representatives. Then, too, as businesses became more litigious, that boosted the size and prestige of litigation departments, raider enclaves within the large firms.

Interior design tells the tale. Gone are the faded carpets, the well-worn wooden desks, the smell of old books, the scarred library worktables, the nondescript plainness that bespoke trader disdain for ostentation. Firm reception areas have been adorned with "corporate art," and lawbooks have been rebound to blend with the colors of carpets and drapes. Professional decorators have scrapped the chairs and engravings that served for generations. Partisans of thrift and modesty put up a struggle, but lost out everywhere to colleagues who insisted that clients would be turned off by an establishment that looked as though it hadn't changed in seventy-five years. Like the nobles of San Gimignano with their rival towers, law firms tried to outdo each other in splendid accommodations. Lawyers hired after the 1980s would have difficulty discerning the vestiges of the older way of life. Pomp and display, the raider's insignia, became the order of the day.

The freakish law boom of the 1980s contributed to other sorts of excesses—the extravagant wooing of summer associates, inflated starting salaries, overstaffing cases, and "Pig Pools." Eventually, the binge of the 1980s gave way to the hangover of the 1990s. But, as Jacobs says, "water over the dam carries debris." Many law firms, like many of the corporate clients they served, came under the control of people with a raider mentality. But the decline of trader culture did not signal the emergence of a new guardian culture with its characteristic, coherent group ethic. What happened in many firms was more like an outbreak of uncontrolled individual raiding behavior, a mutually destructive war of all against all.

In fact, the mingling of trader and raider ways in law firms provides support for Jacobs's theory that confusion of two distinct ethical systems can lead to the undoing of both. Guardian sanctuaries, like the Cook County courts, were corrupted long ago when they became host to trading in what should never be for sale. In the 1970s, encroaching raider ethics wreaked havoc in trader enclaves where relationships depended on trust and reliability. Raider firms, too, were undone as lawyers forgot how to distinguish between the tactics and values appropriate for raiding and trading. There was fine irony in the power struggles that took place after Skadden, Arps's takeover business crashed. One of the arguments that defeated a proposal for democratic participation in the firm's management was that the reform scheme might lead to vote selling![37] Raiderdom had dissolved into mutually suspicious individualism; and all that was left of traderdom was the ability to corrupt guardianship.

Consider the demise of Shea & Gould. The 1964 merger between litigator Milton Gould and lobbyist William Shea was a classic raider alliance. The firm grew and flourished until the mid-1980s, when the two aging chieftains had to turn over the reins of management to an executive committee. Almost immediately, the partners fell to bickering. In 1994, after all efforts to save the firm had failed, the 230-lawyer firm disbanded. Yet, economically, the firm had weathered the decline of its corporate takeover business reasonably well. By the time it folded, Shea & Gould had no serious debt and its financial problems were no more grave than those of many other large firms.[38] Its partners just could not cooperate in running the firm, nor could they agree on dividing the profits. Lawyers came and went, taking clients with them when they defected. Toward the end, the quarreling partners called in an outside consultant to help, but his efforts failed. One member of the executive committee admitted, "There was nothing that man could have done to save us from ourselves."[39] Another partner remarked, "We became a firm of solo practitioners."[40] So might Ik elders have spoken among themselves. With the passing of the canny custodians of their raider culture, Shea & Gould lawyers destroyed themselves with uninhibited individual raiding.

Today, as always, most lawyers are still engaged in unglamorous, steady, useful trading activities. Some areas of practice have an especially strong trader cast; in others raider ideas prevail. But though one ethos or the other usually predominates, most lawyers must wear multiple hats. The criminal defense bar, as a group, is probably the purest raider culture. But most legal roles require considerable versatility. Office lawyers frequently find themselves in adversarial situations; litigators must often be counselors and peacemakers. As lawyers' roles have become more specialized and complex, members of the profession seem ethically to be ever more at sea. Whence cometh their help?

Legal Ethics, Anyone?

The field known as "legal ethics" has only a tenuous relation to the systemic difficulties currently afflicting the legal profession. For one thing, formal codes of ethics never aimed at capturing the entire ensemble of understandings that lawyers observe in their dealings with one another, with clients, and with the courts. The codes mainly set forth a small body of fairly obvious duties with which lawyers must comply on pain of discipline or disbarment.[41] Where ethical problems of great complexity are concerned, formal canons afford little guidance. They are often least helpful where most needed.

The American Bar Association's current Model Rules, adopted in 1983, explicitly recognize that the moral tone of the legal profession depends primarily on a great web of informal understandings.[42] Within the framework of a general obligation to represent the client zealously while remaining within the bounds of the law, one is free (but not required) to advise clients to comply with the spirit as well as the letter of the law. One is equally at liberty to press the letter to its limits. If the great web does not hold, the individual lawyer is essentially in free fall.

Recent changes in the rules actually seem to go with the flow of systemic problems in the profession rather than helping to counter them. In the 1983 Model Rules, for example, almost all of the language of moral exhortation that had characterized previous codes of lawyer conduct has been removed. Just when lawyers were coming under exceptional ethical stress, the Model Rules eliminated such words as "right," "wrong," "good," "bad," "conscience," and "character," and replaced them with words like "prudent," "proper," "permitted."[43]

Also dropped in 1983 was a series of illustrative discussions that used to follow the cryptic rules and canons. The Preamble to the previous code had highlighted these "Ethical Consider-ations": "[They] are aspirational in character and represent the objectives toward which every member of the profession should strive. They constitute a body of principles upon which the lawyer can rely for guidance in many specific situations."[44] The apparent explanation for deleting the Ethical Considerations is that, once you get beyond such obvious no-nos as stealing clients' funds, consensus on what is right and wrong for lawyers is diminishing. In other words, the more moral confusion there is, the less guidance one should expect from formal codes of ethics.

Consider, too, the amazing shrinking concept of the lawyer as independent counselor. The first ABA Canons (adopted in

1908) held up a robust model of a lawyer who was no mere tool of the client: a lawyer "advances the honor of his profession and the best interests of his client when he renders service or gives advice tending to impress upon the client and his undertaking exact compliance with the strictest principles of moral law."[45] In the 1960s, old-fashioned terms like "honor" and "principles of moral law" vanished, but the role of adviser and co-deliberator was still promoted: "A lawyer should exert his best efforts to insure that decisions of his client are made only after the client has been informed of relevant considerations. A lawyer ought to initiate this process if the client does not do so. Advice of a lawyer need not be confined to purely legal considerations. . . . In assisting his clients to reach a proper decision, it is often desirable for a lawyer to point out those factors which may lead to a decision that is morally just as well as legally permissible."[46] In 1983, however, that mild encouragement to moral deliberation with clients was scrapped in favor of a provision that merely permits lawyers to refer to "relevant" factors: "In rendering advice, a lawyer may refer not only to law but to other considerations such as moral, economic, social and political factors, that may be relevant to the client's situation."[47] Like Betty Crocker, the wise counselor has gotten slimmer over the years.

As they stand, the current Model Rules are capacious enough to permit the kind of intelligent flexibility about roles that generalist lawyers may once have possessed. The Rules recognize that different tasks and roles (counselors, advocates, advisers, negotiators, intermediaries, evaluators, litigators) may involve somewhat different ethical considerations. Within their framework, a lawyer could make subtle adjustments in the course of moving from one role to another, more or less consciously shifting priorities depending on the setting. Some legal ethicists now push for more guidance along those lines, calling for more precise attention to the different ethical considerations pertaining to the different contexts in which lawyers operate.[48]

But the current Rules also lend themselves to a simpler

"solution" of complex ethical problems: when in doubt, go with client loyalty, safely earning the support and sympathy of the profession. The most hotly debated issue in connection with the 1983 Rules, in fact, was whether a lawyer should be required, rather than merely permitted, to disclose information he has reason to believe is necessary to prevent a client from causing death or serious bodily harm to another person. The proponents of mandatory disclosure lost out to the advocates of ironclad client confidentiality, striking an unusual balance between client confidentiality and the victim-to-be of a serious crime.[49]

The apparent advance of the client loyalty ideal at the expense of the independent counselor and court officer roles may mask a systemic version of an old problem: a de facto priority for the lawyer's own concerns. Contingent fees do provide many people with access to justice, but frequently make the lawyer the real party in interest. Corporate lawyers have complex loyalties, but many seem far more concerned to satisfy the company managers who hire and fire lawyers than to protect the interests of scattered shareholder-owners. Particular overriding interests of lawyers are not always economic. They can, for example, involve the promotion of a cause at the expense of an individual client, as happened in the case of Norma McCorvey, the unhappy plaintiff in *Roe* v. *Wade*, whose lawyers helped her neither to have the abortion she sought nor to keep the baby to which she eventually gave birth.[50]

San Francisco attorney Alan Marks recently broke the taboo on discussing problems of that sort, charging that ethical rules leave the most severe ethical dilemmas untouched. The "real" dilemmas, Marks alleged, arise mostly from "the powerful compulsion of self-concern."[51] While lawyers argue in public about what constitutes overzealous representation, he claims, they are in practice often engaged in underrepresentation.

Is Marks right? In one sense, the problem of faithless representation is an old one. But the appearance of so many lawyers operating *openly* on their own account is something quite new.[52] Members of the new breed often portray themselves as rebels against the notion that law is not a business. Ironically, the wholehearted embrace of self-interest on the part of some lawyers may have been facilitated by the old mindset that equated "commercialism" and the "marketplace" with unbridled acquisitiveness. Now that lawyers are beginning to say that they want to run their "business as a business,"[53] many seem to suppose they are exempt from ordinary decent behavior. Or they imagine that business ethics are something like the adversarial tactics of criminal defense lawyers. They're like the teenage rat in one of Gary Larson's *Far Side* cartoons who says, when his mother tells him to clean up his room: "Criminy! It's *supposed* to be a rathole!"

What seems to have gotten lost somewhere is Lincoln's down-to-earth, unpretentious attitude toward decency in business, rooted in the trader understanding that any business, including law, thrives best on cooperation and honesty. And the companion understanding that raider lawyers' deception for the sake of the task must be carefully limited to certain litigation and negotiation settings. And Llewellyn's insight that the many competing claims on a lawyer's loyalty are what make the life of a lawyer much more complicated than that of an ordinary businessman.

Academic debunkers of "professionalism," preoccupied with their "discovery" that high-minded lawyers have frequently failed to live up to their professed ideals, have not been helpful in the current period of turmoil. Friendly reminders of practitioners' shortcomings might once have served to puncture the balloon of smug professional self-satisfaction. But the professorial fire brigade arrived with their pails of cold water just when the embers of professional pride need to be coaxed back to life. The scholarly orgy of debunking has obscured the importance of the facts that such ideals were professed at all, and that debate about them helped to focus the attention of a large, diverse professional community on the question of what kind of life a lawyer ought to try to live.

The old moralistic codes of ethics were often cynically derided in the academy as self-serving attempts to fend off tighter regulation. But if mixed motives condemn reform movements, few human efforts to improve our collective condition could pass the test. It is precisely because most of us need lots of help and support in finding an upright path that the exercise of stating professional ideals serves an important function. Retelling the old stories and exploring their implications for new circumstances helps to orient and reinforce each lawyer's quest for a morally coherent professional life. That's why, as Archibald Cox has pointed out, even much-maligned ethical codes are not completely useless. We need them, he says, "both to express our moral sense and sharpen our awareness of its applications."[54] The ideals held up by the pre-1983 codes invited any lawyer to choose them, practice them, and by regularly engaging in a certain kind of conduct, to make himself (and eventually herself) into a certain kind of person.

Today's lawyers wander in an increasingly impersonal, bureaucratized legal world, where neither honesty-based nor loyalty-based systems seem to be operating very well. The families, communities, neighborhoods, and schools that once served as seedbeds and anchors for personal and professional virtues are themselves in considerable disarray. Clients, whether corporate or individual, are in the grip of the same maladies.[55] New recruits to today's profession often have no solid base of old world, old Wasp, or any other culture to fall back on—and no coherent professional culture to embrace. Emancipated from the old ways, they soldier on, with few examples, sketchy guidance, and little reinforcement. In such circumstances, is it remarkable that short-term self-interest often prevails?

The legal ethos that is emerging is very different from a world in which most lawyers were at least oriented toward visions of lawyering that demanded a considerable degree of self-subordination, whether of the guardian or trader variety. Just as sexual self-expression has few limits in a culture where chaste behavior is mocked, lawyers' self-interest is apt to run amok when anyone who places court and client above profit is branded a hypocrite or a chump. Moreover, a lawyer who takes his duties to the court and the legal system seriously will often be at a disadvantage against a less scrupulous adversary. Many lawyers are fearful that in today's competitive environment, contrary to what Lincoln said, good ethics may not make for good business.

Why, then, should we be astonished if some parts of the legal profession begin to resemble the ill-fated Ik tribesmen, neither hunting nor farming, but preying on everyone in sight, including one another? Many lawyers, whether spurred by fear or desire, seem to have concluded that the best survival strategy is not ethical adaptability in Jane Jacobs's sense, but mere ethical agility. The patron saint of these lone raiders is not honest, versatile Abe Lincoln. Nor is it loyal, single-minded Perry Mason. It is the chameleonlike Talleyrand, the all-time champion at reinventing one's self.

The collision and disintegration of old guardian and trader understandings have had personal as well as professional consequences. Transported from their communities of origin to membership in America's deracinated technocrat class, liberated from old world and old WASP values, many lawyers are now free, self-determining, and miserable. Like the displaced Machiguengas in Mario Vargas Llosa's *The Storyteller*, they've lost their myths about where they came from, who they are, and where they are going. They can no longer make sense of their lives. The stories they heard in law school about independence, public service, and professionalism don't match up with their everyday experiences. Many are dispirited. Some of the most affluent and successful lawyers feel bad when they should be feeling good. Others, caught up in one form of misfortune or another, inexplicably feel good when they should be feeling bad.

5

Feeling Bad When One Should Be Feeling Good; Feeling Good When One Should Be Feeling Bad

I really thank God for Watergate. If it weren't for that, I might be back practicing law. —CHARLES COLSON[1]

Charles Colson is not the only lawyer who has come to regret his initial choice of vocation. A California Bar Association survey in 1992 indicated that 70 percent of those polled would choose another career if they had the opportunity and that 75 percent would not want their children to become lawyers.[2] Other recent polls reveal that nearly a quarter of New Jersey lawyers are planning to leave the practice of law before retirement, while the same percentage of North Carolina respondents say that they would not become attorneys again.[3] In a Maryland Bar Association study, almost a third of the respondents were not sure they wanted to keep on practicing law.[4]

Long before postmodern tristesse crept over the American bar, serious people sometimes wondered whether the practice of law was compatible with a good life. Oliver Wendell Holmes, who had spent almost fifteen years in private practice, worried aloud about the problem on a number of occasions. "How," he once asked, "can the laborious study of a dry and technical system, the greedy watch for clients and the practice of shop-

keepers' arts, the mannerless conflicts over often sordid interests, make out a life? Gentlemen, I admit at once that these
questions are not futile, that they may prove unanswerable,
that they have often seemed to me to be unanswerable. And
yet I believe there is an answer."[5]

Holmes's somber public ruminations about the legal profession are as remote from the boosterism of his contemporaries
as they are from the bland pieties spouted by most professional
leaders today. The honoree at a contemporary bar association
dinner might conceivably confess, as Holmes once did, to "long
years of doubt, self-distrust, and solitude."[6] But few speakers
today would look an audience of well-fed colleagues in the eye
and remark, offhandedly, "We are all very near despair."[7] On
one long-ago occasion, Holmes, then a state judge in his fifties,
mused, "I ask myself, what is there to show for this half a
lifetime that has passed? I look into my book in which I keep
a docket of the decisions of the full court which fall to me to
write, and find about a thousand cases, many of them on
trifling or transitory matters, to represent nearly half a lifetime!"[8]

An eminent jurist today might well begin a talk to prelaw
students, as Holmes once did, with a stern warning not to
suppose that the legal profession is "a place where brilliant
results attend your work, which shall be at once easy and new."[9]
Few, however, would share Holmes's idea of an upbeat ending.
Certain intellectual satisfactions are obtainable in law, Holmes
finally assured his young listeners, but "only when you have
worked alone—when you have felt around you a black gulf of
solitude more isolating than that which surrounds the dying
man." To a Chicago bar group, Holmes administered another
stiff dose of Beacon Hill existentialism. "Most of us find it easy
to despond," he began chummily.[10] The lawyers must have
reached for their after-dinner brandies as he warmed to his
theme, speaking of "the rats that gnaw at one from within,"
and concluding, in his usual manic way, that "succeed or fail,
the fight is joy."

What, one wonders, would that Brahmin desperado make

of the spreading misery that now afflicts the legal profession? What are *we* to make of the results of a 1990 follow-up to the ABA's 1984 national survey of lawyer satisfaction? In that six-year period, there has been a drop of 20 percent in the number of lawyers who say they are "very satisfied" with private practice, with twice as many women dissatisfied as men.[11] In corporate legal departments, regarded by many as safe havens from the frenetic pace of law firms, dissatisfaction rates are even higher than among private practitioners. According to a Johns Hopkins University survey, lawyers are more than three times as likely to suffer from symptoms of depression as adults among the general population.[12]

More disquieting still are findings indicating that, even among lawyers who like their work, trouble is brewing. There has been a marked rise since 1984 in symptoms of physical and mental distress in the lawyer population as a whole. About half the lawyers in private practice say they do not have enough time to spend with their families; nearly three-quarters of all lawyers say they "frequently feel fatigued or worn out by the end of the work day." Alcohol and drug abuse among lawyers is significantly higher than in the population at large. While the proportion of problem drinkers in the labor force as a whole is estimated at approximately 10 percent, as many as 13 to 18 percent of lawyers are believed to abuse alcohol.[13] The picture is chillingly similar to the epidemiology of what the Japanese call *karoshi*, death from overwork.[14]

No segment of the profession has remained untouched by spreading malaise. Large firms (housing about 10 percent of private practitioners), small firms, corporate counsel, and government attorneys are experiencing discontents in their own fashion. Solo practitioners, the largest single category, report more often than other lawyers that the practice of law has given them a sense of personal accomplishment, but they also report more anxiety about money.[15] The strain falls on the mighty and the low alike, affecting partners as well as associates. Relative newcomers to the profession—women, blacks, Hispanics—and graduates of lower-status law schools seem to be most affected.[16] Even those for whom "the fight is joy" may pay a stiff price for victory. Peggy Kerr, when she was a high-powered litigating partner at Skadden, Arps, told one interviewer, "I thrive on pressure."[17] But on another occasion, she stated, "I have no doubt that, had I had the wonderful husband and two adorable children I thought I wanted years ago, I would not be a partner today." Kerr eventually realized part of her dream by becoming an adoptive single parent and relying heavily on domestic help.[18]

The stark statistical portrait of dissatisfaction in the profession shades into softer focus for me when I get together with other lawyers who left Chicago's law school with high hopes in the early 1960s. In many ways we were exceptionally fortunate, entering the profession in a season of unusual prosperity and stability. Our expectations were not much grander than Roscoe Pound's idea that law offered a way to make a decent living in the spirit of public service. Now at the age where we wonder about the paths not taken, some of us worry about whether we struck the right balance between work and family. For many, just keeping afloat in our chosen profession exacted a high personal cost—not only from ourselves but from others close to us. Women, especially, found marriage and child raising hard to reconcile with the demands of a legal career, and almost impossible to combine with the fast track in law firms. All of us, within a few years after graduation, came to realize that survival in a changing legal world required different qualities from those we had been encouraged to cultivate in the waning days of the "golden age."

Dissatisfaction is more widespread and acute among our successors, the lawyers who entered practice from the late 1960s onward. In the two decades between 1965 and 1985 the size of the profession doubled (from 300,000 to more than 600,000) as upwardly mobile young men and women swarmed to the nation's law schools. But changes throughout American society during those years unsettled middle-class expectations regarding many things—job security, family life, morals, and manners. Perhaps reflecting the disappointment of a generation that dreamed of having it all, nearly a third of the post-1967 cohort reports being dissatisfied in private practice, as compared with 19 percent of private practitioners generally.

Even in the midst of the fat years, Thomas Geoghegan recorded how he and other "Warren Court children" began to feel bad when they should have been feeling good:

> Many of my friends, if they are still in law practice, now hate it. "The world's most overrated job," one of them says. Lined up at motion calls: a lost generation, the Warren Court baby boom, the flood of us who went to law school in the late 1960s and early 1970s. . . . Back then, the law seemed like a romance. Go to a big New York firm, make tons of money, save the world in your spare time, *pro bono.*
>
> Now, in those corporate firms, people look up for the first time after law school, the clerkship, the years of apprenticing as an associate, and ask: "My God, what am I doing? How can I get out?" And those are the plodders. The smart ones bailed out years ago for investment banking.[19]

The normal drudgery that attends legal work may have seemed especially oppressive to Geoghegan's generation because their expectations were so high. The law business was booming. Second-year law students were being lavishly wined and dined by prospective employers. Large firms were offering astronomical starting salaries. For a time, until house counsel blew the whistle, the big firms spared no expense in staffing a case. At the same time, elite law schools were devoting less and less attention to preparing their students for the inherent difficulty and complexity of much legal work. No wonder many members of that cohort developed a sense of entitlement—not only to affluence but to interesting and "important" work.

The boredom of ambitious young lawyers in private practice began to seem like a luxury, however, when profits leveled off or declined in the 1990s.[20] To the distress of many who had seen their law degrees as passports to social prestige and comfortable living, even unglamorous jobs grew harder to get. While more than 93 percent of 1977 law graduates found legal employment within six months after graduation, fewer than 84 percent of 1992 graduates had done so.[21] In the large firms, associates' salaries were stagnating and the odds against making partner were getting steeper.

The discomfort arising from heightened insecurity is compounded by the fact that many young men and women now emerge from law school heavily burdened by student loans. It is not uncommon for a new lawyer to owe more than $100,000 for combined college and law school expenses. Law school recruiters may be correct when they claim legal education is a good investment. (Where else could you get a better return for your initial outlay? they seductively inquire.) But such indebtedness can weigh heavily on a young lawyer, especially if he or she wishes to begin a family. For some students, certain job options are practically ruled out. A starting public defender or legal services attorney in most cities makes less than $30,000 a year; a new prosecutor less than $40,000. The best-paid jobs —those in large firms—are now among the most precarious. The gilded cage has a trapdoor.

Recently an eminent federal judge speculated, as Holmes had done long ago, about lawyers and their discontents. Richard Posner's economic theory has a great deal of explanatory power. The legal profession of the so-called golden age was "an intricately and ingeniously reticulated, though imperfect cartel" which began to disintegrate in the 1960s.[22] Changes in lawyers' work over the years can be likened to the process through which artisans organized in guilds were rendered obsolete by the methods and structures of modern mass production. Posner, who welcomes that development as healthy and long overdue, numbers among its potential blessings: benefits to the consumer resulting from competition among providers of legal services; eventual free entry to paralegals and others who have been excluded from competing directly with lawyers; and the disappearance of the cartel's self-serving concept of what it means to be a professional. The dissatisfaction afflicting many individual lawyers, Posner observes, is in large part a consequence of competitive pressure to work harder. "Naturally [the practice of law] is less fun," he has written. "Competitive markets are no fun at all for most sellers; the effect of competition is to transform most producer surplus into consumer surplus and in more or less time drive the less efficient producers out of business."[23] Moreover, like the alienated industrial workers of whom Marx and Engels wrote, few modern lawyers can enjoy the satisfactions of craft in an age where so much of their work has become routinized.

Whether one denounces them as "commercialism" or lauds them as "competition," no one can deny that economic changes have transformed the legal landscape. Beneath intensified pressures attributable to competition, however, simmers a deeper misery rooted in meaning. The stories lawyers have always told themselves about professionalism were not just self-serving facades. They were efforts to answer Holmes's question of questions (by no means unique to lawyers): Does all this "make out a life"? But the old incantations aren't as comforting as they once were. Routinization has increased the drudgery that has always been inherent in most legal work. Many lawyers are suffering alienation akin to that experienced by manual laborers whose crafts were superseded by mass production.[24] How can we maintain that we belong to a "learned calling" when so many of us are so narrowly specialized that we work on only one part of a large task? How can we claim to be learned in a broader sense when long hours scarcely leave us time to read a novel or attend a concert? The traditional claim that we pursue our livelihood "in the spirit of public service" often has a hollow ring.

The Answer to Holmes's Question

In truth, the professionalism story was always thin. That's probably why Holmes, who detested conventional pieties, never answered his own question in those terms. Though he nearly died for the Union cause, and though he willed the bulk of his estate to the United States of America, he would have gagged on the notion of "public interest" law. He would have seen that label as a mask for doing whatever you want (taking a government job, saving trees and animals, battling government regulation) while claiming to serve the common good. Lawyers, as he said with brutal frankness, study a "dry and technical system"; they practice "shopkeepers' arts"; and engage in unseemly battles over "often sordid interests." So much for the "learned" calling, the idea that law is not a business, and the zealous defense of individual rights. What, then, was Holmes's answer to the question lawyers still ask themselves—how can one "make out a life" from practicing law?

On various public occasions, he mentioned a number of ways to fend off "the rats that gnaw at one from within." For one thing, he pointed out, the practice of law immerses a lawyer in an ever-changing variety of human situations and legal issues. "But what other [profession] gives such scope to realize the spontaneous energy of one's soul? In what other does one plunge so deep in the stream of life,—so share its passions, its battles, its despair, its triumphs, both as witness and actor?"[25] Another source of satisfaction, according to Holmes, was the sense of contributing one's best efforts to a great whole. A lawyer's monument, he said in a tribute to a deceased colleague, "is the body of our jurisprudence . . . to which the least may make their contribution and inscribe it with their names. The glory of lawyers, like that of men of science, is more corporate than individual. Our labor is an endless organic process."[26]

Finally, there was what Holmes and Learned Hand called "jobbism." Often, the best way to find one's purpose in life, Holmes claimed, is just "to do one's task with one's might."[27]

Holmes nevei spoke more movingly about jobbism than in replying to a letter from a young man about to enter Harvard Law School in the fall of 1927. "What do you have to say to someone embarking on a legal career?" brash young Charlie Wyzanski had written the great Supreme Court justice. Holmes, nearing the age of ninety, wrote back:

> However a man feels about his work nature is likely to see to it that his business becomes his master and an end in itself, so that he may find that he has been a martyr under the illusion of self-seeking. But we rank men partly at least by the nature of their dominant interests, and we think more highly of those who are conscious of ulterior ends—be those ends intellectual ideals, to see the universal in the particular, or the sympathetic wish to help their kind. For your sake I hope that when your work seems to present only mean details you may realize that every detail has the mystery of the universe behind it and may keep up your heart with an undying faith.[28]

In March 1930, Learned Hand took the occasion of the presentation to Harvard Law School of a portrait of Holmes to explain what it meant to be a jobbist.

> Are you a member of the Society of Jobbists, or do you know the guild? If not, let me tell you of it. All may join, though few can qualify. Its president is a certain white-haired gentleman, with a keen blue eye, and a dangerous turn for dialectic. But the other members need not and do not fear him, if they keep the rules, and these are very simple. It is an honest craft, which gives good measure for its wages, and undertakes only those jobs which the members can do in proper workmanlike fashion, which of course means no more than that they must like them. . . . It demands right quality, better than the market will pass, and perhaps it is not quite as insistent as it should be on standards of living. . . . But the working hours are

Learned Hand (right) with Roscoe Pound on the occasion of Hand's dedication of the Holmes portrait: "Are you a member of the Society of Jobbists, or do you know the guild?" *(Courtesy Harvard Law School)*

strictly controlled, because for five days alone will it labor, and the other two are all the members' own.[29]

Though Holmes earnestly urged others to appreciate the austere satisfactions of practice, they do not seem to have been enough to sustain his own interest. Perhaps, after all, the noted judge and scholar was not the best person to answer his own question. We know that, in spite of everything, the contemporary lawyer's cup of satisfaction is far from empty. Though one in five professes to be dissatisfied, 43 percent describe themselves as "somewhat satisfied," and one in three reports being "very satisfied" with professional life.[30] What is going on among that fortunate one-third?

There is, regrettably, little social science data to help us find out. Finding one's niche may be important. Though lawyers cherish and law schools promote the fond belief that a good legal education equips one to perform any type of legal work, the facts are otherwise. The talents and temperament that make for success and personal satisfaction in one branch of the profession do not guarantee distinction or even survival in another. The growing ranks of lawyers in private industry and government include many men and women for whom the rewards of private practice do not outweigh its pressures and risks. Many able judges, such as Learned Hand, were not particularly happy or successful as practitioners. Many gifted practitioners, such as Robert Jackson and Thurgood Marshall, were more comfortable with their roles as advocates than with the public service they gladly rendered as Supreme Court justices. (Jackson, a former Solicitor General and Attorney General, took an extraordinary leave of absence from the Supreme Court in 1945 to become Chief Prosecutor in the Nuremberg trials. Later, he said he considered "the hard months at Nuremberg" to have been "the most important, enduring, and constructive work of my life."[31])

Anecdotal evidence suggests that the sense of having made a difference for the better still ranks high among lawyers' satisfactions. Consider Victor Covalt, Thomas Geoghegan, and Ronald Pohl.

Victor Covalt, a Nebraska bankruptcy lawyer, feels good when he should be feeling bad. Covalt was a most unlikely person to be appointed to represent a black man sentenced to die for killing a white woman. He had never handled a criminal case. The task of pursuing post-conviction remedies for Harold Lamont Otey fell to him, he admits, because "they didn't have anybody else to do it, basically."[32] In the course of his assignment, Covalt became convinced that his new client was "a changed man" since the crime, and that the sentence should be commuted to life in prison. He soon found himself caught up in a blizzard of motions, hearings, stays, and petitions, inventing a series of long-shot legal maneuvers, bearing many of the expenses out of his own pocket. His life changed in other ways, too: the publicity given to his efforts to save the life of a convicted murderer has made Covalt himself the target of public fury and contempt. Still, when a reporter spotted him running through the Omaha District Court building in search of a judge to grant a last-minute stay, and called out: "Is this any way to practice law?" Covalt shouted back: "I've never felt more like a real lawyer." At this writing, Otey is still alive, and Covalt—frantically shuttling back and forth between attempts to save Otey and to rescue faltering businesses—still feels great.

Many aspects of Thomas Geoghegan's litigation and labor practice in Chicago in the 1980s gave him a full-blown case of "mid-life angst."[33] There were long stretches of days filled with trivial or unpromising cases. But one of the most hopeless put him back in touch with what he loved about the legal profession. After a Teamster pension fund cut the benefits of some two hundred retired workers by nearly two-thirds, an elderly truck driver came to see Geoghegan and asked for help. The chances of winning seemed remote, but the old man was so persistent that Geoghegan finally gave in. For four years, they lost every single legal skirmish. Then, suddenly, in a last-minute reversal of fortune, the firm won a clear and decisive victory, worth millions of dollars to the pensioners. Afterward, as Geoghegan tells it, the client kept calling him up: "[H]e says in his thick mountain drawl, 'Well, now, the men are very well pleased.' Then, tickled to death, he starts to laugh. And laughs and laughs. And in the great tradition of our profession, one that I find irresistible, I start laughing too."

When Manhattan probate lawyer Ronald Pohl interviewed ailing ninety-two-year-old Julius Burger, in preparation for drafting Burger's will, he learned that Burger's possessions included sheafs of unperformed musical compositions written long ago in Germany before Burger fled to escape Nazi persecution.[34] In the United States, Burger found work as an assistant orchestra conductor, but his own music remained tucked away in the closets of his Queens apartment. To give Burger the pleasure of hearing his old works just once, Pohl persuaded a friend to play one of the pieces, a cello concerto, in the old man's apartment. Then, convinced that the music was exceptionally good, Pohl investigated the possibility of public performance. Within a year, five of Burger's compositions were played at Lincoln Center, to rave reviews. Pohl's services to his client did not end there. He helped Burger buy new glasses, a hearing aid, dentures, and a new suit. According to David Margolick of *The New York Times*, much of Pohl's work for Burger was done for free, because Pohl "has come to love him."

Many lawyers continue to flourish in the role of peacemaker. In Middlebury, Vermont, Bill van Zyverden practices what he calls "holistic law" out of a former department store.[35] He questions his clients to discover the roots of a conflict, tries to promote their own understanding of the situation that brings them to a lawyer, and encourages the use of informal methods, arbitration, or mediation rather than litigation. Though that sounds a lot like the Abe Lincoln method, van Zyverden's hero is another famous lawyer, Mahatma Gandhi. Much of Gandhi's practice as a solicitor consisted in settling hundreds of cases, and in his autobiography he wrote that he had lost "nothing thereby—not even money, certainly not my soul." Ted Hobson,

a general practitioner who answers his own phone at Linton &
Hobson in Williston, Vermont, says holistic law is just a new
name for "what responsible lawyers do."

Becky Klemt in Laramie, Wyoming, thinks incivility must be
a big-city lawyers' problem.[36] "I don't deal with a lawyer one
time and think, 'I'll never see you again,' nor do I go into court
before a judge, thinking, 'I'll never see you again.' I practice
before these people day in and day out. If I don't treat them
civilly in this case, they won't treat me civilly in the next."
Studies corroborate Klemt's perceptions. Not only "small-town"
lawyers but lawyers in other settings where they have regular
and repeated dealings with the same people tend to be reluctant
to use hardball tactics and to be able to cooperate in ways that
are beneficial for their clients.[37]

It would be pleasant to think that the legal profession is
composed of thousands of lawyers like Covalt, Geoghegan, van
Zyverden, Hobson, Pohl, and Klemt. For them, it has not been
a calamity to admit that law is a business, nor that morality for
lawyers may not be much different from the common decency
that ordinarily guides people when they act on behalf of others.
They are lawyers in the tradition of the Boston attorney whom
Holmes eulogized as one of the vast legal tribe whose finest
works are known to few. Mr. Shattuck, Holmes said, liked to
take his clients' burdens onto himself. "How often have I seen
men come to him borne down by troubles which they found
too great to support, and depart with light step, having left
their weight upon stronger shoulders."[38] Not one to mention
the satisfactions of such a career without noting the personal
costs, Holmes added, "He never shunned anxiety, and anxiety
is what kills."

But if the backbone of the profession is the small entrepre-
neur, its muscle and voice are located in the big firms and the
American Bar Association. In those precincts of professional
power, there are also occasional gusts of fresh air. John J.
Curtin, Jr., for example, in his August 1991 presidential
message to the ABA, went right to the heart of the matter:
"The question each lawyer must answer for himself or herself

remains the same: What kind of lawyer do I want to be?"[39] Only a few days later, Curtin gained national notoriety for lashing out at Vice President Dan Quayle, who had made lawyers a target in the 1992 presidential campaign. In fact, Quayle's criticisms echoed many that Curtin himself had made in speeches exhorting his fellow lawyers to renew their commitment to civility and service. But Curtin, a longtime litigator, instinctively rose to the defense when "his" group was publicly attacked.

Curtin's presidential messages were concerned with the profession's responsibility for its own future. He wanted lawyers to ask themselves: What is excellent in a lawyer? How does one become excellent? While he insisted on each lawyer's personal responsibility for what he or she makes of a life in the law, Curtin implicitly acknowledged that few individuals can go it alone. He called on the bar to repair or reconstruct the shared understandings that shore up the moral courage of individual practitioners, to pull together in setting examples of "the service to others that is the true distinguishing mark of our profession."

Was Curtin whistling in the wind? It does not seem unreasonable to believe that most practitioners are still possessed of the deep desire of which John W. Davis once spoke: to conduct themselves in such a way that the profession will be strengthened by their passage through its ranks and so that they will leave the law a better instrument of justice than they found it.[40] If that is so, the profession's best hope for renewal may reside in those yearnings—and in the current sadness of those who sense that the legal world has spun out of control. Several hundred thousand men and women in search of a meaningful life will not be denied forever.

Even supposing that among thousands of lawyers "very near despair" there is a strong will to renewal, the obstacles are forbidding. Many of the problems are as old as the profession itself. For Karl Llewellyn was right—one thing that does differentiate the lawyer from other skilled workers who exchange services for fees is the presence of an unusually large number of conflicting claims on his or her loyalty. But other stumbling blocks are peculiarly modern. For the legal profession is not the only American institution in disarray. The past thirty years have also witnessed the weakening of leading corporations, financial networks, political parties, labor unions, religious organizations, neighborhoods and families. Americans in all walks of life have experienced a similar sense of release from constraint coupled with anxiety and isolation. As the dam of civil society crumbles, the tides of opportunism are rising in the legal profession as elsewhere.

The same disintegration of informal understandings that has undermined the cultural supports of formal codes of ethics has left many lawyers feeling unable to make sense of their lives. The whole profession is in the disoriented "castaway" state described by Walker Percy: "What does a man do when he finds himself living after an age has ended and he can no longer understand himself because the theories of man of the former age no longer work and the theories of the new age are not yet known, for not even the name of the new age is known, and so everything is upside down, people feeling bad when they should feel good, good when they should feel bad?"[41]

Lawyers and the Republic

The disoriented state of the country's legal profession cannot help but have consequences for our law-dependent democratic experiment, as well as for individual attorneys and clients. Lawyers of all sorts, for better or worse, will continue to have much influence on how America deals with the great issues of our time—the deterioration of natural and social environments, crime, poverty, education, race relations, the plight of child-raising families, decaying infrastructure, intense international competition, and so on. Traditionally, the country has depended on the legal profession to supply most of our needs for consensus builders, problem solvers, troubleshooters, dispute avoiders, and dispute settlers. The country's need for talented persons in such roles is greater than it has ever been. The opportunities for satisfaction and a sense of personal accomplishment are unparalleled. The potential of the alternative dispute resolution movement, for example, has barely been tapped. For some thirty years, however, those creative and useful activities have been devalued while litigation has been exalted.

It will not do to say the profession has always been a mixed bag, for the proportions in the mix are of far-reaching significance, as is the relative prestige of various legal activities. Imagine the American legal profession spread out in the manner of a weather map. If we color its order-affirming activities yellow and its adversarial activities blue, the map will be a study in chartreuse. But the shades of green will vary. The yellowish "trader" hue (to reprise Jane Jacobs's heuristic) will be predominant, because (contrary to television images) most lawyers, most of the time, are engaged in planning, prevention, and problem solving. Relatively close-knit legal communities like Becky Klemt's will be brightest. Several parts of the profession, however, will have a more bluish "guardian/raider" tinge: litigators and those who work in specialties such as plaintiff's personal injury, domestic relations, and criminal law.

Now place our map next to one reflecting the proportions of order-affirming and adversarial activities, say, thirty years ago. Over time, the yellow-green areas have shrunk somewhat and dimmed in brightness. The spread of blue pigments is striking, but equally striking is the fact that the sunny trader hue still predominates. What the maps do not reveal is that the prestige of adversarial activities has risen at an even greater rate than the numbers of lawyers engaged in them. True, those activities have come under intense criticism in recent years. But the profession's connoisseurs of conflict have also been lionized more than ever. Their more numerous brothers and sisters, the artisans of order, receive little recognition from their colleagues or the public. That interesting situation has important personal and political consequences.

Consider first the political implications. The legal profession has always needed its innovators nipping at the heels of its traditionalists, and its heroic advocates alongside its peace-makers and preventive planners. But if Tocqueville was right that lawyers' special attachment to formality, order, and con-tinuity made the legal profession a linchpin of democracy's social checks and balances, a major shift in the proportion and prestige of lawyers who share that attachment is admonitory. It is difficult to say more. History affords no example of what happens to a highly law-dependent polity when the traditional predominance of counselors, planners, and problem solvers is challenged by swelling ranks of innovators, iconoclasts, and adversarial advocates. We are the example.

The declining prestige accorded to order-affirming and peacemaking activities of lawyers has personal effects as well. Few lawyers are virtuoso courtroom performers or full-time vindicators of political and civil rights. Sadly, in recent years, the artisans of order in small and large firms, in government agencies, in corporate legal departments, have received little encouragement and respect. They lack even the cold comforts held out to their ancestors by Holmes, who understood a practitioner's fears and doubts, and respected the dignity of the legal craftsman's everyday labor. No wonder many are dejected.

Yet competent accomplishment of the everyday tasks of lawyers deserves to be celebrated in our complex, pluralistic nation oriented to the rule of law, representative government, and fundamental freedoms. Lawyers cannot claim to have a monopoly on any of the following qualities, but no other occupational group in American society displays the ensemble to the same degree. For that reason, no other group has more to offer American society simply by building on what it has always done best.

The Eye for the Issue. Lawyers like to think—and often it is true—that their training and experience make them handy to have around when people are deliberating about how to reach a common objective, or when they are at odds but need to go on living together—in the neighborhood, workplace, club, church, city, or nation. What makes a lawyer a skillful collaborator or consensus builder is more than just the clean mental slate of any intelligent onlooker. It is his practice in discerning the precise issues in controversy, whether the disagreement is about means to an end or about ends themselves. A trained eye for the issue enables lawyers to constructively disagree with their own clients as well as to narrow the scope of conflict between antagonists. It suits lawyers for the increasingly important roles of mediators. "Can any discipline be more valuable today," constitutional scholar Paul Freund once asked, "than one that teaches us to look through the great antinomies that present themselves like gladiators for our favors—individualism and collectivism, liberty and authority, secularism and clericalism—to look through these in order to discover the precise issue in controversy, the precise consequences of one decision or another, and the possibility of an accommodation by deflating the isms and narrowing the schisms?"[42]

The Feel for Common Ground. The lawyer's experience in delineating the issues that divide people, and in grasping just what is essential or expendable to each party in a discussion, also gives her a feel for the common ground that even determined opponents may share—and the ability to frame a settlement in terms that antagonists can accept. Often it is a lawyer who, in public or private negotiations, comes up with the face-saving compromise that everyone can live with. Effective mediation in situations where deep grievances prevent the partisans from thinking clearly requires mastering the facts, listening exhaustively to all sides, understanding the positions, and patient searching for the scraps of territory on which accord can be constructed. Interestingly, regular users of mediation services are finding that lawyers with extensive practice backgrounds often make better mediators than long-time judges.[43]

The Eye to the Future. When issues are clarified and agreements reached in principle, someone still has to give inchoate understandings a concrete form that will stand the test of time. By training and experience lawyers are accustomed to making shrewd guesses about where trouble is most likely to arise in the future, and adept at creating arrangements to avoid those situations or minimize harm if they occur. As Yale's Anthony Kronman puts it: "The ability to fashion hypothetical cases and empathically to explore both real and invented ones is the lawyer's professional forte."[44] A specialized, cultivated foresight often helps a lawyer to supply the right words, the time-tested formula, the reliable procedural safeguards, the safe passage through stormy straits.

Mastery of the Apparatus. "So what is it that lawyers and judges know that philosophers and economists do not?" former Solicitor General Charles Fried once asked rhetorically. "The answer is simple," he said. "The law."[45] Fried was not being a smart aleck. There's no getting around the fact that a regulatory state with a complex economy requires an array of specialists in interpreting, explaining, applying, and coordinating the rules, principles, and standards emanating from sources as diverse as the local zoning board and the United States Congress. Obvious? Yes, but sometimes we lose sight of the obvious—especially as some law schools begin to neglect the teaching of law in favor of philosophy, economics, and other subjects that are useful adjuncts to, but no substitutes for, legal training. Mastery of the apparatus includes care for the apparatus, its history, its maintenance and proper functioning; awareness of its range of uses; and understanding of its limitations.

Legal Architecture. Without institutional structures and frameworks, the torrent of laws, regulations, and decisions spilling out from legislatures, courts, administrative agencies, and private associations would not constitute a legal system, but only a regulatory deluge. A country's constitution, of course, provides the basic framework. But the never-ending legal construction that goes on within that framework requires architects as well as carpenters. The authors of well-crafted corporate charters and bylaws, collective bargaining agreements, leases, trusts and estate plans, parliamentary procedures, constitution-like regulatory schemes, and so on, have extraordinary opportunities to affect for better or worse the quality of everyday life in our large commercial republic. Theirs is the delicate job of providing structure and order while leaving as much room as possible for spontaneity and creativity. That's why an older generation of legal educators had such great respect for those who negotiate and draft such instruments. Only someone who has never negotiated a long-term agreement and tried to reduce it to writing can regard the exercise as an easy one. It is this aspect of legal work, Paul Freund once wrote, that "most nearly resembles the enterprise of the artist."[46]

Procedure. The history of law, to a great extent, is the record of a search for means to enable people to order their lives together according to principles that can be understood and accepted by affected parties and onlookers—even when the outcomes go against their interests or desires. Disputes must not only be settled, but settled in such a way as to minimize festering resentment and the renewed eruption of conflict. Good lawyers will try hard to accomplish this result without ever going to court. But when all other methods of dispute resolution fail, the legal system is our alternative to private force. Adjudication in advanced societies means, at a minimum, a commitment to hearing both sides, impartial judges, reason-giving in arguments and judgments, and procedures that help to minimize arbitrariness. Though lawyers did not invent procedure, they have become its high priests and protectors. It was lawyers who developed reliable procedures in place of ordeal and torture for the investigation and trial of facts; courtroom protocols for the presentation of arguments; and the law of evidence with its ever more sophisticated understanding of relevance, probability, and human cognition. Procedure pervades the lawyer's world. Love of procedure makes the most diverse members of the legal profession cousins, if not siblings, under the skin. Proceduralism radiates from the law to every corner of American business, political, and associational life.

Problem Solving. Many of the most rewarding moments of law practice occur when a lawyer devises a viable solution to a problem that has brought a client to wit's end, or when lawyers for antagonists resolve the conflict in a way that expands the pie for all concerned. Even in nonlegal settings—the PTA, the corporate boardroom, the town finance committee, the church council—when everyone else has given up, it is often the lawyer who fashions the strategy that works. If the key to success in problem solving were individual ingenuity or common sense, lawyers would be of no special use. The added value that lawyers bring to the table, besides specialized training, is a vast fund of inherited experience. The humble form book (or the firm's computer bank) is every lawyer's endowment, a record of the trials and errors, successes and failures of others in a huge range of variants on recurring human problems. Faced with a new variant, a lawyer typically invents little, but adds, adapts, and rearranges much. Some of the most ingenious legal devices from the medieval trust to the Uniform Probate Code, from the United States Constitution to the federal securities legislation, have been produced in just that way.

Strong Tolerance. Representing other people, in both friendly and adversarial situations, promotes in lawyers an ability to enter empathically into another person's way of seeing things while retaining a certain detachment.[47] That cast of mind in turn fosters a sturdier form of tolerance than that produced by mere relativism or pacts of nonaggression. Strong tolerance can be attentive, protective, and respectful to the other person without being "nonjudgmental." Some such qualities, Learned Hand thought, would greatly aid the country's adjustment to a larger and more varied population. No one can say for certain whether the American design for government will weather the twin challenges of bigness and heterogeneity, but it would help if the sails of the ship of state were billowed by the spirit of which Hand wrote: a "temper which does not press a partisan advantage to the bitter end, which can understand and will respect the other side, which feels a unity between all citizens —real and not the factitious product of propaganda—which recognizes their common fate and their common aspirations."[48]

Incremental Change. As a great lawyer once pointed out: "A state without the means of some change is without the means of its conservation."[49] Nevertheless, Edmund Burke went on, "it is with infinite caution that any man ought to venture upon pulling down an edifice which has answered in any tolerable degree for ages the common purposes of society, and on building again without a pattern." The American Founders, most of them steeped in the same legal traditions as Burke, designed durable political institutions that contained within themselves the means of change. For two hundred years, the American legal profession has provided the polity with a reliable supply of citizens especially attuned to the twin necessities of conserving hard-won achievements and imaginatively adapting old arrangements to new circumstances. Like architects, lawyers are usually at their best when working with existing materials —reshaping, recycling, reshuffling, and adding to the usable past, rather than destroying and starting afresh. In Anthony Kronman's words, they "know how to extend and revise the traditions of their craft in ways that are faithful to the meaning and spirit of those traditions themselves."[50]

Now, returning to the problem of feeling bad when one ought to be feeling good, an attentive reader may have noticed that all of the foregoing traits have one feature in common. The more fully a lawyer excels in them, the less likely it is that his or her work will receive acclaim beyond the circle of those immediately benefited. Peacemaking, problem-solving lawyers are the legal profession's equivalent of doctors who practice preventive medicine. Their efforts are generally overshadowed by the heroics of surgeons and litigators. The plain fact is that much of what lawyers do best is exacting, unglamorous, and unadvertised—the reasonable settlement that averts costly litigation, the creditors' arrangement that permits a failing business to regain its health, the patient drafting of model legislation within the National Conference of Commissioners on Uniform State Laws and the American Law Institute.

The exaltation of litigation, moneymaking, and efforts to

achieve social transformation through law in recent years has been at the expense of the useful services that have always given lawyers in the aggregate their best chance to achieve personal satisfaction while contributing to the well-being of their fellow citizens. The law schools and the organized bar have responded only slowly to the need to develop lawyers' capacities for creative problem solving.

Meanwhile, the current devaluation of the ordinary activities to which most lawyers still devote most of their attention, day in and day out, must be an important reason why so many lawyers feel bad when they should be feeling good. They are torn between their complex obligations to client and court, on the one hand, and their fear, on the other, of being blindsided by competitors, adversaries, and even colleagues, who no longer acknowledge those obligations. Attorneys in all sorts of roles are under pressure to transform themselves on the model of hardball litigators. Many transactional lawyers now want to be participants in deals, rather than advisers to deal-makers.

Yet why should a lawyer not take pride and pleasure in achievements akin to those of a skilled practitioner of preventive medicine, a builder whose house will last for generations, or a parent whose children grow into happy adults and productive citizens? The question that is so often debated—whether the United States has too many lawyers—is the wrong question altogether. Whether a society has too many lawyers depends entirely on what its lawyers are doing and how they imagine the good life. If all lawyers followed Lincoln's advice to be peacemakers among neighbors, there could never be too many lawyers. And there would still, as Lincoln said, be business enough.

PART II

THE WAYS AND TASTES
OF MAGISTRATES

Why, in the branch of government considered "least dangerous" by the Founders, have Supreme Court opinions taken on an imperious tone?

Why, when American judges at all levels exercise more power than judges in any other liberal democracy, are many of the nation's best lawyers declining to be considered for judicial appointments, or resigning from the bench?

Why, as American society becomes more heterogeneous than ever, has the idea of judging "without respect to persons" (without deference to a litigant's wealth, power, ethnicity, or other personal characteristics) come into question?

What do the nation's 27,000 judges believe and teach about law?

How do they envision their own roles in the legal system and the polity?

6

Cracks in the Classical Façade

His influence extends far beyond the precincts of the courts; the American judge is constantly surrounded by men accustomed to respect his intelligence as superior to their own, whether he is at some private entertainment or in the turmoil of politics, in the marketplace, or in one of the legislatures; and apart from its use in deciding cases, his authority influences the habits of mind and even the very soul of all who have cooperated with him in judging them. —ALEXIS DE TOCQUEVILLE[1]

When Tocqueville described the American people as having the "ways and tastes of a magistrate," he was paying our forebears a high compliment. The prestige of American judges in the world outside the courtroom, as he saw it, arose mainly from qualities of a type that require careful cultivation—a particular sort of trained intelligence, a superior ability to set aside personal biases and consider all sides of a question, a knack for explaining positions in terms that make sense even to those who disagree. It would never be easy to find such individuals, Alexander Hamilton remarked in *Federalist* No. 78, for "there can be but few men in society . . . who unite the requisite integrity and the requisite knowledge." Yet, starting in the 1960s, the task became simpler, in a sense. It was not that the country had a sudden boom in intelligence or rectitude. Rather, traditional ideas of what it took to be a good judge were giving way to a new ideal of judicial boldness, energy, and compassion. Court watchers and commentators began to shower attention on judges who were making their influence felt through fiat and rhetoric, rather than craftsmanship, good sense, and steadiness of temperament. Like flowers turning toward the sun, more and more of the nation's magistrates lifted their eyes from the tasks before them to the dazzling light of power and celebrity.

In the early morning on the last Monday of June 1992, crowds gathered outside the Supreme Court building to await the announcement of a decision in the most highly publicized case in years. Justice Anthony Kennedy gazed down at the throng from the window of his chambers. Turning to a reporter from his home state of California, he said, "Sometimes you don't know if you're Caesar about to cross the Rubicon or Captain Queeg cutting your own tow line."[2]

It was the day of an anxiously awaited ruling on the constitutionality of Pennsylvania's abortion regulations, and the Californian seemed to be in an expansive mood. He had come a long way from the Sacramento days when, stuck in a lawyer-lobbyist job he disliked, he began to render services to Governor Ronald Reagan and Reagan's aide, Edwin Meese.[3] Kennedy's loyalty was rewarded in 1975 when President Gerald Ford, on Reagan's and Meese's recommendation, appointed him to the Ninth Circuit Court of Appeals, the nation's largest federal appellate tribunal. With little to set him apart from other federal judges, he probably expected to remain there for the rest of his days. In 1987, though, lightning struck. The nominations of Robert Bork and then Douglas Ginsburg to fill the Supreme Court seat vacated by Lewis Powell had gone down in flames—Bork's after a bitter confirmation battle and Ginsburg's after he admitted that he had used marijuana occasionally in the 1970s. On his third try to find a judicial conservative who could secure the approval of the Democrat-controlled Senate, Reagan turned to Anthony Kennedy. According to the President's White House and Justice Department advisers, the California jurist possessed neither the dynamic brilliance of Bork nor the finely honed legal acuity of Ginsburg.[4] But, unlike them, he was confirmable.

Within a few years, Kennedy became part of an influential

group of centrist justices, aligned neither with judicial liberals like Blackmun and Brennan nor with conservatives like Rehnquist and Scalia. Along with fellow Republican appointees Sandra Day O'Connor and David Souter, Kennedy had begun to be lauded by journalists and academics for his independence. He was said to have "grown." On the day of the decision in *Planned Parenthood* v. *Casey*,[5] he granted Terry Carter of *California Lawyer* the privilege of observing a day in the life of a Supreme Court justice. As the time for announcing the Court's decision approached, Kennedy broke off the interview and asked Carter to leave him alone for a while. "I need to brood," he explained.[6]

A few minutes later, the justices strode in to take their assigned seats. Kennedy read aloud a section of the joint plurality opinion he had co-produced with O'Connor and Souter. The decision itself did not raise many legal eyebrows. As expected, the Court upheld Pennsylvania's informed consent and parental consent provisions and struck down its requirement of spousal notification. The Court's treatment of *Roe* v. *Wade* (affirming it in principle while modifying its scope and basis) was a familiar way of reshaping broadly drawn precedents. But the section read (and presumably authored) by Kennedy was startling. It had a Caesarean—or at least an imperious—ring. It guaranteed that *Casey* would be remembered less for its result than for its grandiose portrayal of the role of the Supreme Court in American society.

Kennedy began by asserting the need to clarify the relationship of the "Court's authority" to "the country's understanding of itself as a constitutional Republic."[7] He then went on to inform the American people that their very "belief in themselves" as "people who aspire to live according to the rule of law" was "not readily separable from their understanding of the Court."[8] The Supreme Court, Kennedy continued, has the authority to "speak before all others" for the "constitutional ideals" of Americans. The people, for their part, were to be "tested" by following the Court's articulation of their ideals.[9]

Afterward, back in chambers with Terry Carter, Kennedy still had Roman generals, obsessive ship captains—and his own place in history—on his mind. Repeating his earlier remarks, he said, "You do wonder if you're Caesar at the Rubicon or Queeg cutting your own tow line. But only history can tell."[10]

Few people outside legal circles read Supreme Court opinions, but the joint opinion in *Casey* would likely strike the average layperson as more than a little presumptuous. Are our civic aspirations, indeed our very belief in our political selves, so bound up with our understanding of the Supreme Court? Americans do hold the Court in relatively high esteem. But it's quite a leap from John Marshall's emphatic insistence on the Court's power and duty "to say what the law is"[11] to the notion that the Court should tell us what our constitutional values should be. Ultimately (or so the Framers repeatedly insisted) the voice that is privileged "before all others" in our system of government is the voice of the people, expressed in a variety of republican ways. Did Justices Kennedy, O'Connor, and Souter, one wonders, consider how their fellow citizens might regard the news that they were to be "tested" by accepting ideas contained in a murky opinion in which two members of the five-person majority did not even join and with which four dissenters vigorously disagreed?[12]

On past occasions when the Supreme Court has stepped into bitter social and political controversies over issues like slavery, economic regulation, segregation, and abortion, it has been not the people's subservience but the Court's wisdom that has been put to the test. The decisions in *Dred Scott* that a descendant of African slaves could not be a citizen of the United States,[13] in *Hammer* v. *Dagenhart* that child labor restrictions violated the freedom of contract,[14] and the early New Deal cases invalidating economic recovery legislation not only failed to command a following but eventually brought the Court itself into disrepute. It was, precisely, the constitutional *ideals* of Justice Taney in *Dred Scott* and of the laissez-faire justices in cases like *Hammer* that Americans eventually rejected. The Warren Court's condemnation of public school segregation in *Brown* v. *Board of Education*,[15] on the other hand, both reflected and promoted the gradual formation of new social ideals and practices. *Brown* was a perfect illustration of Alexander Hamilton's point that the judicial branch does not gain a following by fiat: it has "neither Force nor Will but merely judgment."[16]

It was that elusive quality, judgment, that eventually won acceptance for *Brown* among friends and foes alike of judicial "activism." The members of the Court showed their good judgment not only in the decision itself but in the way they comported themselves. It is inconceivable that any of the justices who participated in *Brown* (Chief Justice Warren, Justices Black, Burton, Clark, Douglas, Frankfurter, Jackson, Minton, or Reed) would have invited a reporter to follow them around on the day they announced such a momentous decision. To be sure, the nine justices who spoke with one voice on that day were trying every bit as hard as the *Casey* plurality to give direction to the nation's constitutional ideals. They must have hoped, by their stern denunciation of the "separate but equal" doctrine, to inspire in their fellow Americans a heightened dedication to racial justice and tolerance. But they were too prudent to claim such moral authority as their due.

Many of the factors that will determine the ultimate reception of a constitutional ruling are beyond the Court's control. But the chances that a particular decision will win respect are increased by: the prestige that unanimity or near-unanimity can lend to an opinion, the soundness and persuasiveness of the Court's reasoning, the opinion's effectiveness in demonstrating to the losing side that their best arguments have been understood and fairly considered, and the moorings of the decision in constitutional text, structure, and tradition. In *Brown*, Chief Justice Earl Warren worked hard to bring his colleagues together in the historic unanimous opinion. His fellow justices, who included some of the most formidable legal minds in the country, lent their talents to make that opinion powerful and persuasive.[17] *Brown*'s authority was further bolstered by the majestic pedigree of the equality principle itself: by adopting the Civil War amendments, the people of the United States had ended the original Constitution's compromise with slavery, repudiated the infamous *Dred Scott* decision, and renewed their commitment to the proposition Lincoln had called a "tough nut to crack": that all men are created equal and endowed with certain inalienable rights. In *Brown*, nine justices of widely differing backgrounds and views called the nation to take up the challenge of a color-blind Constitution.

Contrasts between *Brown* and *Casey* are revealing of several large changes that took place in judicial ethos during the years that separated the two decisions. *Casey*, with its five opinions, smacks more of straight voting than collegial deliberation.[18] Only two years earlier, retired Justice Lewis Powell had chided his former colleagues for deciding too many cases without a clear majority opinion. Decisions by a fractured Court, Powell warned, not only give too little guidance to lower courts and future litigants but invite "perpetual attack and re-examination" of whatever principles the Court is trying to establish.[19] It is quite likely that Justice Powell had in mind the 1989 case in which five members of the Court, including Justice Kennedy, accorded First Amendment protection to flag burning against the overwhelming weight of American opinion.[20]

The plurality's opinion in *Casey* (upholding Pennsylvania's requirements of parental consent for minors, informed consent followed by a twenty-four-hour waiting period, and data reporting) bears the telltale signs of another bad habit for which Powell had scolded his former colleagues: excessive delegation of research and drafting to the bright but inexperienced recent law graduates who serve as clerks to the justices.[21] Overly long for what it has to say (thirty-five double-column pages in the *Supreme Court Reporter*), the opinion is wooden, disjointed, and padded with extraneous material. Chief Justice Warren's opinion for the unanimous Court in *Brown*, by contrast, is short, and stark in its simplicity—a mere five and half pages in the *Supreme Court Reporter*.[22] The threads that connect *Casey*'s reasoning to constitutional text and tradition are slender and wavering, compared to *Brown*'s sturdy anchor in the equal protection language of the Fourteenth Amendment.

How did it come about that "conservative," "moderate" justices on today's Supreme Court are often more assertive and arrogant in their exercise of judicial power than the members of the "liberal," "activist" Warren Court? Part of the answer is that the decades between *Brown* and *Casey* have witnessed a struggle on the Court between competing conceptions of the judicial role, a struggle that is being replicated with varying degrees of intensity throughout the nation's state and federal judicial systems. That contest has contributed to the altered judicial ethos that is so evident in the *Casey* opinions: less collegiality, candor, prudence, and dignity; more dissension, digression, arrogance, and expedience. Those who describe the decisions of the current Court as activist, politicized, or conservative have overlooked the main lines of the Court's trajectory. Both *Brown* and *Casey* were activist decisions; both were inescapably political; and both furthered a liberal social agenda. What has been changing in the years since *Brown* is the way that judges and the legal community in general think about judicial excellence and about the role of the judiciary in American society. Two sets of ideals for judicial behavior are now vying for dominance, one that we may call classical and the other romantic.

For most of American history, the qualities of a good judge seemed written in stone. The classical judicial virtues have been elaborated in loving detail by generations of contributors to what we may call the praise literature of the bench and bar. Tributes offered when a judge retires or dies are notoriously untrustworthy as biographical sources, but they offer marvelous windows onto the changing landscape of legal culture. Set pieces, prepared for ceremonial occasions, disclose not only what qualities the speaker or writer admires but also what sorts of excellence he expects his audience to appreciate. We read Pericles' Funeral Oration, not for its portrayal of Athenian life, but for its evocation of Athenian ideals. A browser in the American legal literature of praise (testimonials, eulogies, dedications) cannot help but notice intriguing recent changes in the judicial qualities that judges, scholars, and practicing lawyers profess to admire and hold up for the admiration of others.

At least until the 1970s, judicial hagiography emphasized impartiality, prudence, practical reason, mastery of craft, persuasiveness, a sense of the legal system as a whole, the ability to preserve principled continuity while adapting the law to changed social and economic conditions—and above all, self-restraint. Three distinct concepts of self-control can be discerned: structural restraint (respecting the limits on judicial power imposed by federalism, the separation of powers, and a court's position in the judicial hierarchy); interpretive restraint (observing the bounds imposed on judicial discretion by precedent, statute, or constitutional text, design, and tradition); and personal restraint (avoiding distortion of the decision-making process by one's own opinion of the parties or the issues).

Some famous judges are specially associated with particular classical virtues; a few seem to combine many of them. John Marshall, who shaped the course of the nation in decisive respects as Chief Justice from 1801 to 1835, is as celebrated among lawyers for his prudence and craft as for the pathbreaking decisions that entitle him to be numbered among the Founders. In *Marbury* v. *Madison*, the historic case in which the Supreme Court first asserted judicial power to review executive and legislative action for conformity to the Constitution, Marshall was exceedingly careful to avoid direct confrontation with the other branches of government.[23] His Court was as "active" as any in American history, establishing the supremacy of federal law and the power of the federal government over interstate commerce. But Marshall secured acceptance for those bold decisions through his consistent acknowledgment of the Court's limited role within the constitutional regime—and by persuading his fellow justices to unite (as a rule) in a single opinion for the Court. His matter-of-fact recognition of the inescapably political role of the Supreme Court was accompanied by a firm insistence that its justices should remain aloof from partisan politics. Historians will long quibble about how well Marshall practiced what he preached, but as Lawrence Friedman has written, the restrained, independent image of the judiciary fostered by John Marshall "had enough truth, and enough hypnotic force, to influence the role-playing of judges" for many years after his own departure from the scene.[24]

Marshall was the very incarnation of the classical republican virtue of love of regime, a form of patriotism that manifests itself as pride in the American form of government.[25] He also took a craftsman's pleasure in the lawyerly arts. He was unsurpassed at separating the key issues from the peripheral, distilling an argument to its essence, trimming his generalizations close to the facts, and maintaining continuity between the decision in a particular case and the great principles of the legal order.

Marshall's example and leadership, at a time when the American judiciary was actively fashioning law for a young nation, helped to bring into being a most un-English model of judging. His personality seems to have been as distinctively American as his jurisprudence. Unlike his bewigged, aloof British counterparts, the Chief Justice of the United States could often be seen marketing, or fetching firewood, or just passing the time of day with strangers in the street.[26] He was noted for his informality—to the point where his carelessness about his dress and personal appearance sometimes drew comment. He seems to have been the kind of person cultivated Europeans regard as a special American type—amiable, intelligent, unpretentious, sociable, an amusing companion, and not quite presentable in the best society.

Marshall's prudence in exercising a judicial power he had fathered established a climate that outlasted his own tenure. During the first seventy-five years of the Republic, the Court held only two federal laws invalid, one being the Missouri Compromise of 1820 (prohibiting slavery in certain of the new territories) in the *Dred Scott* decision.[27] Beginning at the turn of the century, however, the Supreme Court embarked on its first sustained adventure with judicial review. Invoking the Due Process Clauses of the Fifth and Fourteenth amendments, the justices struck down the precursor of the federal income tax,[28] as well as a variety of statutes designed to protect women and children and to improve conditions for the nation's factory workers.[29] That period of activism lasted until the New Deal era, when the Court temporarily resumed a more deferential posture toward legislative action, especially where economic regulation was concerned.

Vigorously challenging judicial inroads on the province of legislation from the moment of his appointment to the Supreme Court in 1902 until his retirement in 1932 was one of the most brilliant and colorful figures in American legal history. Oliver Wendell Holmes was a Civil War hero, the son and namesake of a celebrated writer-physician, and the author of an iconoclastic treatise on the common law. Part of his larger-than-life quality was that he filled so many legal roles—partner in a Boston law firm, Harvard law professor, pathbreaking scholar, Chief Justice of the Massachusetts Supreme Judicial Court, and Associate Justice of the United States Supreme Court. That's something like being drafted into professional football, then becoming a chess master, and finally switching to baseball and ending up in the World Series.

No shrinking violet in any sense, he nevertheless personified the classical judicial virtues of structural and personal restraint. Throughout the years when Court majorities were striking down social legislation left and right, Holmes steadfastly insisted that the Supreme Court must not sit as a super-legislature and that unelected justices must not substitute their views for the judgments of the people's elected representatives. Associated with Holmes in many of those dissents was Louis D. Brandeis, who joined the Court in 1916. The two eventually saw their position prevail when a changing Court began to uphold regulatory legislation—tentatively in the 1920s and regularly in the 1930s.

Oliver Wendell Holmes (1841–1935): "About seventy-five years ago, I learned that I was not God. And so, when the people . . . want to do something I can't find anything in the Constitution expressly forbidding them to do, I say, whether I like it nor not, 'God-damit, let 'em do it!' " *(Portrait by Charles Hopkinson; courtesy Harvard Law Art Collection)*

Unlike Brandeis, who had been a Ralph Nader–like social and political reformer, Holmes personally disapproved of the popular legislation he repeatedly voted to sustain. From his voluminous correspondence, it is plain that Holmes was a social Darwinist who considered most of the protective laws and economic regulations of his time foolish and unsound. "Of course I enforce whatever constitutional laws Congress or anybody else sees fit to pass—and do it in good faith to the best of my ability," he wrote to Sir Frederick Pollock in 1910, "but I don't disguise my belief that the Sherman Act is a humbug based on economic ignorance and incompetence."[30] When his fellow justices pulled property and contract rights out of the Due Process Clauses like rabbits out of a hat, Holmes refused to go along. As a Supreme Court justice, he continued on the course he had established for himself as a member of the Massachusetts Supreme Judicial Court, not only regularly voting to uphold such statutes but giving them generous interpretations.

Holmes's explanations of his reasons for deferring to the judgments of the elected branches on controverted social and economic issues (when there is no solid guidance in constitutional text, design, or tradition) remain canonical. The best-known appears in his dissent in *Lochner* v. *New York*, in which the majority had struck down—as a violation of freedom of contract—a New York State law establishing a maximum sixty-hour workweek for bakery employees.[31] In refusing to join the decision, Holmes explained:

> This case is decided upon an economic theory which a large part of the country does not entertain. If it were a question of whether I agreed with that theory, I should desire to study it further and long before making up my mind. But I do not conceive that to be my duty, because I strongly believe that my agreement or disagreement has nothing to do with the right of a majority to embody their opinions in law. . . . The Fourteenth Amendment does not enact Mr. Herbert Spencer's Social Statics. . . . [A]

constitution is not intended to embody a particular economic theory. . . . It is made for people of fundamentally differing views, and the accident of our finding certain opinions natural and familiar or novel and even shocking ought not to conclude our judgment on the question whether statutes embodying them conflict with the Constitution of the United States. . . . I think that the word liberty in the Fourteenth Amendment is perverted when it is held to prevent the natural outcome of a dominant opinion, unless it can be said that a rational and fair man necessarily would admit that the statute proposed would infringe fundamental principles as they have been understood by the traditions of our people and our law.[32]

Holmes's frequent deference to the more representative branches was neither reflexive nor mechanical, but guided by his sense of the Court's appropriate place in a constitutional design that both distributes and limits governmental powers, and that simultaneously promotes and checks popular rule. Neither liberal nor conservative as those terms are now used, he could be as vehement in defending the political and civil liberties of individuals against majoritarian infringement[33] as in protecting the freedom of electoral majorities to act within the limits imposed by "fundamental principles." He adhered to the view of judging set forth in his *Lochner* dissent with impressive consistency over his long career. His occasional lapses (commentators still argue over what counts as a lapse) are less remarkable than his overall obedience to a principled, restrained approach to adjudication.

There are so many instances of restraint or post-appointment evolution in the history of the Supreme Court that it is commonplace to observe that a nominee's background and personal opinions are unreliable guides to how he or she will decide cases as a judge. Justice Joseph Bradley, who had represented railroads and other corporations for thirty years, regularly voted to uphold restrictions on corporate activity; Confederate drummer boy Edward D. White lined up against

states' rights more often than did Union soldier Holmes.[34]
Felix Frankfurter, ardent champion of Sacco and Vanzetti, civil
liberties, and the infant labor movement, strove mightily, if not
always successfully, to master his passionate nature when he
became a judge.[35] Thurgood Marshall, described by his close
friend Carl Rowan as having once been something of a male
chauvinist,[36] consistently voted to support women's rights.

For obvious reasons, however, the Supreme Court is not the
ideal place to search for judges who display the full range of
classical judicial qualities. That body, after all, occupies a unique
position in the American polity, and those who have been
appointed to its ranks have seldom been chosen mainly for
their outstanding judicial virtues. That's why, within the profession, it generally has been judges more removed from the
vortex of politics who are most admired for their impartiality,
interpretive skill, and self-discipline—judges like Benjamin N.
Cardozo, Learned Hand, and Henry Friendly.

Although Cardozo did become a Supreme Court justice near
the end of his life (he was appointed to fill the seat vacated by
Holmes in 1932), his reputation mainly rests on his work as a
member of the highest court of New York State and on lectures
concerning the judicial process that he delivered during the
1920s. A shy, reclusive descendant of Sephardic Jews prominent in American public life since the eighteenth century,
Cardozo was a judge's judge. To men like Learned Hand and
Felix Frankfurter he represented the very embodiment of the
quality they professed to honor most: humility.

The humility admired by these proud men had nothing to
do with timidity or self-abasement. It was, rather, the attitude
of a person conscious of heavy responsibility. Felix Frankfurter
explained it this way:

> What is essential . . . is that you get men who bring to
> their task, first and foremost, humility and an understand-
> ing of the range of the problems and of their own
> inadequacy in dealing with them, disinterestedness, and
> allegiance to nothing except the effort, amid tangled words

"A runner stripped for the race": Benjamin Nathan Cardozo, as rendered by Sergei Konenkov with an assist from Karl Llewellyn *(Courtesy Harvard Law School)*

and limited insights, to find the path through precedent, through policy, through history, to the best judgment that fallible creatures can reach in that most difficult of all tasks: the achievement of justice between man and man, between man and state, through reason called law.[37]

That special kind of humility goes along with a particular sort of pride—the pride one takes in mastery of one's craft and in the tradition of which one feels a part. Unlike vanity or hubris, the traditionalist's pride rests heavily on the shoulders of those who bear it, like a burdensome legacy.

Frankfurter and Learned Hand outdid one another in praising Cardozo's detachment and "the priestlike disinterestedness" of his mind.[38] Those qualities, according to Hand, did not denote mere aloofness from "grosser interests" like money and personal ambition. (Hand said he "dared to believe" that most judges could be, and were, detached in that sense.) What was infinitely harder was to bring one's own ingrained convictions to the conscious level, and to prevent them from distorting the impartial decision-making process that every litigant has a right to expect. This was a constant struggle for men like Hand and Frankfurter. Neither haughtily aloof from politics as was Holmes nor as retiring as Cardozo, Hand and Frankfurter remained deeply involved with the events of their day, even after appointment to the bench. Viennese-born Frankfurter had been an enthusiastic New Dealer and had an intense interest in Jewish affairs.[39] Hand, scion of an upstate New York family with a long tradition of public service, ran (unsuccessfully) for Chief Judge on the Progressive Party ticket and was an early, vehement critic of McCarthyism.[40]

Complete self-mastery is, of course, impossible. But to some who knew him, Cardozo seemed to be in a class by himself. He had a special incentive to strive for an impeccable reputation, for his father, also a New York State judge, had been caught up in the doings of Boss Tweed's machine. The elder Cardozo, to the family's intense shame, had left the bench in disgrace amidst charges of corruption.[41] The son seems to have spent a lifetime trying to restore the family honor. He succeeded so well that the Cardozo name became synonymous with a certain type of judicial excellence. Here is Learned Hand's tribute upon Cardozo's death:

> [I]nto our past have been woven all sorts of frustrated ambitions with their envies, and of hopes of preferment with their corruptions, which, long since forgotten, still determine our conclusions. A wise man is one exempt from the handicap of such a past; he is a runner stripped for the race; he can weigh the conflicting factors of his problem without always finding himself in one scale or the other. Cardozo was such a man . . .[42]

In the legal world of the 1990s, to speak without irony of judicial detachment as Hand did is to invite a knowing smirk. When Clarence Thomas used the image of a runner stripped for the race in his stormy 1991 nomination hearings,[43] the halls of legal academia buzzed with derision. Apparently unaware that Thomas was invoking Hand and Cardozo, the cynics of the corridors asked one another how any judge could possibly rise above his experiences and prejudices. And Clarence Thomas of Pinpoint, Georgia, and Yale Law School—self-made, religious, and Republican—clearly had the "wrong" experiences and prejudices.

Thomas's detractors seemed oblivious to the fact that they were rolling out a very old chestnut. Judges like Holmes, Cardozo, Frankfurter, and Hand were as conscious of the mental baggage we all carry as any law professor who discovered the unconscious mind in the 1930s or false consciousness in the 1960s or deconstruction in the 1970s. Cardozo had written, "Try as we might, we can never see . . . with any eyes except our own."[44] And Frankfurter had acknowledged, "Of course, a judge is not free from preferences or, if you will, biases."[45] Moreover, he admitted, "reason cannot control the subconscious influence of feelings of which it is unaware."[46]

Holmes had summed up the situation with his usual crispness

decades ahead of anyone else. Judges, he famously wrote, cannot help but be affected by "the felt necessities of the time, the prevalent moral and political theories, intuitions of public policy, avowed or unconscious, even the prejudices which judges share with their fellow-men."[47] All the great classical judges were openly resigned to the fact that total objectivity is an unattainable goal. But they also knew (to borrow Clifford Geertz's analogy) that a doctor who cannot have a completely sterile operating field does not need to perform surgery in a sewer.[48]

The classical judges were hardheaded realists, but they insisted that the impartiality promised to litigants by our government (and by judicial oaths and ethical codes) is not a sham. Frankfurter's response to the cynics of an earlier generation went to the heart of the matter:

> It is asked with sophomoric brightness, does a man cease to be himself when he becomes a Justice? Does he change his character by putting on a gown? No, he does not change his character. He brings his whole experience, his training, his outlook, his social, intellectual, and moral environment with him when he takes a seat on the supreme bench. But a judge worth his salt is in the grip of his function. The intellectual habits of self-discipline which govern his mind are as much a part of him as the influence of the interest he may have represented at the bar, often much more so.[49]

In other words, a lawyer's self-discipline in general, and restrained view of the judicial role in particular, can be as much a part of her character as her views on crime, race, religion, ethnicity, abortion, or redistribution of wealth.

Frankfurter's knockdown argument to the cynics does expose a flaw, though, in Hand's metaphor of a runner stripped for the race. For Frankfurter is surely right that a good judge surmounts bias (to the extent she can), not by stripping on the day of the race, but through sustained "habits of self-discipline."

The classical judicial virtues and skills cannot be donned and shed like a black robe or a running suit. Like a runner's endurance, the judge's impartiality, interpretive skills, and self-control are acquired only through long practice and training, and through emulating the work of others who excel. Without the support of a professional community oriented toward similar values, moreover, it is hard to stay the course.

Today, one cannot read what judges steeped in the classical tradition have written on the judicial process without the sense that the best of them approached the task of judging in fear and trembling, with acute awareness both of their own limitations and of the awesome power they wielded over the lives, liberties, and fortunes of others. They took for granted that a person with a vigorous intellectual life will revise and even repudiate some of his earlier views as his knowledge increases and his character develops. They brooded—not before publicly announcing their decisions—but before making them, and sometimes long afterward. When Learned Hand was asked about his judicial philosophy, he liked to say it was summed up in Oliver Cromwell's admonition to the Kirk of Scotland: "I beseech ye in the bowels of Christ, think that ye may be mistaken."[50] Those words, said Hand, should be inscribed on the portals of every courthouse in the nation.

How did it come to pass that the austere classical ideals lost much of their power over the past three decades? There can be no simple answer, but one can point to certain developments in legal culture that played significant roles. Our examination of one of these developments, a sustained scholarly attack on the very idea of objectivity, must await our discussion of legal education and scholarship. First, we need to consider the way in which social and economic transformations in the twentieth century made judging a very different enterprise from what it seemed to Hamilton, Marshall, and Tocqueville. By the 1970s, it was clear to all concerned that the rules, the playing field, and the players would never be the same again.

7

The New Ball Game

[T]he last quarter century has witnessed an astonishing rise in the amount of litigation in the country (including a tenfold increase in the number of cases filed annually in the federal courts of appeals), to which the legal profession has responded with all the imagination of a traffic engineer whose only answer to highway congestion is to build more highways, or of a political establishment whose only answer to increased demands for government services is to print more money. —JUDGE RICHARD A. POSNER[1]

An adventurous concept of judging has infiltrated judicial mentalities just as the routine business of the courts has become more complex and demanding than ever before. The drab fact is that most judges have to spend most of their time on the humdrum but crucial tasks of finding facts and interpreting laws in cases that hold little drama except for the immediate parties. American judges are unique, however, in that every single one of them possesses extraordinary powers that have no place in the job descriptions of most of their counterparts in other nations. The increasingly ambitious deployment of those powers as our judges have spread their constitutional wings has produced subtle changes in judicial culture. The combination of a crushing workload and grandiose yearnings has not been a happy one for what the Founders called "the great cement of society," the regular administration of justice.[2]

It is only in recent years that the problems have come to a head, but their roots are deep. The United States is set apart from most other liberal democracies by the fact that the awesome power of judicial review belongs not only to the Supreme Court but to every judge in the land. Because the power to annul executive or legislative acts by declaring them unconstitutional is widely regarded as too mighty a weapon to be entrusted to ordinary judges, most countries have created a special tribunal to handle constitutional controversies.[3] Only a handful of nations—notably Canada, Japan, and the Republic of Ireland—have embraced the American system of permitting any judge to rule on constitutional questions in a regular lawsuit. And even within that small group, the United States stands alone. For American state and federal judges have exercised their powers of constitutional review with much greater frequency and boldness than judges elsewhere.

Excellent Judicial Adventures, Part I

American judicial assertiveness is traceable to a variety of factors. Foremost, perhaps, is the historic role of our early judges in adapting English law, first to the circumstances of a new continent and then to a wholly new type of political regime. Our Supreme Court not only laid claim to the power of judicial review at an early date but began to exercise it vigorously in the early years of the twentieth century, before it even existed in most other nations. Important, too, is an Anglo-American peculiarity—the ancient system of "equity" courts where the King's chancellor, in his discretion, dispensed relief to litigants whose remedies in the regular "law" courts were inadequate. When equity tribunals were eventually folded into the regular court system, ordinary judges acquired the chancellor's extraordinary powers to issue remedies such as injunctions commanding or prohibiting certain acts. Thus, the toolbox of every American judge has always contained some highly potent instruments.

American judges began to use those special powers with increasing frequency as the pace of social and economic change quickened. For most of the nineteenth century, the process of judicially adapting the common law (judge-made case law) to new conditions had taken place, as a rule, in gradual increments.

In 1917, Oliver Wendell Holmes could still describe judicial creativity as highly circumscribed. It was hemmed in by the facts of concrete cases, and confined to "molecular motions" within the limited spaces left open by previous court decisions (precedents), statutes, and state and federal constitutions.[4] As time went on, however, the gaps widened. It became increasingly difficult to stick to molecular motions while adapting traditional property, tort, and contract law to the legal conundrums created by the growth of cities, heavy industry, mass transportation, and instant communications.

Judges cannot refuse to decide disputes merely because the problems have never arisen before, or because legislatures have failed to deal with the larger underlying policy issues. Thus, American judges found themselves in a new ball game. Some of the equipment that had served them well for centuries now seemed as out of place as a cricket bat on a baseball field. How was one to develop principles for big-city landlords and tenants in the interstices of agrarian land law? For injuries from automobiles and defective manufactured products in the nooks of preindustrial tort law? For transactions involving corporate entities in the crannies of principles developed for flesh-and-blood buyers and sellers?

It was the gift of Benjamin Cardozo to accomplish such leaps by making the resolutions of novel problems seem to flow naturally from well-established principles. Recalling his early years on the bench, Cardozo admitted he had been initially distressed to find "how trackless was the ocean on which I had embarked."[5] "As the years have gone by," he went on, "I have become reconciled to the uncertainty, because I have grown to see it as inevitable."

That uncertainty, however, did not suggest to Cardozo that all bets were off. It did mean that a judge's job was more demanding than ever. Over his eighteen years of service in the New York State courts (1914–32), Cardozo wove webs of practical reason amidst the gaps, silences, and ambiguities of the sources in such a way as to provide guidance for judges across the country. With one luminous opinion after another, he served as progenitor and midwife to much of twentieth-century contract and tort law, striving to maintain predictability, coherence, and continuity while making the law responsive to the needs of a changing society. Though his motions were hardly molecular, his stitches were neat, his seams nearly invisible. The results he achieved were usually plausible, if not inevitable, unfoldings of familiar doctrines. His legal skills were of such a high order, and his writing style so graceful, that the full extent of his innovations often went unnoticed.

Cardozo's accomplishments owed much to the circumstances of time and place. New York City was the hub of the nation's commercial and financial life, and the New York Court of Appeals was a tribunal with a long and distinguished history. Into it flowed a steady stream of important and challenging cases, briefed and argued by some of the finest lawyers in the country. The issues were discussed and deliberated by some of the best judicial minds, for Cardozo was but the most famous of several able judges on that exceptional bench.

Cardozo contributed relatively little, however, to the resolution of the novel legal dilemmas that arose in connection with the advent of the regulatory state. As a state judge for most of his career, he was mainly occupied with the (then) largely judge-made law of torts and contracts and with traditional criminal law. During his brief tenure on the U.S. Supreme Court (1932–39), the vast apparatus of federal statutory and administrative law had only just begun to take shape.

Federal judges like Learned Hand, August N. Hand, and later Henry Friendly did for regulatory law what Cardozo had done for private law. Their task was even more difficult than his, for little in their training had prepared them to deal with the legal aspects of the country's transformation from a minimalist "night watchman" state into a proactive social welfare state. In their professional lifetimes, administrative agencies wielding enormous rule-making and discretionary power emerged as virtually a fourth branch of government, and statutes became the most important starting points for judicial reasoning (especially in the federal system). But judges were handicapped by the fact that the science of legislation—drafting and interpretation—had always been the Achilles' heel of the Anglo-American legal tradition.

Amidst the confusion, Learned Hand set to work. He had enjoyed, by all accounts including his own, no great success as a practicing lawyer. By the end of his long career, however, he was (in the words of a judge who was in many ways his opposite) "universally acknowledged as the greatest living judge in the English-speaking world."[6] That reputation rested mainly on some 3,000 influential opinions that helped to shape and maintain coherence in fields as diverse as antitrust, trademark, patent, admiralty, and commercial law. His skillfully crafted opinions cut paths through the jungle of burgeoning federal law that many fellow judges were glad to follow. After Hand's death in 1961 at the age of ninety, Judge Charles E. Wyzanski, Jr., wrote, "No lower court judge was so often cited by name in opinions of the Supreme Court of the United States or in academic publications. None in so few strokes could etch the growth of a legal principle, or reveal, without massive, pretentious quotation, its cultural and philosophical import. Justice Holmes had written that he would have welcomed Hand as a colleague; and the press spoke of him as the Tenth Justice of the Supreme Court."[7]

Augustus N. Hand was less celebrated than his cousin Learned, but was even more admired by some who knew them both. "Quote Learned, but follow Gus," it was sometimes playfully remarked. As boys, the two had been close companions, roaming the woods and countryside together near Elizabethtown, New York, where among their forebears had been many lawyers and judges.[8] Despite contrasting temperaments, they remained best friends for life. Learned was mercurial, impatient, profoundly skeptical, and subject to mood swings. Augustus was calm, steady, a staunch churchman, and modest—priding himself on nothing but the care he lavished on the most ordinary cases. Both counted it as great good fortune that they were able to serve together for a time as trial judges in the Southern District of New York, and that later they were reunited on the Second Circuit Court of Appeals. The judicial style of Augustus Hand was neatly captured in a tribute by Wyzanski, who served as clerk to both men: "Judge Hand's intended audience was not the bench, bar, or university world in general, but the particular lawyer who was about to lose the case and the particular trial judge whose judgment was being reviewed and perhaps reversed. And it is because of their direction toward this specialized audience that Judge Hand's opinions so often deserve the adjective 'thorough'—the adjective which he chose to describe that part of Justice Brandeis's work which he most admired."[9]

Neither Augustus nor Learned Hand delegated much work to clerks, even though "law secretaries" in the early years had to be paid out of the judge's own pocket. Both took it upon themselves, rather, to continue the education of the carefully selected young men who came to them for a year between law school and practice. Learned was the more intimidating taskmaster, but provided occasional comic relief in the form of ribald sea chanteys and Gilbert and Sullivan solos. Augustus was more sedate, bent on impressing each clerk with the importance of every case, no matter how commonplace. His conversations with his assistants were punctuated with tart admonitions such as "You had better stick to your job and not become an asteroid."[10]

Cardozo and the Hands, extraordinary individuals on strong and influential courts, could venture competently into uncharted territory because they were securely rooted in a centuries-old, fertile, dynamic tradition. All over the nation in the early decades of the new century, judges were faced with similar challenges. Not all of them, however, had well-stocked libraries, learned colleagues, and the benefit of briefs and arguments prepared by able and experienced practitioners. Judges in the far western states, separated by only a few decades from the relative lawlessness of the frontier, had to work under more challenging conditions. California, for example, was a brand-new game.

In 1848, when Mexico ceded that sparsely settled province

to the United States, California barely had a legal system. In the courts, such as they were, American judges succeeded traditional *alcaldes* who, according to Samuel Eliot Morison, had been administering "any sort of law they pleased—the code of Mexico or of Napoleon, common law, or lynch law."[11] At first the judiciary could do little more than try to maintain minimal law and order. That this was no easy task, even among the judges themselves, is evident from the career of California Chief Justice David S. Terry. Terry killed a U.S. senator in a duel in 1859. Years later, he was shot dead himself by a deputy marshal when he assaulted U.S. Supreme Court Justice Stephen J. Field in a train station. There is some reason to believe that Field, who had been feuding with Terry ever since they served together on the California court, planned the whole thing.

California was legally unprepared for its sudden development from a frontier outpost into a major center of agricultural, mining, commercial, and industrial activity. Its population grew from 15,000 to 300,000 in the seven years between 1849 and 1856. State legislators reached for a ready-made European-style solution in 1872 by adopting four codes drafted by Stephen Field's brother, David Dudley Field. Those civil, penal, procedural, and political codes were designed to provide judges with a comprehensive set of new starting points for legal reasoning. But California judges and lawyers never really acquired the Continental knack of working with a code. Most of the time they treated the codes as a kind of overlay on the skimpy case law rather than as a framework replacing the common law. Often they simply ignored relevant code provisions and proceeded, as they always had, by looking for a reported case with facts similar to the one at hand. California entered the twentieth century as a common-law state, but without a common-law tradition.[12]

Against that background, California Chief Justice Roger Traynor and his colleagues in the 1940s and 1950s dealt with the legal aspects of California's emergence as the country's most populous and prosperous state by developing the case law with great energy and imagination. Traynor, a former

Berkeley law professor, frequently drew on theories and ideas gleaned from academic writing. His opinions were in turn much admired and discussed by the professoriat, foreshadowing the synergy that currently exists between certain judges and scholars. Relatively unencumbered by tradition, Traynor paid less attention than most eastern judges to continuity in the state's case law. He saw the judge's role as that of an active partner with the legislature in lawmaking and policymaking.[13] His bold opinions began to attract attention, as Cardozo's more craftsmanlike ones had once done, from judges in other states confronted with similar problems.

Few American judges have been as proficient, imaginative, and persuasive as Cardozo, the Hands, and Traynor. Yet every twentieth-century judge has been obliged to handle novel and complex problems with uncertain guidance. It was mainly out of necessity, rather than through lust for power, that judges at all levels moved increasingly into areas where their legitimacy was weakest and their traditional skills of least use. They found themselves doing things that legislatures are better equipped to do, such as making judgments about broad social and economic facts rather than just finding the facts at issue in the case before them. In weighing and balancing competing social interests (as distinct from merely resolving the concrete dispute at hand), they began making the types of decisions that a republic ordinarily entrusts to elected representatives.[14]

Excellent Judicial Adventures
Part II: Constitutional Law

Contrary to popular belief, the Warren Court (1953–69) did not invent, but simply took to new heights, the freewheeling approaches to adjudication that were gaining ground here and there among state court judges. The initial justifications offered for the Warren Court's expansive readings of constitutional language were similar to those employed by defenders of the role state court judges had assumed in modernizing tort and contract law: if legislatures cannot or will not address a problem, then the courts should not hold back; if the house is on fire, it makes no difference who puts out the blaze; the branches of government should be partners, cooperating in the solutions of new social and economic problems; courts and legislatures should be in "dialogue" on vexing issues. In California, Roger Traynor had already made the leap from modernizing private law to ambitious constitutional interpretation.[15]

The problem with the model of cooperation and dialogue, as applied to constitutional law, however, is that legislators cannot talk back when the courts speak in their constitutional voice. It is never easy to marshal a legislative majority to modify or override a court decision, but if legislators deem the matter important enough, they can do so. When the courts hang their rulings on constitutional pegs, however, the "dialogue" is over and the ordinary political process comes to a halt. The broader the court's ruling, the less room is left for future exchanges. The matter is off the table—unless the Constitution is amended or the court changes its mind. Political energy, lacking its normal outlets, flows into litigation and the judicial selection process.

That's why most other liberal democracies have been reluctant to confide the power of judicial review to their ordinary supreme courts, and why John Marshall, once he had secured that power, was highly circumspect in its exercise. That's also the reason Justice Ruth Bader Ginsburg has been critical of the Supreme Court's 1972 abortion decision, *Roe* v. *Wade*—to the puzzlement of many who know of her work as a women's rights advocate. That decision was so broadly drawn, she points out, that it "invited no dialogue with legislators. Instead it seemed entirely to remove the ball from the legislators' court."[16] The Court's desegregation decisions took the initiative in an area where ordinary democracy was not working. But *Roe* v. *Wade*, Ginsburg observed, "halted a political process that was moving in a reform direction and thereby, I believe, prolonged divisiveness and deferred stable settlement of the issue." The Court would have done better, she went on, to proceed as it had done in sex discrimination cases, confining itself to instructing Congress and state legislatures to reexamine old classifications, and throwing the ball "back into the legislators' court, where the political forces of the day could operate."

It was out of a similar concern for the regime effects of constitutional decisions that judges like Holmes and Learned Hand counseled prudence in constitutional interpretation, though they accepted a relatively robust judicial role in other areas. Hand in his youth had witnessed and deplored the aggressive use of the Due Process Clauses in the service of laissez-faire capitalism. In middle age, he applauded the Court's more deferential approach to the popular branches of government in the New Deal era. In later years, he sniffed trouble when he sensed the Court was poised for new forays into legislative and local territory. When he was invited in 1958, at age eighty-seven, to give the Oliver Wendell Holmes Lectures at Harvard Law School, Hand was like an old warhorse rallying to familiar trumpets.

"I cannot frame," he said in those lectures, any definition of the Court's power under the Due Process Clauses "that will explain when the Court will assume the role of a third legislative chamber and when it will limit its authority to keeping Congress and the states within their accredited authority."[17] When the Court takes the former course, Hand confessed, "I have never been able to understand on what basis it does or can rest except as a *coup de main*." To the dismay of many in the audience, Hand expressed reservations about the then-recent desegregation decisions. Nothing in the Warren Court's opinions in those cases, it seemed to him, suggested that the Court had not been acting on the basis of "its own reappraisal of the relative values at stake."

Yet, characteristically, as he neared his conclusion, he confessed his doubts about his own reservations. Quoting Benjamin Franklin, Hand said, "[H]aving lived long, I have experienced many instances of being obliged by better information or fuller consideration to change opinions even on important subjects, which I once thought right, but found to be otherwise. It is therefore that the older I grow, the more apt I am to doubt my own judgment, and to pay more respect to the judgment of others." In the case of *Brown* v. *Board of Education*, Hand's self-doubts were grave enough that he did not want his lectures to be cited in the Senate by attackers of the Court that had decided them.[18] But he could not prevent his critique of *Brown*'s reasoning from being exploited by segregationist enemies of its substance.

Today, *Brown* is virtually immune from substantive criticism. But with hindsight, Hand's concern that *Brown* signaled the beginning of more audacious and less justifiable displacements of local and legislative authority seems prescient. As Judge Wyzanski, a wholehearted enthusiast for most Warren Court decisions, already acknowledged in 1963: "[Hand] is chiefly concerned to keep out of the law avowedly political choices lest . . . judges come to regard themselves as free of any restraint except to follow their private notions of justice. Such absence of restraint he rightly regards as arbitrary despotism. Nor will any studious observer of the current judicial scene say that Judge Hand's fears are groundless."[19]

But in 1954, when *Brown* was decided, few observers suspected that the Supreme Court was about to start substituting its own judgment for state and local decisions on a wide range of social issues. Segregation, after all, was the legacy of slavery, and race relations were a grave "American dilemma." There was no reason to think that the school desegregation cases would be followed by extensive judicial foreclosure of local self-determination on matters ranging from defamation, the details of capital punishment, and exclusion of evidence obtained in warrantless searches to pornography, abortion regulations, Christmas displays, and school curricula. *Brown* and the one-man, one-vote cases might well have gone down in history as an extraordinary constitutional moment. They might have been remembered, as are the Marshall Court's historic cases on the broad contours of federalism, as great decisions that made up in statesmanship what they lacked in legal authority. The Warren Court, following John Marshall's example, might have charted the new course with a few bold strokes, and left the rest to the political branches and the American people. But in the 1960s the judicial genie refused to go back into the lamp.

Sociologist Nathan Glazer got it right when he wrote that the Warren Court's desegregation decisions represented "a heroic period in the history of the court. But even heroes may overreach themselves."[20] The impulses that the Court unleashed proved difficult to contain. Many lawyers and laypeople began to imagine that wise judges in black robes could cure social ills, and many unwise judges down the line began to believe they had the magic touch. Interest groups of many sorts seized the opportunity to advance their causes by taking them to the courts rather than to the people. The litigating branch of the legal profession was off to the races.

The Warren Court (no longer unanimous) began to scrutinize and invalidate state legislative and judicial decisions in many areas, while expanding the categories of persons to be afforded protection against democratic decision making. Whereas *Brown* and the voting cases had been a response to insufficiently representative political processes, many later decisions seemed antagonistic to democratic decision making as such. The flight from politics turned into a stampede, as courts became alternatives to legislatures, and judges began acting like executives and administrators. Lower federal court judges, with the Supreme Court's approval, began issuing orders that involved them in the day-to-day administration of schools and then of other public institutions—deploying their ancient injunctive powers in the service of the Supreme Court's new constitutional agenda.

As time went on, it became apparent that the rising tide of rights was not lifting all boats. Some rights were more important than others. The Warren and Burger Courts paid particular attention to freedom of the press and expression, certain aspects of privacy, reproductive freedom, and the rights of women, racial minorities, and criminal defendants. Property rights, however, were left pretty much where they had been since the New Deal—in the realm of the legislative process. Religious freedom remained a relatively low priority. The right of local self-determination within constitutional limits took a beating, for nearly every advance of individual and minority rights is at the expense of another core constitutional value: democratic decision making.

The Rehnquist Court has not rejected the adventurous decisions of the Warren and Burger Courts so much as it has called a halt to further expansion. On some fronts, however, the current Court has sanctioned uses of judicial power as startling as any of those of their predecessors. What would Alexander Hamilton, who believed the judiciary had "neither purse nor sword," have made of the 1990 decision authorizing a lower court, as part of a desegregation plan, to direct a local school district to raise taxes?[21]

Meanwhile, in one of the most far-reaching judicial developments of the 1980s, state supreme courts in many parts of the country began to imitate and even outstrip the Warren and Burger Courts in their zeal for selected rights. State trial judges, like their federal counterparts, experimented with new uses of their injunctive powers. By the early 1990s, judges had established varying degrees of administrative control over public housing authorities, mental health and youth correction facilities, union locals charged with racketeering, and so on. Through court orders, federal and state judges were overseeing the operations of over 500 school districts and were supervising prison facilities in nearly forty states.[22]

The wheel thus came full circle. The Warren Court, importing practices developed by state supreme court judges, used open-ended constitutional concepts like due process and equal protection as points of departure for journeys to the outer frontiers of judicial power. When the Supreme Court's zeal for further exploration began to fade with changing personnel, state supreme courts mounted their own expeditions. Meanwhile, at all levels of the nation's judicial system, the ordinary business of the courts was becoming steadily more difficult and demanding—and not only because so many areas of law had been "constitutionalized."

The Judge's Lot Is Not a Happy One

While ambitious judicial review was enjoying an Indian summer in the nation's high courts, the daily work of every federal and state judge in the land was being transformed by a changing and rapidly expanding caseload. By the 1980s, the situation had reached crisis proportions. Some court systems were in gridlock. The causes included the increasing resort to litigation by previously court-shy businesses; the war on drugs; the green light the courts had given to rights-based claims; a host of other new judge-made and statutory causes of action; the creation of new crimes; and mass tort actions such as the asbestos and Dalkon shield litigation. Federal courts have had to cope, in addition, with an avalanche of new regulatory law as Congress and administrative agencies moved into areas such as environmental protection, occupational health and safety, pensions, medical care for the elderly and poor, food and product safety. Today's judges are so busy that, as one federal district judge has remarked, even a Learned Hand could no longer be Learned Hand.[23]

Heavier caseloads in turn have led to expansion of the judicial corps and to the creation of more positions for staff assistants of various sorts. The evolution of the federal judiciary from an elite judging corps into a layered bureaucracy was complete in less than two decades. Between 1961 and 1980, the number of federal trial judges, after remaining stable (relative to the U.S. population) from 1900 to 1961, expanded from 227 to 483,[24] and by 1993 was approaching 600, while the total number of federal judges was 846 (authorized).[25] The growth in the staff of the federal courts was even more dramatic—from 6,887 employees in 1970 to 14,261 in 1981[26] and 22,399 in 1991.[27] Ironically, the expansion of court staffs

to deal with the growing workload turned judges into supervisors, saddling them with distracting new duties.[28] Even with
more judges, staff attorneys, and clerks, the courts have not
been able to keep up.

An early warning was sounded in 1981 by former Solicitor
General Wade H. McCree, Jr., who predicted that the caseload
crisis and bureaucratizing trends would undermine the legitimacy of the entire American court system.[29] Four years later,
Judge Richard Posner of the Seventh Circuit Court of Appeals
called attention to spreading disarray in the ordinary noncriminal business of the federal courts.[30] In 1992, in an open letter
to Congress, a member of the Ninth Circuit bench candidly
acknowledged what many judges are still reluctant to say in
public: "Those who believe we are doing the same quality work
that we did in the past are simply fooling themselves. We adopt
more and more procedures for 'expediting' cases, procedures
that ensure that individual cases will get less attention."[31]

The problems fall into three broad categories: outright
neglect, inappropriate delegation, and erosion of institutional
checks on the arbitrary exercise of discretion. Neglect occasioned by crowded dockets takes the form of delay in getting
one's day in court and assembly-line treatment when that day
finally arrives. Conditions are worst where the courts touch the
lives of average citizens most closely—in state trial courts. The
shabby disrepair of courthouses that once gracefully adorned
the nation's public squares is all too often the outward symbol
of the slapdash administration of justice by demoralized men
and women within. Many conscientious judges are anguished
at not being able to give litigants the time and attention to
which they are entitled. Stepping down from a New York State
trial court after nearly a decade of service, Harold Baer, Jr.,
said in 1992 that his "crushing caseload" of over 800 pending
cases (as compared to the hefty average of 400–450 per federal
judge) made it impossible to do his job properly: "Even a
moment for contemplation and thoughtful decision-making is
sheer fantasy."[32]

Equally troubling is what happens behind the scenes at the

appellate level—the transfer of judicial work to nonjudges. Trial judges often delegate responsibility, too, but usually with the consent of the parties, as when an outside expert is appointed to supervise fact finding in a complex patent case. It is quite a different proposition when appellate judges farm out to assistants the jobs of reading briefs, summarizing arguments, and preparing draft decisions. According to Judge Posner (who clerked for Justice William Brennan), "today, a judge-written opinion, at any level of the American judiciary, is rare."[33] The assignment of such tasks to staff attorneys and law clerks is the equivalent of replacing an experienced surgeon with a resident or intern after the patient is anesthetized. As Posner has pointed out, the problem is hard to remedy, for few other parts of an overworked appellate judge's job are delegable.[34]

While extensive delegation at the appellate level can be explained, it is hard to square with any legitimate conception of the administration of justice. Courtroom protocols and rituals encourage citizens to have confidence that each and every case receives the personal attention of experienced judges who study the facts and law, and wrestle with the issues and arguments. But the public symbolism of the courtroom is often belied by the reality of chambers. In all too many cases, litigants get no more from the judge than supervision—sometimes very light—of the work of a twenty-four-year-old.[35] Law clerks are usually drawn from the top law graduates at good schools, but few have any legal experience, and most have received an education in which, as we will see, many aspects of law are shockingly neglected.[36] Yet, frequently, a clerk's initial "screening" of a case will be decisive on such matters as whether the lawyers are permitted to make oral arguments, or—in the Supreme Court—whether the case will be reviewed at all.

Another common response to heavier workloads has been to decide "routine" cases summarily without opinion or with cryptic unsigned opinions issued by "the Court." Since no lawsuit is routine to those involved, a litigant who gets a mere thumbs-down may understandably feel frustrated and resentful. Losing parties (and lawyers who have worked hard on briefs) are apt to wonder what goes on behind the scenes. Why didn't the judge buy the argument they thought was a clincher? Did the judge read the briefs at all? Judge Reinhardt of the busy Ninth Circuit has made no bones about the reality behind the appearance: "In place of the traditional oral argument and written opinions that we used to provide in most instances, we now all too often give cases second-class treatment. We merely look at the files and then issue unpublished memorandum dispositions or orders. The use of these makeshift procedures ensures that many cases do not get the full attention that they deserve, and the quality of our work suffers."[37] Heavy caseloads, according to federal District Judge Robert Keeton, are casting judges in the role of "Terminator"—just get it over with and don't worry too much about terminating justly.[38]

As Professor Joseph Vining points out, many time- and labor-saving practices fly in the face of what judging is all about. Judges, more than any other officials, are expected not only to listen but to show that they have listened; not only to reason their way through to the decisions they reach but to expose their reasoning processes to the parties and the public.[39] Those functions cannot be delegated without crossing the line, as Vining puts it, from the authoritative to the authoritarian.[40]

Not even the Supreme Court of the United States, with its relatively small caseload, has remained immune from bureaucratizing change. In 1933, Justice Brandeis proudly told a young New Dealer, "The reason they think so much of the Justices of the Supreme Court in Washington is that we are the only people who do our own work."[41] Today, with up to four law clerks apiece, few Supreme Court justices can be heard to make that claim. Only Justices Scalia and Stevens are said to take a leading role in crafting their own opinions. Supreme Court clerks are often amazed at the extent of the responsibility handed to them. As one described the experience to Nat Hentoff: "You go back to your office, you take a deep breath, you stare at your computer screen, and you go, 'Holy shit, I'm going to write the law of the land.' "[42]

Of equal concern is the extent to which the Supreme Court justices rely on their clerks to determine which of the approximately 6,000 petitions for certiorari that arrive at the Court each year will be among the 120 or so cases the Court elects to hear and decide. In that process of picking and choosing, the Court is no longer the relatively weak, reactive body the Founders envisioned, but has considerable power to shape its own agenda.[43] In making those crucial decisions, it is said, all of the justices except Justice Stevens (a longtime practitioner) base their sense of the case and its importance on memos prepared by clerks.[44]

Former Solicitor General Kenneth Starr blames insufficient judicial involvement for a disturbing pattern of certiorari denials in cases involving "important but unglamorous business-related issues."[45] The "Bermuda Triangle" into which such petitions have fallen, he speculates, is the pool of smart, easily bored young clerks "who typically have never practiced law or otherwise been involved in the world of free enterprise." How else explain, he asks, how the Court came to agree to determine whether 2 Live Crew's raunchy parody of "Oh Pretty Woman" infringed Roy Orbison's lyrics, while refusing to resolve a serious conflict among lower federal courts' interpretations of trademark law in the context of the largest trademark judgment in history? Since many rejected petitions involve questions on which lower courts have reached differing results, federal law is losing the coherence and uniformity that was once the pride of the federal judiciary. In Starr's view, it is as though the Court has said, "The system will simply have to tolerate greater instability and uncertainty."[46]

As for the work of a Chief Justice, one wonders what sort of opinions John Marshall would have written if (like Warren Burger and William Rehnquist) he had had to oversee the administration of a vast network of federal courts? Being a Chief Judge on any court these days is a dubious honor.

Finally, the caseload crisis and bureaucratization have eroded certain traditional checks on arbitrariness in the judicial process. The discipline of writing out the reasons for a decision and responding to the main arguments of the losing side has proved to be one of the most effective curbs on arbitrary judicial power ever devised. (Many are the stories told by judges of how they changed their minds after they realized that an initial hunch just "wouldn't write.") An equally useful constraint has been the practice of collegial deliberation before voting. In a full and frank exchange of views, individual appellate judges can test their own and each other's reasoning; together they may spot issues or problems that escaped everyone's individual attention.[47] Those important safeguards are lost when, as is increasingly the case, decisions are rendered without written opinions and judicial panels vote after little or no discussion.

Amidst all these changes in the world of judging, there are disquieting signs that the judiciary is losing some of its ability to attract and retain highly qualified men and women. Today, many capable lawyers no longer regard appointment or election to the bench as the capstone of a distinguished career.[48] It is not uncommon, when a judgeship is being filled, to hear that prominent attorneys have declined to have their names placed in nomination—or that a firm is angling to relieve itself of an unproductive partner by touting him or her for a judicial appointment. Sitting judges, meanwhile, are resigning in record numbers, often after a relatively short tenure.[49] Many return to practice, citing financial reasons.

Not only are there great disparities between judicial salaries and the annual draw of partners in large firms, but the average associate's pay in a corporate firm exceeds the typical judicial salary. Nevertheless, modest judicial pay scales are not the only explanation for the diminishing attractiveness of these once-coveted positions to able, ambitious men and women. For one thing, a judge's pay with benefits compares favorably with the median income of lawyers in the aggregate. (The typical salary of a state judge is $70,000 to $100,000; federal judges make $129,500 at the district level, $137,500 at the Courts of Appeals, and $159,000 on the Supreme Court, with excellent retirement benefits.) Furthermore, many successful practitioners within recent memory willingly traded significant reductions in income for the prestige of a judicial appointment. The appeal of the prestige factor, however, has decidedly dimmed with changes in judicial work and working conditions, especially in the state court systems.

Even the job of a federal judge is not as attractive as it once was to practitioners. In 1980, when Susan Getzendanner became the first woman to be appointed to the federal bench in Chicago, it seemed like a natural advance in a career that had taken her from the top of her law school class to a partnership in one of the city's most respected law firms. Seven years later, though, Getzendanner resigned from the U.S. District Court to join the high-powered takeover firm of Skadden, Arps. Discussing her move with a reporter from the *National Law Journal*, she explained that the courtroom is "not where the action is."[50]

Most people, including many lawyers, might find that statement astonishing. If presiding over a federal trial court in Chicago is not an exciting job, what is? It is not yet widely realized that, over the past few years, many of the nation's federal trial courts have been transformed primarily into criminal courts flooded with drug cases and habeas corpus petitions.[51] Because district judges are required by federal law to deal promptly with such matters, they often fall seriously behind in their noncriminal cases. The nation's drug problem has wreaked havoc in the courts. Narcotics cases account for nearly half of all federal criminal trials; while two out of three criminal cases in some states involve drugs.[52]

In sum, the rise of the judge militant has proceeded from the 1960s onward in lockstep with bureaucracy rampant. By degrees, American judges, long distinguished by their independence and prestige from Continental civil service judges, are coming to resemble harried bureaucrats. But unlike their European counterparts, American judges receive no particular training for, or supervision in, their delicate and important roles. The country is thus beginning to experience the disadvantages of a bureaucratized judiciary, without the advantages.

Alarmingly, some judges seem to have found consolation by

turning the judicial role on its head—lifting their eyes from the tasks at hand to the audience beyond the courtroom. Some launch one-man crusades into law reform and contrive to be frequently in the public eye. Others strive to gain recognition, not among their peers for a lifetime of impartial judging and fine craftsmanship, but in the media and the academy for making a splash in a big case or for leaving a "personal mark" on the law. According to Federal Judge Andrew J. Kleinfeld, "Any judge knows that if he or she cares to be famous, widely praised in universities, the object of adulation among the greatest number of law clerk applicants, and invited to speak at the largest number of universities, the most efficient means is a novel and creative opinion favoring the interests of those groups that are now favored in the universities."[53]

A few judges have discovered television. Patrick Kelly, a federal district judge in Wichita, Kansas, went on *Nightline* in August 1991 to discuss with Barbara Walters his annoyance with the Justice Department for intervening in an Operation Rescue case then pending before him. He repeated the performance the following evening on the *MacNeil/Lehrer NewsHour*. Though judicial ethics forbid a judge to make any public comment that might reasonably be expected to prejudice the outcome of pending litigation, Kelly did not recuse himself.[54] Another media-struck magistrate earned the *National Law Journal's* 1992 "Mirror, Mirror, on the Wall Award" for permitting television coverage of the Woody Allen–Mia Farrow child custody case, even though attorneys for both sides had agreed to keep cameras out of the courtroom.[55]

An increasing number of judges have taken up their pens to write op-ed pieces, columns, and articles of a sort that once would have been generally frowned upon—one to defend his mandated breakup of AT&T, another to criticize the Supreme Court's handling of a capital punishment case, one (at the height of the Clarence Thomas nomination hearings) to urge President Bush to withdraw the nomination, and another presuming, in a patronizing tone, to tell Justice Thomas how to decide cases. There is no longer any solid consensus among judges about the precise application, scope, and limits of the principle that judges should be circumspect about public comments that may create doubts about their own impartiality.[56] Many judges still try to follow Francis Bacon's counsel: "Judges must be as chaste as Caesar's wife, neither to be, nor so much as suspected in the least to be unjust."[57] Others dream of being Caesar.

One exasperated federal judge broke ranks in 1992 to take fellow judges to task for unseemly grandstanding. Judge Laurence Silberman of the U.S. Court of Appeals for the District of Columbia charged that the desire for media approval was actually influencing the decisions of some judges.[58] Amidst the heated denials that followed Silberman's accusation, *Legal Times* journalist Tony Mauro wrote that his own off-the-record interviews had convinced him that Silberman's concerns were privately shared "by many judges throughout the federal judiciary."[59]

Some of the very traits that horrify tradition-minded judges, though, are part and parcel of a new, attractive concept of the judicial role. At the same time that the job of a judge was becoming more complex and burdensome, many judges began to chafe at traditional constraints. The classical conception of the judicial role, by their lights, was too confining, boring, unrewarding, or insufficiently responsive to social problems. They began orienting themselves toward more gratifying models of excellence. The new judicial ideal that has been taking shape has had wide appeal, not only among judges but within other relatively unaccountable institutions such as the press and the universities. Many academics and journalists, too, were beginning to bridle at the discipline of subordinating their personal views to the demands of scholarly or reportorial detachment. The new academy and the postmodern fourth estate helped to make heroes and heroines of the romantic judges to whom we now turn.

8

The Extra Man on the Field: Hey! Wasn't That the Umpire?

There is a sense among judges that there are wrongs to be righted and that it is their responsibility to do it.

—D.C. TRIAL JUDGE SYLVIA BACON to the American Society for Public Administration (1976)[1]

As more judges began to taste and enjoy the once-forbidden fruits of emancipation from the constraints of statute, precedent, Constitution, or tradition, the classical ideal associated with modesty, impartiality, restraint, and interpretive skill has been rivaled by an image of the good judge as bold, creative, compassionate, result-oriented, and liberated from legal technicalities. In contemporary praise literature, new heroes have emerged, judges celebrated for their daring, imagination, sensitivity, and zeal for fairness—William O. Douglas, Earl Warren, Thurgood Marshall, J. Skelley Wright, William Brennan. Some are especially noted for one romantic trait or another, while a few seem to possess the full range. Elements of the new ideal achieved official status in 1988 when the American Bar Association's powerful Standing Committee on the Federal Judiciary added "compassion" and "sensitivity" to "integrity" and "competence" on the list of traits it would consider in rating candidates for federal judgeships.[2]

Romantic Heroes

Between John Marshall's time and Earl Warren's, exceptional adventurousness in a judge, even a Supreme Court justice, was little admired. Justice William O. Douglas, for instance, was a romantic judge ahead of his time. His contempt for form was regarded by many observers as sloppiness; his visionary opinions were seen as evidence he was angling for the presidency; and his solicitude for those he considered underdogs was perceived as favoritism. In the 1990s, he would surely have basked in the "Greenhouse Effect"—a term (named after the *New York Times*'s Linda Greenhouse) for the warm reciprocity between activist journalists and judges who meet with their approval. But in the 1950s and early 1960s, Douglas was widely considered to be unprincipled.

The appointment of Earl Warren as Chief Justice in 1953 would eventually change all that. President Eisenhower's choice of the California governor was an unusual move, for Warren had spent almost all his professional life in electoral politics. After serving as California's Attorney General, he became a power in the state Republican Party and a popular chief executive. He was Tom Dewey's running mate in 1948, and a serious contender for the Republican presidential nomination himself in 1952. What made Warren's political career remarkable was that, as legal historian Edward White has put it, "he seemed to have succeeded by virtue of characteristics long thought to be incompatible with public office: integrity, nonpartisanship, honesty, humanity. He appeared to have acquired prominence and power simply by being a good man."[3]

Though he had little else in common with John Marshall, Earl Warren was a statesman. He came to the Court, White recounts, "imbued with self-confidence in his ability to persuade others, possessed of a strong belief in the worth of active government, secure with power and unafraid of controversy, and eager, as in the past, to make his influence felt."[4] Where American race relations were concerned, statesmanship was

Classic-romantic handshake: Learned Hand and Earl Warren at ceremonies marking the judge's fifty years of service in the U.S. courts, April 11, 1959 *(Courtesy the Bettmann Archive)*

sorely needed. President Truman had taken a giant step with his executive order desegregating the armed forces in 1948. Under Warren's leadership, the Supreme Court moved even more dramatically toward making race an unacceptable basis for official classifications.

Unlike John Marshall, however, Warren was relatively un-concerned about the regime effects of his pathbreaking deci-sions. Nor had anything in his background prepared him for the fine-gauge work of opinion writing. He was impatient with the need to ground a desired outcome in constitutional text or tradition. As described by an admirer in the 1960s, Warren was a man who brushed off legal and historical impediments to the results he felt were right; he was not a "look it up in the library" type.[5]

It took a former Warren clerk, John Hart Ely, to articulate a technically satisfactory rationale, long after the fact, for most, but not all, of the Warren Court's controversial decisions. Their constitutional grounding, Ely contended, was not so much in any particular provision as in two fundamental values that permeated the entire structure of the Constitution—access to political processes and representative government.[6] The decisions that broadened access to schooling and voting were in furtherance of the fundamental value of "representativity" inherent in the constitutional design. Precedential support for refusing to defer to majoritarian arrangements in cases like *Brown*, Ely pointed out, could be found in a 1938 case where the Court in a footnote had announced its willingness to closely scrutinize statutes "directed at particular religious, or national, or racial minorities" where prejudice "tends seriously to curtail the operation of those political processes ordinarily to be relied upon to protect minorities."[7]

Although scholars may argue about its foundations in text and tradition, the Warren Court's decision in *Brown* v. *Board of Education* is widely recognized as a great act of statesmanship. Those academics who downplay the importance of *Brown* in the struggle for racial justice have underrated two aspects of the landmark decision, one influencing the legal profession and the other affecting popular culture. *Brown*, to my generation of lawyers (entering practice in the early 1960s), was a sign that law (and therefore we) could play a part in building a better society. To many of us who worked in the civil rights movement of the 1960s, educational opportunity and participatory politics seemed to be the two principal paths to realization of the American dream for everyone. Even if the courts could do little more than clear away official roadblocks, that was no small achievement.

Second, and of at least equal significance, *Brown* contributed to substantial, if unmeasurable, effects on attitudes about race relations—effects that in turn helped to bring about important political changes like the Civil Rights Act and voting rights legislation.[8] The Warren Court laid its prestige on the line in a bid not only to dismantle official segregation but to delegitimate racially discriminatory attitudes.

That wager was successful. Though racial prejudice has not been eradicated, it has no respectability whatsoever in contemporary American society. In *Praying for Sheetrock*, an inspiring account of the gradual political empowerment of the black community in McIntosh County, Georgia, Melissa Fay Greene wrote: "Of course, it is not enough, but it is a beginning. The descendants of the Scottish settlers start to view the descendants of the African slaves not as aliens in their midst, and not as servants, but as neighbors, colleagues, partners, fellow Americans, and increasingly, as leaders."[9]

Greene's dream of the day when African Americans would be accepted, easily and naturally, as leaders was already advancing. The very year her lines were published, a black Georgian from the nearby Pinpoint community became the second member of his race to be appointed to the nation's highest court. Thirty-seven years after *Brown* v. *Board of Education*, and thanks in part to its role in changing American sentiments, Clarence Thomas, sharecropper's son and admirer of the great classical judges, took the seat vacated by Thurgood Marshall. At the same time, another African American, General Colin Powell, was Chairman of the Joint Chiefs of Staff and was beginning to be widely mentioned as a possible presidential candidate.

If *Brown* v. *Board of Education* represented the summit of romantic judging, it was William Brennan, appointed to the Supreme Court by President Eisenhower in 1956, who incarnated the full spectrum of romantic judicial qualities. Like Clarence Thomas, Brennan was of humble origins. The son of Irish immigrants, he made his way to Harvard Law School—encouraged by his trade-unionist father, who told him that a lawyer could do a lot for working people.[10] Brennan did go into labor law, but enlisted on the other side of the cause that had meant so much to his father. After some years as a successful corporate practitioner in New Jersey, he became a trial judge and rose in time to the New Jersey Supreme Court. On the U.S. Supreme Court, he became a towering hero to those who shared his view that the Court not only had the power but also had the duty to use its power to effect social and political change. When several hundred state and federal judges were asked in 1987 to name the judge they most admired, Brennan was mentioned more often than any other.[11]

In many ways, Brennan dominated the Court during his long tenure through sheer energy, personality, and political savvy. Described by biographer Kim Eisler as neither the most brilliant nor the best writer on the Court, Brennan nevertheless may have had the most influence on the general direction of its decisions.[12] Few lawyers would disagree with *The New Yorker*'s evaluation, on Brennan's retirement in 1990, that the affable and determined justice had come "to personify the expansion of the role of the judiciary in American life."[13] He played a major role in decisions that effected a major transfer of power to the federal government from the state and local levels.

Even toward the end of his career, as the composition and mood of the Court changed, Brennan was often able to beat the odds and further his vision. As former Solicitor General Rex Lee has put it: "This was largely because he was so skillful at doing those things that were necessary, both theoretically and in personal kinds of ways, to marshal five votes."[14] As portrayed by Woodward and Armstrong in *The Brethren*, Brennan "cajoled in conference, walked the halls constantly and worked the phones, polling and plotting strategy with his allies."[15] Upon returning from one of these sorties, he would often tell his clerks, "Well, guys, it's all taken care of."[16] Thurgood Marshall recalled that Brennan "was always ready to prune a paragraph here or recast a thought there in order to accommodate a colleague's concerns."[17] In later years, when his colleagues on a changing Court declined to follow him on such excursions as judicially banning capital punishment or abolishing the custom of prayer at the opening of legislative sessions, Brennan went out on the hustings, calling on state courts to take up the cudgels.

In speeches and writings, Brennan encouraged state judges to exercise their powers of constitutional review in new and creative ways, as California's Roger Traynor had once done. State courts, he pointed out, could interpret their own constitutions so as to provide even more rights than are afforded under the federal Constitution.[18] Like the fox in Aesop's fable, the wily Brennan cajoled whole flocks of jurists into dropping their reserve. "State courts cannot rest," he wrote, "when they have afforded their citizens the full protections of the federal Constitution. State constitutions, too, are a font of individual liberties, their protections often extending beyond those afforded by the Supreme Court's interpretation of federal law."

Brennan's retirement in 1990 did not mark the disappearance of his notion that the Supreme Court should provide ultimate resolution of a wide range of controversial social questions. The grandiose claims of Justices Kennedy, O'Connor, and Souter in *Casey* are witness to the persistence of what Yale's Robert Burt calls the "Court's chronic conceit, that its constitutional command should be the last word on fundamentally disputed issues"—a conceit which "recurrently stumbles over the order implicitly established by the Constitution itself."[19]

Unlike many adventurous judges, Brennan had well-developed views of judging and did not mind discussing them. Here is Brennan in a 1988 essay:

> The Constitution is fundamentally a public text—the monumental charter of a government and a people—and a Justice of the Supreme Court must apply it to resolve public controversies. For, from our beginnings, a most important consequence of the constitutionally created separation of powers has been the American habit, extraordinary to other democracies, of casting social, economic, philosophical, and political questions in the form of law suits, in an attempt to secure ultimate resolution

by the Supreme Court. . . . Not infrequently, these are the issues on which contemporary society is most deeply divided. They arouse our deepest emotions. The main burden of my twenty-nine years on the Supreme Court has thus been to wrestle with the Constitution in this heightened public context, to draw meaning from the text in order to resolve public controversies.[20]

That passage can instructively be compared with the view often expressed by Justice Holmes that "legislatures are the ultimate guardians of the liberties and welfare of the people in quite as great a degree as the courts."[21] Although one of the opinions of which Brennan was proudest was on legislative reapportionment,[22] he maintained an uncharacteristic silence on the role of the elected branches in resolving the issues on which "society is most deeply divided." The reason must be that the way he saw his own life's work, as indicated in the above passage, put him in direct competition with the popular branches. Later in the same essay, he made no bones about his position that, right or wrong, the Court is to have the last word: "The justices are certainly aware that we are not final because we are infallible; we know that we are infallible because we are final."[23]

Brennan's approach to judging could not be more remote in spirit from Holmes's structural restraint. As Brennan admirer Professor Bert Neuborne has noted: "Brennan's legacy is a legacy of overruling majoritarian judgments that violate constitutional norms."[24] Nor did Brennan have much use for John Marshall's prudent avoidance of the appearance of judicial imperialism. In the passage above, he did not hesitate to claim, regarding the Court's powers: "The course of vital social, economic, and political currents may be directed."[25]

Energized and prodded to no small degree by Brennan, majorities on the Warren and Burger Courts actively pursued a high-minded vision of empowering those individuals and groups they perceived as disadvantaged. As the ACLU's Norman Dorsen put it, Brennan's judging was characterized by "a sensitive, consistent and courageous concern for the individual, and particularly the underdog, in American society."[26] When deference to the elected branches served those ends, as in many affirmative action cases, Brennan deferred as humbly as any classical judge. When the decisions of city or town councils or state or federal legislatures got in his way, he invoked expansive interpretations of constitutional language to brush them aside. Brennan, unlike many of his imitators, was fully aware of the tradition he had rejected. According to Woodward and Armstrong, Brennan often told his clerks that John Marshall Harlan had been "the only real judge" on the Court in the Warren years, the only one who weighed the issues dispassionately.[27]

While Brennan was not one to let text or tradition stand in the way of a desired result, he knew how to turn his corners squarely. But he did not share the devotion to craft values that characterized the work of judges like Harlan or Byron White. Nor did he show much concern about the probable side effects of a desired result in a particular case on the separation of powers, federal-state relations, or the long-term health of political processes and institutions. With respect to such matters, he was one with Warren and Thurgood Marshall, impatient with what he considered to be abstractions and technicalities.[28]

As for compassion, Brennan had plenty for those he made (or wished to make) winners, but he showed little sensitivity toward those he ruled against. His heart went out to Native Americans when a Court majority permitted the federal government to build a road through sacred Indian places on public land.[29] But in striking down a long-standing and successful New York City program providing remedial math and reading teachers to poor, special-needs children in religious schools, Brennan was pitiless.[30] It took dissenting Justice Sandra Day O'Connor to point out that the majority ruling, written by Brennan, had sacrificed the needs and prospects of 20,000 children from the poorest families in New York, and thousands more disadvantaged children across the country, for the sake of a maximalist version of the principle of separation of church and state.[31]

Brennan was not much given to doubts and self-questioning. Shortly after his retirement, the justice reminisced with journalist David O. Stewart about his long judicial career. Stewart reminded Brennan of retired Justice Lewis Powell's admission that with hindsight he regretted voting to uphold Georgia's sodomy law. Had Justice Powell's second thoughts prompted Justice Brennan to think of any cases over his thirty-three years on the Supreme Court where he wished now that he had voted differently? Stewart asked. "Hell no," Brennan replied, "I never thought I was wrong."[32]

The model of bold, assertive judging has also had its exemplars in the lower courts. One federal appellate judge famed for his crusading decisions on civil rights and tenants' remedies was the late J. Skelley Wright. Looking back on his role in expanding landlords' liability for the condition of leased premises, he wrote in 1982, "I didn't like what I saw, and I did what I could to ameliorate, if not eliminate, the injustice involved in the way many of the poor were required to live in the nation's capital. I offer no apology for not following more closely the legal precedents which had cooperated in creating the conditions that I found unjust."[33]

The romantic ideal also fired the imaginations of judges in the capillaries of the legal system, the sites of the everyday administration of justice described in *The Federalist* as "the great cement of society."[34] A longtime District of Columbia Superior Court judge, Sylvia Bacon, told the American Society for Public Administration that judges have a sense that there are "wrongs to be righted" and that it is their job to put matters in order.[35] As for the role of the Constitution and the law in guiding the judge's sense of right and wrong, Judge Bacon brusquely remarked, "Legal reasons are often just a cover for a ruling in equity (basic fairness)." By "fairness," Judge Bacon apparently did not mean anything so prosaic as keeping an open mind to the arguments and applying the relevant law without regard to the identity of the litigants and without regard to a particular outcome. Her notion was more visceral: "Plain and simple sense of outrage by the judge." Such views were no impediment to Judge Bacon's election to a seat on the American Bar Association's Board of Governors in the 1980s.

As new ideas about judging have spread from the Supreme Court's most momentous decisions to the regular business of the Court, and filtered downward through the nation's ordinary courts, several questions arise: What judicial qualities are best suited for the needs of a nation whose diverse people increasingly have little in common but a love of individual liberty and a commitment to the rule of law? Of a country with an ever more complex legal system? Of an economy that requires a measure of legal stability and predictability? Of a polity that aims to be a democratic republic? Is judicial self-abnegation outdated? Should Americans be seeking more judges who are assertive and compassionate, rather than restrained and impartial? How much has romantic judging contributed to the cracks and potholes that are appearing in the "great cement"?

Judges for a Pluralistic Republic

To the Founders, impartiality was the sine qua non of judicial justice. Massachusetts, adopting John Adams's words, built the concept into its Bill of Rights: "It is essential to the preservation of the rights of every individual, his life, liberty, property, and character, that there be an impartial interpretation of the laws, and administration of justice. It is the right of every citizen to be tried by judges as free, impartial and independent as the lot of humanity will admit."[36] From the early years of the Republic to the present day, every American judge has taken a solemn vow to carry out his or her duties without fear or favor: "I do solemnly swear that I will administer justice without respect to persons, do equal right to the poor and to the rich, and that I will impartially discharge and perform all the duties incumbent upon me, according to the best of my abilities and understanding agreeably to the Constitution and laws of the United States, so help me God."[37]

Have the old ideals of judicial independence and judging "without respect to persons" become obsolete in a country where diverse ideas of justice compete among an increasingly heterogeneous population? Should we, perhaps, revise the oath to read: "I affirm that I will administer justice with careful attention to the individual characteristics of the parties, that I will show compassion to those I deem disadvantaged, and that I will discharge my duties according to my personal understanding of the Constitution, the laws of the United States, and such higher laws as may be revealed to me"?

Some critics of the worldview implicit in the present oath say that judging "without respect to persons" can lead to inhumane results by ignoring important differences—between men and women, rich and poor, black and white, strong and weak. Besides, they observe, impartiality is often just a mask covering various sorts of bias. They point to historical research that has found more than a little clay on the feet of classical idols. It may well have been Holmes's obnoxious eugenic views, for example, rather than his vaunted restraint, that prompted him to uphold a state statute providing for the forced sterilization of mental patients—with the cruel comment that "three generations of imbeciles are enough."[38] Even Cardozo seems to have had his weakness, a zeal to "improve" the law that sometimes overwhelmed his concern for fairness in the actual case at hand.[39]

But are judicial compassion and responsiveness viable substitutes for the elusive ideal of impartiality? Few would dispute that judges should be able to empathize with the men and women who come before them. But in the early years of this century, adventurous judges were extremely tenderhearted toward big business, while showing little compassion for women and children working long hours in factories. Or consider Ronald Dworkin's grim judgment on another subjective judge, William O. Douglas: "[T]he conclusion is tempting, suggested by well over a dozen incidents, that his final and long alliance with civil liberty and the cause of the poor was based at the start not on any moral conviction or natural sympathy, but on a much cooler assessment of where, on the day, the action was."[40]

Let us acknowledge that, until someone figures out how to make judges from other than human material, neither classical nor romantic feet will be a pretty sight. The real question then is which judicial attributes, systematically cultivated, are best suited for the needs of a modern republic. Which traits offer the most protection against arbitrariness and bias? Whatever one may conclude about the right mix of qualities for the special circumstances of the Supreme Court, it is hard to imagine that the routine administration of justice can benefit from an increase of compassion at the expense of impartiality. Impartiality does not exclude the ability to enter empathically into another person's point of view. The virtue of "disinterest," as understood by the Founders, is the antithesis of partiality or self-interest.[41] It does not mean indifference to the parties and their dispute. It means: "I'm not doing this because of what's in it for me."

Far from being outmoded, that cultivated self-restraint is more essential than ever under modern American conditions. A close-knit, relatively homogeneous community can get along (perhaps) with a system where village elders reach decisions on the basis of their personal sense of fairness and their informed concern for the parties and the community. But that pastoral model cannot serve for an ethnically and ideologically diverse nation where litigants are strangers to the judge and often to each other. The liberties and fortunes of citizens cannot be left at the mercy of each judge's personal sense of what procedures are fair, what outcome is just, who needs protection, and who deserves compassion.

The combination of subjective judging and an elected judiciary is an especially unhappy one. In the forty states where elections play a role in selecting or retaining some or all judges, the American Judicature Society reports, problems related to campaign advertising and financing are serious and worsening.[42] What does it portend for a judge's impartiality when his election ads look just like a district attorney's: "Tough on

Crime"?[43] Or for her independence when she accepts large campaign contributions from lawyers who regularly appear in her court?[44]

For cynics who maintain that judicial independence and impartiality are simply a sham, the logical move is to select judges according to their ideological leanings. But that's a dicey business—and not only because "sensitivity" and "compassion" are easier to fake than intelligence and integrity. The problem with subjective judging is that, sooner or later, the tables are apt to be turned when ambitious judges with the "wrong" ideas ascend to the bench.

That's why many journalists and legal academics who once cheered the progress of assertive judging on the Supreme Court had second thoughts as the composition of the Supreme Court changed. When William Brennan retired in 1990, *The New Republic* nervously editorialized:

> [Brennan's] passionate judicial activism was unafraid, in a pinch, to leave constitutional text, history, and structure behind. When liberals like Brennan held sway in the courts, judicial activism often led to liberal results; now that "conservatives" are the ones ignoring legislative history and congressional intentions, Brennan's legacy makes it harder for liberals to cry foul.[45]

But why should the country's response to the old problem flagged by Alexander Hamilton (the scarcity of individuals with the requisite skill and integrity) be to accept a thoroughly politicized judiciary? One alternative that has worked well for some liberal democracies is a meritocratic civil service judiciary, staffed with graduates of judicial training academies. But we need not depart so radically from our own traditions. Surely our wise course is to insist on judges who have demonstrated a capacity for self-restraint (structural, interpretive, and personal) as well as a commitment to the time-honored judicial practices that help to promote those qualities.

What are those practices? The Pavlovas and DiMaggios of

judging are those who are most skilled in maintaining principled continuity in the system, while deciding particular cases in a way that even the losing party can accept as fair. But no one is born with that sort of virtuosity. Anglo-American judges over centuries have developed numerous safeguards against lapses and partiality. Chief among them is the requirement that a judge expose his or her reasoning processes in a written opinion. Since a perfectly reasoned opinion may rest on arbitrarily chosen premises, a judge is also expected to explain the facts and principles on which each decision is based. He or she is expected to follow those principles consistently in future cases. Some judges impose upon themselves the discipline of addressing their explanations to the losing party, or to the judge below whose opinion is being reviewed. Through such practices, and through thousands of small daily acts and choices, a man or woman constitutes himself or herself as a certain kind of judge. Therein lie the hope and the danger.

Judges for a Complex Society

No one seriously disputes the proposition that current economic and social conditions demand a high degree of technical skill in the judiciary. Senator Roman Hruska's famous remark that mediocre people ought to be represented on the Supreme Court was rightly derided. The supply of competent judges at all levels is indirectly threatened, however, by several habits associated with adventurous judging.

As every lawyer knows, part of an appellate court's work involves maintaining a reasonable degree of coherence and predictability in the law. If that unglamorous but crucial task is not performed well, the courts falter in their fundamental obligation to decide like cases alike. Practitioners then stumble, too, for they cannot give reliable advice to clients who are trying to plan for the future, or to decide whether to prosecute, defend, or settle claims.

Yet, over the past fifty years, it has become steadily more difficult for appellate judges to ensure reasonable reckonability and coherence in the legal system. Legislatures and administrative agencies rarely take the trouble to fit new statutes and regulations into the framework of existing law. Rather, they leave it up to judges to make some sense of a welter of federal, state, and local enactments that are often conflicting or overlapping—some overly detailed, others airily vague. The intellectual difficulty of many of these cases surpasses anything that ever came before John Marshall's Court. In consequence, the quality most required of an appellate judge is often a craftsman's art and painstaking care.[46]

Thus it is a cause for concern that specialists in areas like tax, antitrust, labor, pensions, maritime law, insurance, social security, patents, trademarks, and copyrights increasingly complain of a decline in judicial workmanship. After all, what would be left of the principle that like cases should be decided alike if every judge felt free to brush aside precedents, statutes, and bargained-for contractual provisions as mere technicalities? What would be the effect on the economy if our present imperfectly functioning system should degenerate into a nonsystem, a chaotic heap of idiosyncratic decisions? Are we really ready for the rank-and-file judiciary to cast off restraints that rested lightly on the shoulders of men like Holmes and Hand? For judges who slip the mailed fist of power into the velvet glove of compassion?

Judges and the Democratic Experiment

Romantic judging in constitutional cases exacts a toll on the democratic elements in our form of government. As Tocqueville pointed out, those who wish to attack the decisions of the people acting through their elected representatives have only two courses open to them: "They must either change the nation's opinion or trample its wishes underfoot."[47] When

Warren and Burger Court majorities converted the Constitution's safety valves (the Bill of Rights, Due Process, Equal
Protection) into engines with judges at the controls, they
wreaked havoc with grass-roots politics. The dismal failures of
many local authorities in dealing with racial issues became
pretexts for depriving citizens everywhere of the power to
experiment with new approaches to a wide range of problems
that often take different forms in different parts of the country.
Constitutional provisions designed to protect individuals and
minorities against majoritarian excesses were increasingly used
to block the normal processes through which citizens build
coalitions, develop consensus, hammer out compromises, try
out new ideas, learn from mistakes, and try again. Judicially
ordained, top-down regulations are poor substitutes for local
trial and error—especially where knotty problems such as those
related to crime, pornography, education, teenage pregnancy,
and delivery of social services are concerned.[48]

Elected officials have offered little resistance to judicial inroads on their powers. On hot issues, they are often are only
too happy to be taken off the hook by the courts. But each
time a court sets aside an action of the political branches
through freewheeling interpretation, the American experiment
in self-government suffers a setback. Political skills atrophy.
Men and women cease to take citizenship seriously. Citizens
with diverse points of view lose the habit of cooperating to set
conditions under which all can flourish. Tolerance suffers as
communication declines. Adversarial legalism supplants the
sober legalistic spirit that Tocqueville admired. As Abraham
Lincoln warned in his First Inaugural Address, "if the policy
of the government, upon vital questions, affecting the whole
people, is to be irrevocably fixed by decisions of the Supreme
Court . . . the people will have ceased to be their own rulers,
having, to that extent, practically resigned their government
into the hands of that eminent tribunal."[49]

Like deficit spending or toxic-waste dumping, the regime
effects of romantic judging are not easy to discern until the
harm has reached crisis proportions. But just as impartial

judges are beacons, leading public servants of all sorts in the direction of reasoned adherence to principle,[50] romantic judges are pied pipers enticing bureaucrats everywhere to new heights of arrogance and abuse of power.

In Praise of "Ordinary" Judges

In retrospect, one can see that the rise of bold judging proceeded for the most part with good intentions. Earlier in the century, state court judges often had to take the initiative to keep judge-made law abreast of social and economic changes. In the wake of the New Deal, federal judges had to improvise techniques for dealing with regulatory law. In *Brown* and the one-man, one-vote cases, the Supreme Court had to exercise statesmanship in addressing legal aspects of the country's most pressing social problems. The achievements of gifted judges in meeting those challenges made it difficult for some of them—as well as for less capable judges—to resist the impulse to keep on doing justice by their own lights. That those lights were not always powered by authoritative sources was easy to disguise, even from themselves. It was a case of successes leading to temptations, of a good thing taken to extremes.

One can presume that romance in judging will run its course. If so, and if strength begins to return to the atrophied parts of the body politic, perhaps Americans will again honor the men and women who have stood firm for the everyday judicial virtues. The beginning of wisdom would be to recognize that, whatever the pros and cons of adventurous judging by the Supreme Court on momentous occasions, romantic ideals are a poor guide to how judges throughout the system should comport themselves as a general matter. The unique political role of the nation's highest court may require its members at times to show the sorts of excellence that are traditionally associated with executives or legislators—energy, leadership, boldness. But, day in and day out, those qualities are no substitute for the ordinary heroism of sticking to one's last, of demonstrating impartiality, interpretive skill, and responsibility toward authoritative sources in the regular administration of justice.

Few admirers of Earl Warren would want to live in a society where all judges felt as free as he to sweep aside legal "technicalities." William Brennan's most ardent devotees would be dismayed to see the nation's benches crowded with judges as dynamic as he, but in pursuit of, say, a laissez-faire economic vision. In today's society, even more than at the Founding, "considerate men of every description ought to prize whatever will tend to beget or fortify [integrity and moderation] in the courts; as no man can be sure that he may not be tomorrow the victim of a spirit of injustice, by which he may be a gainer today."[51]

It is hard to gauge how deeply the American judicial corps has been affected by the increased respectability of subjective judging. But the same 1987 poll in which William Brennan was "most admired" is illuminating. Though more judges gave Brennan's name than any other, he received only 22 percent of the vote. The next most admired, with 15 percent each, were Chief Justice William H. Rehnquist and former Justice Lewis Powell, followed by former Justice Byron White, with 8 percent.[52] The Chief Justice being a mixed case, those figures suggest that while a substantial segment of the judiciary admires qualities traditionally associated with ambitious executives and legislators, significant numbers of judges are still oriented to the model of pragmatism and restraint represented most clearly by White and Powell.

A recent study comparing the performance of Democratic and Republican appointees on the federal bench suggests that romanticism has made less progress on intermediate appellate courts than among trial judges. Professor Robert Carp found plenty of instances where the decisions of trial judges (who sit alone) seemed to reflect ideology rather than principle. On the other hand, his survey confirmed that collegial decision making on appellate courts (where judges sit in panels) does foster principled consensus. He concluded that, on appeal, "about 90% of the time, in any given case, it makes no difference who the judge is."[53]

The admiration for Powell and White among their peers is all the more interesting when one takes into account that, unlike Brennan, they have seldom been singled out for praise by legal pundits. Indeed, in the topsy-turvy world of legal journalism, a judge may even earn the contempt of reporters for not being interesting enough. When Byron White stepped down from the Supreme Court in 1993, *The New Republic*'s cover story called him "a perfect cipher."[54] Admitting that White was "a first-rate legal technician," a writer for that magazine sneered at him for being "uninterested in articulating a constitutional vision." To *TNR*'s legal analyst, it was evidence of White's "mediocrity" that he was hard to classify as a liberal or a conservative.

What made White hard to classify, of course, were the very qualities that made him an able and conscientious judge—his independence and his faithfulness to a modest conception of the judicial role. His "vision," implicit in nearly every one of his opinions, was not that difficult to discern. As summed up by a former clerk, White's vision was one "in which the democratic process predominates over the judicial; [and] the role of the Court or any individual justice is not to promote particular ideologies, but to decide cases in a pragmatic way that permits the political branches to shoulder primary responsibility for governing our society. Inherent in the more pragmatic and less activist view is a belief that judicial opinions are not a proper vehicle for intellectual pretension and self-promotion. The purpose of an opinion . . . is quite simply to decide the case in an intellectually and analytically sound manner . . ."[55]

White's offense, to many professional Court watchers, was that he was more interested in getting each decision right than in promoting an agenda. Yale law professor Kate Stith, another White clerk, observed on his retirement: "A Supreme Court Justice at some point makes a decision, consciously or not, whether his first loyalty is to his personal place in history or to the institution. . . . Justice White's loyalty was to the institution."[56]

Though White's competence, independence, and integrity did not make lively copy, he was a model of modern neoclassical judging. As for the future, it is heartening that White's replacement, Ruth Bader Ginsburg, took the occasion of a speech shortly after her appointment to embrace the model of the "good judge" as represented by Learned Hand. Quoting Hand's biographer, Justice Ginsburg said, "The good judge is 'open-minded and detached . . . heedful of limitations stemming from the judge's own competence and, above all, from the presuppositions of our constitutional scheme; [the good] judge . . . recognizes that a felt need to act only interstitially does not mean relegation of judges to a trivial or mechanical role, but rather affords the most responsible room for creative, important judicial contributions.' "[57] As Justice Ginsburg's former colleague Robert Bork has observed, the key check on judicial authoritarianism will always be the judge's own understanding of the scope and limits of judicial power—and the insistence of a vigilant citizenry on having judges who will resist the temptation to remake the constitutional design for government.[58]

Is it realistic to hope that we can continue to find, among the hundreds of thousands of lawyers in our vast nation, 27,000 or so men and women who can wholeheartedly comply with the judicial oath's promise to do equal justice without respect to persons? A fair assessment of the current state of affairs, I believe, is that classical and romantic attributes are competing for ascendancy, not only throughout the judicial system but within the psyche of nearly every judge. The synthesis that will emerge, if we are hopeful, may resemble Judge Richard Posner's pragmatic, neoclassical catalogue of judicial virtues: "self-restraint, self-discipline (implying submission to the authority of statutes, precedents, etc.), thoroughness of legal research, power of logical analysis, a sense of justice, a knowledge of the world, a lucid writing style, common sense, openness to colleagues' views, intelligence, fairmindedness, realism, hard work, foresight, modesty, gift for compromise, commitment to reason, and candor."[59] Judges possessing the full range of such qualities will, no doubt, be rare indeed, but with wit and will great numbers of men and women could turn in honorable performances. Much will depend on the state of the profession from which the judiciary is drawn and on the ethos in the academies where they are trained—to which we now turn.

PART III

THE LAMP
OF LEARNING

Why, when record numbers of young men and women flock to law schools for professional training, have so many legal educators lost interest in teaching law?

Why, after the machinery of a modern regulatory state has been in place for nearly a century, do law schools still neglect the subjects of legislation and regulation?

Why, in a society confronted with novel and pressing legal dilemmas, do law courses stress litigation rather than planning, negotiation, and problem solving?

Why, when lawyers bear major responsibilities in connection with maintaining the democratic experiment, do so many teachers of constitutional law ignore the Constitution's design for government?

Why, in an increasingly heterogeneous nation, are institutions dedicated to free-ranging open inquiry becoming ever more intellectually homogeneous?

9
The Ballad of Karl Llewellyn

[T]he business of a law school is not sufficiently described when you merely say that it is to teach law, or to make lawyers. It is to teach law in the grand manner, and to make great lawyers.

—OLIVER WENDELL HOLMES (1886)[1]

On the final day of his Elements of the Law course in the spring of 1959, Karl Llewellyn stumped into the classroom, grasped the podium, and invited us students to join him in singing a ballad of his own composition.

> Come gather and sing to the Common Law
> whose leaf and seed we are,
>
> Whether we live by the waggling jaw or
> counsel, miles from the Bar.
>
> The wood is good and the sap is strong
> that gave us Coke and Hale,
>
> Right is a battle to win from Wrong, in
> spite of contempt and jail.
>
> It calls for brain and it calls for
> will, but an acorn knows his mission:
>
> Law is the Oak of Liberty still, in the
> Common Law Tradition.
>
> Rowdy dowdy doodle-ee-o   In the Common
> Law Tradition.

Rowdy dowdy doodle-ee-o   In the Common
Law Tradition.[2]

He was a sight, with his rumpled tweed jacket a size too small, the traces of a fondness for strong beverages in his complexion, his ferocious eyebrows jutting every which way. Soigné is not a word one would have applied to Karl Llewellyn. To watch his performance that day was sort of discomfiting, like seeing your parents dancing. Yet it was all of a piece with the Elements course, which had been one long paean to the excitement, the struggle, the nobility, the sheer joy of living in the law. This final act was sort of nice, like seeing your parents dancing.

Karl Llewellyn loved the law. He loved it so much and in such a corny way that we of the "silent generation" often felt embarrassed for him. Students in today's legal academy are spared such agonies; few of them will ever hear a teacher sing the praise of the common law tradition or celebrate the lives of its heroes. Professors who share Llewellyn's enthusiasm for training competent practitioners are becoming harder to find, too. Legal scholars, of all intellectual persuasions, have never been more disdainful than they are at present concerning legal traditions, nor more detached from the practice of law.

It is commonplace today for legal academics to say, "We're all Realists now," as a way of acknowledging our debt to Llewellyn and his confreres of the 1930s who challenged simplistic accounts of fact finding and rule application. But in point of fact there are hardly any Realists now. Those rebels of the 1930s were, for the most part, solid craftsmen who would have been repelled by the current vogue for pure theory. Most of them were Progressives and New Dealers who would have been skeptical about their successors' preference for litigation over ordinary politics.

Although my classmates and I squirmed when Llewellyn displayed his heart on his sleeve, most of us did not question the objects of his affection. Nor did the demeanor of our super-cool professors like Edward Levi, Bernard Meltzer, Walter

Blum, Francis Allen, and Soia Mentschikoff disguise the fact that they, too, were passionate participants in the heritage they were inviting us to share. We would have been disappointed if it were otherwise. Since nearly all of us expected to practice law, it was good to know that our teachers regarded the career we had chosen as interesting, useful, and worthy of respect. We did not think to press the question that would have been uppermost in the minds of many students in the years shortly to come: What is there to admire about a tradition so intimately associated with colonialism, slavery, patriarchy, and unreconstructed capitalism? When that question began to be regularly posed, most law teachers could not or would not answer it, and many of the questioners were not really interested in hearing an answer.

A response would have to begin with an adequate concept of tradition and an understanding of Anglo-American law as a tradition animated by a distinctive set of habits and attitudes.

The Common Law Tradition

"A living tradition," in Alasdair MacIntyre's useful formulation, "is an historically extended, socially embodied argument, and an argument precisely about the goods which constitute that tradition. Within a tradition the pursuit of goods extends through generations, sometimes through many generations."[3] The expression "common law tradition" refers to the type of law, and the mode of lawmaking, that historically distinguished the English legal system from the Romano-Germanic legal systems of continental Europe. The common law is an evolving body of principles built by accretion from judicial decisions rendered in the context of countless individual disputes. Because those principles are embedded in concrete cases, they are highly fact-sensitive, and not too general. Until relatively recent times, the common law and the craft techniques associated with it were transmitted from one generation to the next

chiefly by practitioners. Continental law, by contrast, always
had the smell of the lamp—it was developed by Renaissance
scholars of revived Roman law, and scholars again played
leading roles when it was recast in comprehensive legislative
codifications.

Another contrast with the legal systems of continental Europe
is the common law's mode of evolution. Over centuries that
saw the rise and fall of feudalism, the expansion of commerce, and the transition to constitutional monarchy and
representative government, judges and lawyers adapted English law to each new circumstance, neither erasing prior
arrangements completely nor becoming captives of them. Par-
liament made relatively few efforts to hasten or force the
process. Its enactments, for the most part, were like patches
here and there against the background of the judge-made law;
and judges blended them, so far as possible, into the fabric of
the case law. Thus, in 1894, the great English legal historian
F. W. Maitland could look back on centuries of legal evolution
and say, "When we speak of a body of law, we use a metaphor
so apt that it is hardly a metaphor. We picture to ourselves a
being that lives and grows, that preserves its identity while
every atom of which it is composed is subject to a ceaseless
process of change, decay, and renewal."[4]

The key to the common law's ability to change and grow
while maintaining its coherence and continuity was a distinctive
set of habits and practices which its participants learned through
doing and by observing and imitating others. To try to describe
those methods is a bit like trying to describe swimming or
bicycle riding. But the conventional understanding goes something like this: the common law judge is supposed to be a
virtuoso of practical reason, weaving together the threads of
fact and law, striving not only for a fair disposition of the
dispute at hand but to decide each case with reference to a
principle that transcends the facts of that case—all with a view
toward maintaining continuity with past decisions, deciding
like cases alike, and providing guidance for other parties

similarly situated; and all in the spirit of caring for the good of the legal order itself and the polity it serves.

The best times were those marked by what Llewellyn called the "Grand Style." In such periods, he wrote, the outlook and manner of judges and lawyers were characterized by "an as-of-courseness in the constant questing for better and best law to guide the future, but the better and best law is to be built on and out of what the past can offer; the quest consists in a constant re-examination and reworking of a heritage, that the heritage may yield not only solidity but comfort for the new day and for the morrow. . . . It is a way of ongoing renovation of doctrine, but touch with the past is too close, the mood is too craft-conscious, the need for the clean line is too great, for the renovation to smell of revolution or, indeed, of campaigning reform."[5] Judges in the Grand Style (John Marshall, Cardozo, Learned Hand), Llewellyn said, seek to fit rule and decision "with the feel of the body of our law," to assure "that they go with the grain rather than across or against it, that they fit into the net force-field and relieve instead of tautening the tensions and stresses."[6]

Practicing lawyers, as participants in that tradition, framed their instruments and arguments with such habits and attitudes in view. It was that shared legal culture that stood behind Lord Coke's famous insistence: "Reason is the life of the law; nay, the common law itselfe is nothing else but reason."[7] To Coke, "reason" did not mean deductive logic, or self-interested calculation, or any activity of an individual mind in isolation. It was, rather, an extended collaborative dialogue, a group achievement, "an artificial perfection of reason gotten by long studie, observation and experience . . . fined and refined [over the ages] by an infinite number of grave and learned men."[8]

The most impressive accomplishments of the shared legal culture of English and American lawyers took the form of ingenious approaches to new political, social, and economic problems. Where Americans are concerned, the most important of these collective achievements was the American Founding, which gave this country's public law its own unique stamp and character. The Declaration of Independence, the Constitution, *The Federalist,* and the landmark early decisions of the Supreme Court could only have been produced by statesmen who were steeped in the common law tradition and supremely skilled at innovative extensions of established principles. In the very act of breaking with the mother country, the American colonists claimed their legal inheritance ("the rights of Englishmen"), transformed it, and made it into the basis of a new order that remains one of the wonders of the political world. What Ireland did for the English language, America did for English law. Seventy years after the Revolution, Daniel Webster described the process as "a sort of reverse hereditary transmission": "We have seen, in our generation, copious and salutary streams turning and running backward, replenishing their original fountains, and giving a fresher and a brighter green to the fields of English jurisprudence."[9]

Americans also enriched the common law tradition at the humbler everyday level where judges and practitioners, dealing with routine problems of social and business life, were adapting English law to the circumstances of the new continent. Office lawyers framed agreements, bylaws, contracts, deeds, leases, wills, and trusts that, at their best, aided citizens to live together with a minimum of friction, to make reliable plans for the future, and to avoid unnecessary disputes. For the occasions when preventive law failed, American judges and litigators fined and refined their procedures for fact finding and adjudication.

The history of the common law is a textbook example of what Alasdair MacIntyre calls a living tradition, one that is "historically extended" and "socially embodied," whose development constantly points beyond itself. To be a traditionalist in such a tradition is not to be frozen in the past, or mired in the status quo, but rather to participate in an intense ongoing conversation about what it is that gives the tradition its point and purpose.[10] That discussion, carried on across generations, enabled the tradition's participants not only to make useful contributions to society through changing times but to recognize and correct for many of their own shortcomings. Unlike the Revolution in France, upheavals and civil strife in common law countries did not entail root-and-branch rejection of the legal past. The American revolutionaries stood on the ancient rights of Englishmen to shake off colonial oppression; feudal relations of protection and loyalty gradually evolved into rights and responsibilities in the modern state; the Civil War amendments brought the Declaration of Independence's promise of equality into the Constitution.

Toward the end of the nineteenth century, the common law tradition entered a period of severe turbulence. As we have already noted, the method of leisurely judicial adaptation, case by case, was not well suited to many of the new problems generated by rapid urbanization and industrialization. Industrial accidents, for example, required thinking about aggregates rather than isolated instances; about long-range preventive planning as well as after-the-injury compensation. Legislatures—representing more diverse constituencies than ever before—began to move into areas formerly occupied entirely by case law, and to experiment with regulatory techniques like licensing, inspection, delegation of authority to agencies, and administrative rules backed up by civil and criminal penalties.

The courts, understandably, did not know quite how to handle disputes that arose under legislation so different in form and inspiration from the piecemeal statutes to which they had been accustomed. They were like dancers trained for the minuet suddenly whisked into ballrooms filled with the unfamiliar strains of the waltz. They improvised clumsily. The band played on. Case law and legislation, state and federal, grew at an alarming rate. No practitioner or judge could see the law as a whole, much less keep track of developments in all its expanding parts. A major scholarly effort might have helped to maintain some coherence and accessibility in what was becoming a chaotic mass of decisional and legislative law. But until the end of the nineteenth century there were few law schools and few full-time teachers of law.

The stresses and strains on the legal system called for a high degree of skill, imagination, and cooperation among the various branches of the legal profession. Thus it was, or might have been, fortuitous that legal education was moving from the haphazard system of apprenticeship in lawyers' offices and brief training programs in proprietary law schools into universities.[11]

In 1870, Harvard Law School dean Christopher Columbus Langdell began to implement some new ideas about legal education. Contrary to the older English view of law as a form of custom, Langdell taught that law was a science consisting of "principles and doctrines" applied "to the ever-tangled skein of human affairs."[12] The task of the legal scholar and educator, as he saw it, was to extract the principles and doctrines from the court decisions where they had been embedded and to classify them so "that each should be found in its proper place." Since judicial decisions were then the principal source of law, it seemed reasonable to make them the principal basis of legal studies. Written opinions in cases were the legal scientist's specimens or "data." So, instead of textbooks, law students were given "casebooks" in which noteworthy appellate opinions were collected. Rather than passively listening to lectures, students had to be prepared to participate in classroom discussions of selected cases and hypothetical variants introduced by the professors. The Harvard "case method" caught on, and quickly became standard in the law schools that were springing up across the country.[13] University legal training steadily displaced the old apprenticeship system; by 1910, two-thirds of new lawyers held law school diplomas.[14]

Full-time teachers and scholars using Langdell's method synthesized whole fields of law that had never been systematically studied. They summarized the doctrines they found in cases in learned articles and treatises that had enormous influence. Judges and practitioners relied so heavily on standard treatises like Scott on trusts or Williston on contracts that the authors, in an important sense, became lawmakers. Unfortunately, those treatises, each dealing with a single field in isolation, perpetuated a fragmented approach to legal studies. It would be many years before legal scholars would attempt, as Blackstone had done in the eighteenth century, to present all or major parts of the legal system as a whole, systematizing both decisional law and legislation.[15]

The exclusively court-centered focus of Langdellian scholars and educators was another weakness. In practice, judges and lawyers were spending more and more of their time dealing with enacted law. Langdell's theory, if consistently pursued, should have required the law schools to take more account of statutes—the new "data" produced by legislatures. But professors stuck to what they knew best, lavishing most of their attention on court decisions. A notable exception was Chicago's Ernst Freund, who wrote learned and prescient tomes on administrative law and the various modes of legislative regulation.[16] Packed with insights drawn from continental European learning and experience in these areas, Freund's books were treasure troves of information that might have proved useful to lawyers entering the trackless thicket of bureaucratic regulation. But they attracted little notice from insular American academics. Meanwhile, like an untended field gone to brush, legislation continued to proliferate, and the administrative powers of the state continued to expand.

The movement of legal education into university settings had brought together two sorts of learning that did not sit easily with each other: practical vocational training and the freewheeling pursuit of knowledge. Langdell and his followers had foreseen a happy accommodation at a middling level of theory. The better law schools would not be mere trade schools, but neither would they be ivory towers. Law professors would serve the profession and the academy alike by historical investigation, systematization, and explication of the law. That was in fact the path taken by many distinguished law teachers. Monumental "first generation" treatises like Scott on trusts, Williston on contracts, and Beale on conflict of laws organized and explained the principles and doctrines the authors discerned in the case law in their respective fields. The American Law Institute in its early years commissioned teams of scholars to study and "restate" the law in various areas. The finished products had a reassuring solidity. But the scholars of the period achieved their magisterial tone by underemphasizing the areas of uncertainty at the margins of the doctrines they elaborated.

Even as treatise writers were neatly organizing one field of law after another, trouble and excitement were brewing in the academy. Legal theory, together with all the other human sciences, was in the early stages of a historic encounter with modernism. Shortly after Langdell and his colleagues had set about expounding their new "scientific" approach to law, the writer of unsigned book notices in the *American Law Review* began to lob verbal grenades in their direction. The reviewer was a sardonic fellow, but he had a way with words. Langdell, he wrote, was no scientist, but "the greatest living legal theologian."[17] Those reviews were the earliest in a series of writings through which Oliver Wendell Holmes would exert a sway over legal theory as powerful as Langdell's influence on legal pedagogy.

From his early writings, it is clear that Holmes believed, as patrician Romans did, that no one really lives "unless he devotes all his energies to some task and seeks fame by some notable achievement or by the cultivation of some admirable gift."[18] A member of a distinguished Boston family, Holmes was already a war hero (wounded at Ball's Bluff, Antietam, and Fredericksburg) when he had to decide on a career. He settled on lawyering only after he had satisfied himself that "a man may live greatly in the law as well as elsewhere."[19] Once the choice was made, he set out immediately to make his mark. He calculated, according to biographer Mark DeWolfe Howe, "that his best chance of making himself a figure in the profession was through industrious and critical scholarship."[20]

The legal stage was ready for someone with Holmes's ambition and gifts. Tocqueville, a decade before Holmes was born, had found it "strange" that such a legalistic society as the United States had not yet produced any "great writers inquiring into the general principles of the laws."[21] Holmes made that task his own. As a young practitioner, he devoted so much of his spare time to scholarly writing that some of his old friends were put off. William James wrote to his brother Henry that "Wendell" was becoming "a powerful battery, formed like a planing machine to gouge a deep self-beneficial groove through life."[22] But Holmes persevered, and in 1881, at age forty, he published a work that was soon acclaimed as an intellectual tour de force. As if in response to Tocqueville's call, he announced: "The object of this book is to present a general view of the Common Law."[23]

A speech to Harvard undergraduates a few years later affords a glimpse into the intensity of Holmes's ambition. Among the satisfactions that, just possibly, might come to one who pursues a career in the law, he told his young listeners, there was "the secret isolated joy of the thinker, who knows that, a hundred years after he is dead and forgotten, men who never heard of him will be moving to the measure of his thought, the subtle rapture of a postponed power, which the world knows not because it has no external trappings, but which to his prophetic vision is more real than that which commands an army."[24]

American lawyers will long argue about whether it is cause for regret or rejoicing that Holmes's dream came true. But his wish was more than fulfilled, for most of those who march to the measure of his thought also know and honor his name. *The Common Law*, together with various speeches and articles, revolutionized the way American lawyers wrote and spoke about law. Even today, the long shadow of Holmes looms over all contemporary legal scholarship. His writings, studded with quotable aphorisms,[25] set the intellectual agenda of the law for the entire twentieth century. Legal realism, pragmatism, sociological jurisprudence, law and economics, and critical legal studies are all elaborations of themes announced by Holmes. As Karl Llewellyn used to say, "Holmes was the daddy of us all."

Holmes was an odd sort of daddy, though—one who luxu-
riated in the family inheritance while often seeming to disdain
the honest labor of his ancestors. He was a daddy who misled
his dimmer offspring—the ones who listened to what he said
more closely than they watched what he did. Consider how he
spoke of tradition in "The Path of the Law" (a speech which
remains the most widely quoted law review article ever published). Wherever one looks in the law, Holmes complained,
one sees tradition getting in the way of rational policy.[26] The
"tradition" he was attacking on that occasion was an easy mark.
It was not Maitland's living, growing organism, but just the
lifeless, empty husk of the past. "It is revolting," he said, "to
have no better reason for a rule of law than that so it was laid
down in the time of Henry IV."[27]

That reductionist assault on tradition came on the heels of
a similar maneuver against legal reasoning. The opening
sentence of *The Common Law* had been a gauntlet flung down
to Lord Coke's dictum that "reason is the life of the law."
Holmes wrote: "The life of the law has not been logic: it has
been experience."[28] In "The Path of the Law," he returned to
that theme, declaring the need to expose the "fallacy" that
logic is "the only force at work in the development of the
law."[29] The famous first line of *The Common Law* flows so
majestically that a reader may not pause to wonder whether
anyone had actually said that logic *was* the life of the law. The
fact is that even at the height of nineteenth-century legal
formalism, it would have been hard to find any American
lawyer advancing such a proposition. That point was made by
a commentator as soon as "The Path of the Law" appeared in
1897. Jabez Fox wrote that he could not believe "that this
particular fallacy has taken a deep hold on the profession."[30]
Certainly Lord Coke himself had held no brief for logic. His
passion was reason, "fined and refined" in the crucible of
practical experience, a far different idea.

So where were the logic freaks? Far away in Germany there
was a group of lawyers whose work would later be described
by Max Weber as the most perfect expression of the legal style

he called "logical formal rationality."[31] They were the distinguished professors commissioned in the 1870s to draft a civil code for the newly unified German nation. Their avowed aim was to make that code a complete "logically closed system."[32] Among their critics was the formidable modernist Rudolf von Jehring. Recently, a Cambridge University historian called attention to the close resemblance between the opening sentence of *The Common Law* and a passage in a book by Jehring that Holmes checked out of the Boston Athenaeum in 1879.[33]

That discovery does not really impugn Holmes's originality (his formulation was much catchier than Jehring's), but it does illuminate a more important matter. Holmes's aphorism was perfectly aimed at the rigid conceptualism of the Germans who were trying to construct a code endowed with *logische Geschlossenheit* (a self-contained, logically closed system). But it was wildly inappropriate as applied to Coke and other writers on the judge-made, open-textured common law. And as to the weaker sort of formalism that prevailed in America in the 1870s, it fell beside the target. But it was a terrific line.

Holmes was a man on the move. With matchless verbal dexterity, he converted a living "tradition" into fossilized "history" and downgraded Coke's singing "reason" to dry "logic" —a collection, as he put it, of syllogisms, axioms, and deductions. That took the piano out of the *Emperor* Concerto.

There was more. Holmes announced, with all the fanfare of a discovery, what good lawyers have always known: that there are many times when the law is silent or unclear, and that part of a judge's role, therefore, includes a limited lawmaking function. With his flair for sensationalizing the obvious, Holmes mentioned some of the things that judges made law from. Expediency, opinion, and even prejudice, he said, had all played a greater part "than the syllogism" in fashioning the rules by which we are governed.[34] In other words, a judge's mind operates much as everyone else's does.

Revisiting the subject in his "Path of the Law" speech, Holmes told a group of law students: "You will find some text writers telling you that [law] . . . is a system of reason."[35] That, according to the great man, was obfuscation. Laws were nothing more or less than commands backed up by the armed might of the state. In the blunt macho style that was his trademark, he told his young audience that the aim of legal study was simply the science of prediction, prediction of "where the axe will fall."[36] And, in words that every lawyer still knows, he said that if you want to know the law, "you must look at it as a bad man, who cares only for the material consequences which such knowledge enables him to predict."[37] He advised his listeners to use "cynical acid" to wash away all the moralizing language of right and wrong so that they could see the law as it truly is.[38] "For my own part," he opined, "I often doubt whether it would not be a gain if every word of moral significance could be banished from the law altogether."[39]

The "ideal" to be served by banishing the language of morality was, he said, to put the law on a truly scientific basis. That meant clear thinking about means and ends, costs and benefits—not Langdell's pseudoscience of extracting principles from scattered court decisions.[40] Reason might be out, but what Holmes approvingly called "rationality" was in. He especially recommended that every lawyer should acquire a knowledge of economics, for the "man of the future is the man of statistics and the master of economics."[41] A century later, lawyers all over the world are marching to the measure of those thoughts. Interdisciplinary law-and-economics scholarship is one of the most influential forces in legal studies today, the only indigenous American legal "school" to command a significant international following.

With his seemingly cavalier dismissal of reason, morality, and tradition, Holmes helped to prepare the way for the carnival of late-twentieth-century American legal theory. His critique of reason anticipated the fact skeptics and the rule skeptics of the 1930s, who called themselves Realists, and their more radical successors, the critical theorists who came on the scene in the 1970s. His call for a rational science of law was answered by the legal economists. For many of today's law professors, across the political spectrum, the word "tradition" has acquired a pejorative sense—it is merely the debris of old errors, power relations, and prejudices.

With hindsight, though, it is remarkable how deeply Holmes himself drew from the springs of the very heritage he often seemed to be disparaging. The same Holmes who could set his face against tradition could in another mood liken the law to a "magic mirror" in which a suitably trained observer could see a mighty princess eternally weaving into her tapestry dim and distant figures of the ever-lengthening past.[42] The same man who proposed to erase all moral language from the law could observe that legal history is a panorama of the moral development of the human race: "The law is the witness and external deposit of our moral life. . . . The practice of it, in spite of popular jests, tends to make good citizens and good men."[43] The same judge who urged law students to wash the law with "cynical acid" hastened to assure them that he did not mean any disrespect for their common calling. "I venerate the law," he solemnly avowed.[44]

In his complex relation to his métier, Holmes bears a striking resemblance to those of his contemporaries whom Hilton Kramer calls the great "tradition-haunted" artists—Picasso and Matisse, Eliot and Yeats, Schönberg and Stravinsky.[45] With his vision of the mighty princess, with his mastery of his craft, and with his vaulting ambition, Holmes was a Picasso-like figure—larger than life, boldly iconoclastic, yet mindful of his lineage and of the continuity of legal culture. "The Path of the Law" was his *Demoiselles of Avignon*.

If Holmes was the harsh, bold Picasso of legal modernism, Karl Llewellyn was its exuberant Matisse.[46] While Holmes took bleak satisfaction in seeing life as a Darwinian struggle in which the fittest prove their worth by survival and success, Llewellyn marveled at the human capacity for cooperative living, whether in the pueblo, on Main Street, or on Wall Street. Where Holmes saw the armed might of the state poised menacingly behind every judicial ruling, Llewellyn was struck by human success in devising systems to minimize disputes and to settle them without violence when they arise. Where Holmes saw a calculating bad man, Llewellyn saw a hardworking businessman (like his father in Seattle, Washington), trying to make reasonably reliable plans for the future. While Holmes looked down upon the human drama with Olympian detachment, Llewellyn threw himself into a host of projects and causes, from poetry writing and anthropological fieldwork to systematizing commercial law and crusading for civil rights and improved access to legal services. While Holmes pointed a long bony finger at elements of stubborn irrationality in the judicial process, Llewellyn clapped in delight at the ability of that process to yield a remarkable degree of reckonability.

The gusto with which Llewellyn embarked on each of his ventures was perhaps inherited from his mother, an evangelical Congregationalist who took young Karl on marches in favor of woman suffrage and against the evils of drink. (The former cause made a lasting impression.) Karl's father sought to foster his son's development in another way by sending him to Germany for part of his college preparatory education. One consequence of that decision was that Llewellyn, like Holmes, became a war hero. Llewellyn's war experience, though, like many other aspects of his colorful life, was something of an embarrassment—being acquired in Kaiser Wilhelm's army. When the war began, Llewellyn, then a Yale student, happened to be in Paris. He rushed to Germany and, in solidarity with his old schoolmates, fell in with the Prussian infantry on its way to the front. A few weeks later, in November 1914, he was seriously wounded while attacking the English lines near Ypres. As soon as he was well enough to travel, "the fool American" (as the German officers called him) was sent home—with the Iron Cross, a permanent limp, and a lot to explain when the United States entered the war against Germany.

As a young law professor in the 1920s at Yale and Columbia (he switched schools to accommodate his first wife's career), Llewellyn threw himself into the academic movement that came to be known as Legal Realism (after a flurry of law review articles that began with Llewellyn's "A Realistic Jurisprudence —The Next Step"[47]). The Realists were a wildly varied crowd, but they shared Holmes's disdain for Langdellian scholars who took judges' reasoning at face value and who stated the law as a body of clear "black letter" rules. Fact skeptics like Jerome Frank drew on the new field of psychoanalytic theory to elaborate Holmes's insight that legal decision making, especially fact finding, was often influenced by unconscious and irrational factors.[48] Rule skeptics like Llewellyn criticized the older generation of treatise writers for failing to grapple with the uncertainty, ambiguity, and "leeways" of doctrine.

Most Realists were not content to be mere critics. Some responded to the Holmesean call for "men of statistics" and embarked on empirical studies of the "law-in-action." Others sought to understand judicial decision making by looking beyond the written rationales to patterns in results. That led to a new generation of more sophisticated treatises, of which *Corbin on Contracts* was a leading exemplar. Most Realists were actively involved in law reform—some in the New Deal, some in the uniform law movement, and some in the restatement projects of the American Law Institute, which gradually turned from merely restating various areas of law to proposals for revising them.

Llewellyn, curious about everything, had a finger in nearly all of the Realist pies. Feeling his lack of practical experience as a weakness, he took two years off from teaching in the early 1920s to work in a bank and in the Wall Street firm of Shearman & Sterling. Shortly after returning to Yale, he began his long association with the National Conference of Commissioners on Uniform State Laws, a group of practitioners, judges, and scholars founded in 1892 to promote greater harmony among the laws of the various states. At Columbia in the 1930s, his most prolific decade, he was active in the liberal causes of the day, collaborated with anthropologist E. Adamson Hoebel on what is still recognized as a pathbreaking study of the law ways of the Cheyenne Indians,[49] published two books of poems, drafted a couple of uniform laws, prepared teaching materials on sales, wrote articles explaining and defending the Realist perspective on law, and introduced generations of students to the study of law in an entertaining series of lectures published as *The Bramble Bush.*[50]

It was during that period of furious creativity that Llewellyn persuaded the shy and reluctant Benjamin Cardozo to sit for the Russian sculptor Sergei Konenkov.[51] Dropping in on one of the sittings, Llewellyn found the sculptor in distress over the difficulty of capturing his subject. The face had taken on a hard, ruthless expression. Llewellyn went out, bought some modeling clay, and returned the next day with a small head he had fashioned himself. That visual suggestion, apparently, was enough to start Konenkov on a new and more promising course. The result was the fine bust of Cardozo which now graces the Harvard Law School (see p. 125).

In the 1940s, when many of his fellow Realists were active in the Roosevelt administration, Llewellyn concentrated most of his energies on drafting a Uniform Commercial Code designed to replace the varying and often conflicting systems of state law governing sales, negotiable instruments, investment paper, and secured transactions. He was greatly aided in that immense task by his co-reporter, Soia Mentschikoff, a Wall Street lawyer whom he married in 1946. In the 1950s, Llewellyn and Mentschikoff joined the University of Chicago law faculty. They were an awesome duo, two of the most important figures in commercial law since Lord Mansfield. Llewellyn took the lead in draftsmanship, forging a single commercial code out of a chaotic welter of customs, statutes, and decisions. Mentschikoff was primarily responsible for the equally amazing feat of persuading legislators, lawyers, and the affected business communities in every state but Louisiana to accept it! (Llewellyn often told his students that, in oral argument, we could do no better than to emulate the silver-tongued Soia.)

Though the Realists are now often portrayed as rebels and skeptics, that does not do justice to the lawyerly qualities they generally shared. Paramount among those traits was an appetite and energy for creative problem solving that yielded innovative New Deal legislation in the public sector and important model statutes touching many aspects of private law. For the first time

Karl Llewellyn and Soia Mentschikoff, partners in life, law, and the common law tradition *(Courtesy University of Chicago Law School)*

in American history, some of the best legal talent in the nation was being devoted to systems thinking and legislative drafting. Scholarly lawyers in the Roosevelt administration, the American Law Institute, and the National Conference of Commissioners on Uniform State Laws saw statutes, not as legal Band-Aids, but as much-needed frameworks and fertile starting points for fresh legal development. Their interest in legislation led many of them to be interested in ordinary politics and to appreciate consensus building.

The Realists, as a group, were not especially enamored of fancy theory. Llewellyn repeatedly insisted that Realism was not a philosophy, but a set of attitudes—see it whole, see it fresh, see it as it works in practice, come back to make sure, think clearly.[52] When the English legal scholar William Twining studied the Realists, he saw plainly what had escaped many American observers: "Law was their primary discipline and they were proud of it. . . . They have most to teach those who wish to treat law as their primary discipline, while keeping it steadfastly in its place as one of the great humane studies."[53]

The Realists' interest in law and law reform had important implications for their teaching. They took the job of preparing students for practice and public life very seriously. No one put more of himself into that activity than Karl Llewellyn did. His course on Legal Argument, for example, was designed to give would-be litigators practice in brief writing and oral argument. It was full of what students now call "feedback." Few of us will forget the day when he came to class after grading our first written exercises. He threw the blue books down on the desk, glared at us, and said, "When I read your papers, brethren and sistern, I puked."

The class meetings we dreaded and enjoyed the most were the ones where we practiced summations to the jury or appellate arguments. All of us had to come prepared to argue for either side. If called on, one had to go to the front of the room, deliver the argument, and remain standing there until Llewellyn and our fellow students were through critiquing our performance. The students naturally went easy on one another, but Llewellyn did not mince his words. Later, when I argued in front of real juries, it seemed like a breeze in comparison with my reluctant defense of the sinister Dr. Crippen in Legal Argument class.

Llewellyn was the only teacher at Chicago who required first-year students to stand while reciting. Though weak of knee and dry of mouth under his scrutiny, most of us did not resent his strenuous criticisms. They were at least more bearable than the bullying sarcasm that passed for Socratic method with some of the other teachers. It was so clear that he was on our side, wanting each and every one of us to be a wonderful lawyer. There was not a shred of meanness in him.

When I became a teacher myself, I realized how bravely he

had put his own ego on the line in his zeal to turn us into competent professionals. Once, when a student was presenting what seemed like a good summary of the general thrust of Section One of the Sherman antitrust law, Llewellyn interrupted and told the student to sit down. He then lectured us for a while on the importance of the fact that Congress had voted on a particular set of words and no other. "And so," he concluded, "I want you all to repeat after me three times: 'Never paraphrase a statute.'" For a long moment we sat mute, rolling our eyes. He must have read a single thought on a hundred sullen faces: "What an ass!" He held his ground until we grudgingly complied. Afterward we told one another what an old fool he was. I doubt, though, that any of us has ever paraphrased a statute.

On another occasion, one of the bolder students complained about what seemed to be Llewellyn's pettifogging insistence on getting some detail or other exactly right. Crafty Karl had been lying in wait for just such an opportunity to deliver his favorite admonition: "Son, technique without ideals is a menace, but ideals without technique are a mess."

In the early 1960s, the American variant of the common law tradition seemed to be in reasonably healthy condition. The success of the Uniform Commercial Code showed what could be accomplished by years of collaboration between scholars and practitioners, by careful study of the practices and needs of the affected communities, and by patient work with legislators. Harvard's Henry Hart and Albert Sacks had developed an influential set of teaching materials that taught an entire generation of lawyers to work with statutes and to view the whole legal order, with all its interrelated specialized parts, as a functioning system. Energetic and lawyerly academics, with the benefit of their New Deal, American Law Institute, and Uniform Law Commission experiences, were finally beginning to take legislation seriously. Scholars began systematizing fields that had been brought into being by legislation: Loss on securities, Areeda on antitrust, Bittker on tax, Wright and Miller on procedure, Davis on administrative law. Those third-generation treatises were the most sophisticated that had ever been produced, and their writers enjoyed great prestige both in the academy and among practitioners. Legal historians and members of the infant law-and-economics movement were giving lawyers a deeper understanding of the development and operation of American law. *Brown* v. *Board of Education* and the one-man, one-vote cases showed that lawyers could help to open up educational opportunities and political participation to all citizens.

The legal system seemed to be shedding many old biases, and lawyers seemed poised to be more helpful to society than ever in their modest, if somewhat dull, fashion. The marriage between professional training and scholarship appeared on the surface to be a happy one. Learned Hand's evocation of the qualities of great scholars and teachers of law still represented the ideals of a broad cross section of academics: "scepticism, tolerance, discrimination, urbanity, some—but not too much —reserve towards change, insistence upon proportion, and, above all, humility before the vast unknown."[54]

In the spring of 1961, Karl Llewellyn sang for the last time:

Some say our Law's in a sorry plight, and folly its fruition.

The answer to that is to set it right, in the Common Law Tradition.

Rowdy dowdy doodle-ee-o

How did it come about that, within a decade, professional training, the scholarly quest for truth, and the law itself began to lose their appeal among law professors?

10

The New Academy—Look, Ma! No Hands!

The legal scholar may have been certain as he selected his career that the law and the legal system were subjects of central intellectual importance, but now theory tells him that he was wrong.

—GEORGE L. PRIEST, YALE LAW SCHOOL[1]

In the 1960s, the Warren Court went into full swing; the federal courts got busier; the Great Society created government jobs for the children of the middle class as providers of services to the poor; law firms prospered contentedly; and law school enrollments zoomed upward. Between 1962 and 1972, the law student population doubled. A host of new law schools opened their doors. The students who sought legal education in that period were not only among the most talented college graduates in the country but were a marvelously diverse crowd. For the first time, law teachers looked out on a student body that, superficially at least, resembled America. In classrooms that only a few years earlier had been filled mainly with young white men just out of college, there were now many and varied voices, of people who had held real jobs, of members of minority groups, of women who had raised or were raising children, of Vietnam veterans and Vietnam draft evaders. Most of these students, like law students of the past, expected to practice law. But the new mixture also included an increased proportion of men and women who were uncertain, not only about their future plans but about whether they belonged in law school.

The Best and the Brightest

The practice-bound students, on the whole, were more socially conscious than their predecessors had been. They included many Great Society schoolteachers, social workers, and community organizers who hoped that a legal education would enable them to be more effective agents of change. This made for a real difference in atmosphere from the early 1960s, when most of us had our sights firmly set on private practice or government service. One of my classmates had drawn puzzled looks from other students as well as from our constitutional law teacher when he explained a class absence by saying that he had been engaged in a "sit-in" at Woolworth's. It was only after I had joined a large firm, and mainly due to the urging of my classmate Nancy McDermid, that I became involved in the activities of the Chicago branch of the National Lawyers' Guild. By contrast, in the late 1960s, substantial numbers of entering students saw the law as, among other things, a means for transforming "the system."

As for those who were initially unsure whether they really wanted to be lawyers, many took to legal studies with enthusiasm. But others were like tourists in New York City who, hearing that Lutèce is a fine restaurant, and having the luck to get a reservation, find that after all they do not like French cuisine. By the 1970s, there were so many of these lukewarm law students that they acquired clout. For the first time, American law professors found themselves plying their arts before classes with a hefty proportion of students who were not especially keen to acquire specialized professional skills, and not particularly impressed by virtuosity in analogizing, distinguishing, and posing hypotheticals.

An inquisitive reader might wonder why such persons would subject themselves to the expense and drudgery of law school. There were a number of reasons. For some, law school was a temporary solution to a problem. During the Vietnam War years, avoiding the draft was foremost on the minds of many young male college graduates.[2] For others, law school was a distant second choice when their hopes to pursue graduate work in history, sociology, or philosophy had to be abandoned because of limited opportunities in those fields.

All too many young men and women drifted into law school the way that Patrick Griffin did. Looking back ruefully after twenty years of working in various disappointing legal positions, Griffin reminisced recently about why he had been drawn to law. By the 1970s, law school had become the place for a bright, upper-middle-class liberal arts major to go when he still had no idea of what he wanted to do in life. "In an earlier day," said Griffin, "as a promising youngster who didn't promise anything in particular, I suppose I might have ended up a clergyman."[3] "One of the strongest attractions of law school" to such a person, he pointed out, "is that it is, after all, more school." In retrospect, Griffin realized that it had been an "ominous" sign that his courses became less interesting as he passed from the sweeping surveys of the first year to the bread-and-butter courses of the second and third.

With increasing numbers of students like Griffin, American law schools began to resemble the huge law departments in European universities where legal studies are a popular undergraduate major. A big difference, of course, is that American legal education is very expensive—and follows four expensive years of undergraduate education. Law school recruiters claim that a law degree is a path to many careers. But Griffin came to see it somewhat differently. "The law degree has become the degree of choice for all those who would rather not make any irrevocable choices, who lack unshakable convictions about what they want to do with their lives, who could use some time, some room, some psychic slack." At the end of the day, for many of these halfhearted lawyers, the vaunted flexibility of their degrees is not flexible enough. Some swell the ranks of discontented practitioners. Some drift into other fields as they drifted into law school.

As the aims and interests of the consumers of legal education became more diverse, so did curricular offerings.[4] To the old menu of heavy legal dishes, legal educators added many new courses. They experimented with "lite" versions of standard items. The manner of presentation was spiced up for the TV generation. As a beginning law teacher in the 1970s, I read in *The Wall Street Journal* one day of professors who hired professional joke writers to help them improve their teaching evaluations. Walking by the classrooms of other teachers, I began to notice the sounds of laughter and applause. Ever ready to try new pedagogical methods, I experimented with some homemade humor in my first-year property class. That year, one of my course evaluations came back with the verdict: "She laughs at her own jokes, which are not as funny as she thinks."

While law professors were adjusting to their new clientele, major changes were also being made in the law school admission test (LSAT). The LSAT makes no pretense of identifying those men and women who may be well-suited for the practice of law. According to the Law School Admission Council (LSAC), the purpose of the test is to explore the qualities which are important for success in law study, particularly in the first year.[5] In the early 1960s, when first-year courses were training grounds for rigorous case analysis, the LSAT was an all-round examination. Besides testing verbal and logical-analytical skills as it does today, it included spatial and mathematical problems, as well as questions under the heading of general cultural literacy. Then, as law schools made the first year more comfortable for the casual shopper, the LSAC undertook periodically to revise its test. The spatial relations and general background questions were the first to go. Next, all math questions were eliminated. The number of logical-analytical questions was reduced.

When I asked Robert Berry, the former chairman of the LSAC's Test Development and Research Committee, whether he thought the changes in the LSAT had introduced a systematic bias against intelligent people whose verbal skills are good, but weaker than their mathematical and creative right-brain abilities, his answer was: "Definitely." If Berry is right, as he seems to be, we have a situation where a test which makes no pretense of identifying talents relevant to the practice of law plays a significant role, along with college grades, in determining the ultimate composition of the country's lawyer population.

One may speculate further that, while it is true that law schools attract many of the best and brightest college graduates, a certain kind of brightness predominates. In the first place, the law school population is overwhelmingly composed of liberal arts majors. Second, the LSAT ignores certain types of intelligence that become increasingly important when law graduates take their places in a society that has more urgent need for creative problem solvers than for verbal acrobats.

To be sure, all law students and lawyers must be proficient in reading comprehension, writing, and communication. Given the varied responsibilities of lawyers in American society, however, those skills, while necessary, are insufficient. The factors that militate against diversity of intellectual strengths among law students, moreover, are probably responsible for the "prevalent (and disgraceful) math-block that afflicts the legal profession."[6] And they may also help to explain the current dearth of the imaginative innovators who were so much a part of the legal scene in the New Deal period. The most significant right-left imbalance in contemporary law schools, in fact, may not be political, but cerebral.

The New Faculty

For the young men and women who are most adept at the art of being a student, the career of law professor beckons. It is, after all, more school. The old academy, for the most part, welcomed bright new faculty members of the 1960s generation who aspired to build bridges between law and other disciplines and who promised to make law more relevant to social concerns.[7] The influential professors of the day were mainly old-fashioned liberals who respected the erudition of their junior colleagues with Ph.D.s. in history, literature, and economics, and admired the idealism of newcomers with backgrounds in legal services, antipoverty programs, public defenders' offices, and civil rights organizations. The old guard was genuinely bewildered when their tolerance was not reciprocated by many of the people they hired. By the end of the 1970s, like courtly senior partners in large law firms and classical judges in the justice system, legal traditionalists in the academy found themselves, their life's work, and their ideals of excellence under assault.

Who could have predicted, for example, the declining prestige of the legal treatise over the professional lifetime of Louis Loss, the intellectual father of modern securities law? When Loss moved into law teaching in the 1950s, after fifteen years with the Securities and Exchange Commission, it was natural that he should design a course dealing with the field that he had helped to create in the New Deal era. His initial treatise in 1951 gave a name and a shape to a field that had only been a mass of statutes, regulations, and court decisions involving modern finance. Loss's *Securities Regulation* was a godsend to practitioners. His three-volume second edition never left my desk when I worked on securities cases in practice; it was a cornucopia of ideas on hard problems. Up to the mid-1970s, treatises like Loss on securities regulation, Areeda on antitrust, Wright and Miller on civil procedure, and Wigmore on evidence were widely regarded as the highest form of legal scholarship. Their authors were the superstars of the legal academy.

By the late 1970s, however, a new generation of professors, hired by men like Loss and his colleagues, was beginning to exert considerable influence over hiring and tenure decisions. Ambitious candidates for appointment or promotion at leading schools, noting changes in the power structure, began to avoid purely "doctrinal" scholarship. The ratio of "practical" to "theoretical" essays published in leading law journals dropped from 4.5:1 in 1960 to 1:1 in 1985.[8] In 1983, a young legal economist at Yale delivered a harsh judgment on the work of his elders. "Today," wrote George Priest, the preparation and constant updating of works that systematically analyze the various fields of law "has been cast off to practitioners. The treatise is no longer even a credit to those competing on the leading edge of legal thought."[9]

The trend in elite schools away from treatise writing is perhaps only to be expected as so many fields are gobbled up by administrative regulations which are often too arbitrary and short-lived to repay extended study. But what is the audience for the new scholarship that is no longer directed to practitioners, legislators, or judges? Who's supposed to read all that stuff in over 425 (at last count) student-edited law reviews? One plausible answer seems to be that as law professors increasingly come to resemble other university scholars, they have become more interested in writing for each other. Anyone who samples the contents of recent law journals, however, might be forgiven for suspecting that many articles will be read by no one at all, other than the writer's promotion and tenure committee. The dean of Stanford Law School has said it right out loud: "[T]here are now so many law reviews—mostly edited by students rather than refereed by professionals—a perseverent professor who can afford the photocopying and postage can eventually get any article published somewhere."[10] That fact has excited wonder, envy, and other feelings among academics in the fields where tenure pieces must pass blind peer review in order to be accepted for publication.

George Priest's report of the demise of the treatise in respectable academic society was somewhat exaggerated. Treatise writing is still ably carried on by first-rate scholars in many law schools. But it is true that the genre has lost much of its prestige in the elite academy. On the publication of the eleventh volume of the third edition of *Securities Regulation* in 1993, Harvard's Loss, aged seventy-nine, commented: "There are people on this faculty who scorn treatise writing and liken legal treatises to battleships—prime, prestigious stuff in their time, but not really worth their keep in the contemporary world. They prefer to write about the sex lives of caterpillars. But what they don't realize is that these books have shaped the law."[11]

Those who rejected traditional legal scholarship, however, had their own ideas about shaping the law. Attacks on the sort of work at which Loss's generation excelled came from four principal directions: from those who thought the professional training offered in law schools was not practical enough; those for whom the middlebrow theorizing of mainstream legal scholarship was not theoretical enough; those whose allegiance to projects of social transformation trumped scholarly obligations of thoroughness, evenhandedness, and open-mindedness; and those who scoffed at the very idea of a disinterested quest for knowledge. The challenges found their way into the academy under various banners: clinical law, "advocacy" scholarship, the law-and-economics movement, and the critical legal studies movement. The old fault line between professional training and university education opened into a chasm.

Clinical legal education might have helped to knit together university and professional traditions. Like medical interns, students in well-run clinical programs learn by doing, and follow up on their real or simulated practical experiences with classroom reflection and deliberation on the legal, ethical, and human problems they encounter. Such programs have not only filled an educational gap but improved access to legal services for the poor and the middle class.

Clinical programs were bedeviled from the beginning, however, by the difficulty of finding instructors with the requisite combination of practical and academic skills. That problem (which could have been remedied with teamwork) both aggravated and was aggravated by the tendency of law faculties to relegate clinical programs and teachers to second-class status. Many professors initially hired to teach in clinical programs took the first opportunity available to switch to the "core" curriculum. The focus of most clinical programs on litigation and poverty law has been another factor impeding the clinical movement from reaching its full potential to enrich a wide variety of legal fields including the business curriculum.[12]

At its best, clinical legal education has been a valuable supplement to bookish legal education. At worst, the clinics have become clubhouses for the alienated, and cautionary instances of Blackstone's warning about the drawbacks of the old apprenticeship system: "If practice be the whole he is taught, practice must also be the whole he will ever know."[13]

Independently of formal clinical programs, law professors often lend their talents and expertise to parties engaged in promoting this or that objective through litigation or legislation. Like clinical work, these professorial activities in the "real world" can help to bridge the gap between practice and the academy. Students of criminal law, for example, can benefit in many ways from their professor's involvement in an actual case or in drafting model statutes. At their best, such endeavors help a scholar to keep current in his field and to fulfill his responsibility to make the benefits of research available to the wider community.

In certain cases, however, the connection between outside work and one's academic duties is remote. Some professors become consultants mainly to supplement academic salaries. Despite guidelines limiting outside work, the tail sometimes begins to wag the legal beagle. Commenting on reports of hefty fees paid to moonlighting professors, the late Judge Wyzanski wrote to a prominent Washington lawyer, "No one in Hand's day, no one in my day, would have thought that a Harvard professor would charge his client, if he had one, the maximum permissible or even what was the standard of the marketplace. A Harvard Law professor if he had a client had one under very special circumstances. Usually the professor was retained because of the expertness he had in the field which he taught at the law school. His justification for acting as a lawyer in that field was primarily because he would learn as much from doing that kind of work as from writing articles for scholarly journals about the topics covered in his teaching. To charge more than a decent amount would set a very bad example for students as to what was the nature of their calling—a profession to serve the public."[14]

Law professors who engage in outside consulting (as well as many who would have difficulty getting hired as consultants) are often tempted to engage in *advocacy scholarship*. Many legal scholars, of course, write in hopes of furthering definite practical or political objectives. But advocacy scholarship, as that term is understood among law professors, openly or covertly abandons the traditional obligation to deal with significant contrary evidence or arguments. In fact, advocacy scholarship is not scholarship at all, for its research is not conducted with an open mind and its results are not presented with a view toward advancing knowledge about the subject treated. Ironically, it was a paragon of romantic judging who was one of the first people to call attention to the sudden increase of partisan legal literature in the 1960s. Many writers of law review articles, Justice William O. Douglas complained, were failing to disclose that they were "people with axes to grind."[15]

What is novel in recent years is the degree to which one-sided advocacy in the guise of scholarship has gained respectability. In many schools, hiring and promotion committees, the gatekeepers of academic standards, no longer insist strictly on a candidate's duty to master important contributions by others in the field or to fairly appraise the pros and cons of the positions he or she takes. The scholarly enterprise has thus been transformed. Although many legal writers, and especially the authors of widely used treatises, still try conscientiously to deal with all relevant information and points of view, a reader can no longer take that for granted. A law review article, say, on environmental law, may be written by someone who is advancing the same position in a brief as a paid consultant for the National Association of Manufacturers or the Sierra Club.

Learned Hand argued in former times that any scholar who becomes engaged in the controversies of the day is playing a dangerous game: "You cannot raise the standard against oppression, or leap into the breach to relieve injustice, and still keep an open mind to every disconcerting fact, or an open ear to the cold voice of doubt. I am satisfied that a scholar who tries to combine these parts sells his birthright for a mess of pottage; that, when the final count is made, it will be found that the impairment of his powers far outweighs any possible contribution to the causes he has espoused."[16]

For good or ill, that purist view of the scholar's role no longer prevails. Advocacy scholarship at its best adopts the precautions recommended by Judge Posner: the partisan writer candidly exposes his interest and his reasoning processes, and does his best to assess the merits of contested legal doctrines.[17] At its worst, it imports the most debased adversarial litigation tactics into the realm of scholarship. Rambo scholars, like Rambo litigators, engage in no-holds-barred attacks on their opponents' positions, and sometimes on the opponents themselves.

Many legal academics still share with their colleagues in other disciplines the scholar's commitment to pursue knowledge wherever it leads and whatever its unpopularity. But for a growing coterie of professors in the human sciences, including law, that ideal is simply meaningless. In some quarters, notions of knowledge, objectivity, and truth have come under heavy attack. If truth is whatever you want it to be, or the will of the stronger, the distinction between scholarship and advocacy collapses. If all law is radically indeterminate, then all legal scholarship becomes a form of advocacy.

Those esoteric problems do not trouble most members of the influential *law-and-economics* school, which derives its appeal precisely from its reassuring claims to be able to deliver more knowledge, objectivity, and truth than its competitors. In many respects, those who do interdisciplinary work in law and economics are the true heirs of Holmes's most constructive scholarly vision. The form of rationality he prized—functional, instrumental, and utilitarian—is their stock-in-trade. They have helped to explain why many areas of law have taken their present form, and their empirical work has improved our understanding of the practical effects of many legal measures.

At its best, law-and-economics promotes Holmes's ideal of thinking clearly about the structure, operation, and impact of law. Legal economists have revolutionized antitrust law and the proof of damages, and have importantly influenced the way lawyers think about securities regulation, environmental law, and the regulatory activities of the state. The work of judges and lawyers in many fields has been transformed by the insights of the school's members, who include two Nobel Prize winners, Ronald Coase and Gary Becker.

At its worst, law-and-economics replicates the fallacy of the pre-Realist doctrinalists who achieved the appearance of explanatory power by ignoring or assuming away messy facts that gummed up their tidy analyses. It is worrisome, too, that many legal economists are relatively indifferent to the traditions of separation-of-powers constitutionalism, the common law, and craft professionalism. But, unlike the critical legal theorists, few law-and-economics scholars are actually hostile to those traditions.

While the law-and-economics school ran with Holmes's ideal of rationality, the *critical legal studies movement* (CLS) took up that fertile thinker's emphasis on the irrational aspects of lawmaking, giving his skepticism a postmodern twist with the aid of continental literary criticism and neo-Marxist social thought. CLS is a capacious umbrella covering a varied collection of individuals, connected through personal relationships and ideological sympathies, sharing some loosely related ideas and a mood of resentment regarding the distribution of wealth, power, and prestige in society. As one of their leading members has observed, however, most of the movement's political energy has been expended within the relatively cloistered environment of the law schools. "Critical legal studies," writes Mark Tushnet, "is a political location for a group of people on the Left who share the project of supporting and extending the domain of the Left in the legal academy."[18] Unlike members of the law-and-economics school, CLS has had little influence outside the academy, but their impact on legal education has been substantial. To no small degree, that effect can be credited to two charismatic teachers who joined the Harvard Law School faculty in 1971. Roberto Unger and Duncan Kennedy are the John

Lennon and Mick Jagger, respectively, of the form of legal avant-gardism that arose in the late 1960s.

When young Roberto Unger came to Harvard Law School from Brazil for graduate study in 1969–70, the place seemed to him to be moribund. The famed professors of torts, contracts, property, procedure, criminal and constitutional law appeared to be bogged down in "analogy mongering."[19] They bore little resemblance to real intellectuals—not having studied Marx, Freud, Nietzsche, Gramsci, or Foucault. The elders were thus unaware that eighteenth-century constitutionalism was passé, that law was nothing but a historical artifact or the will of the dominant classes, and that the common law existed only in their own imaginations—if the word "imagination" could be used to describe the pedestrian gropings of their narrow minds. Most of them, in Unger's often-quoted description, "dallied in one more variant of the perennial effort to restate power and preconception as right. . . . When we came, they were like a priesthood that had lost their faith and kept their jobs. They stood in tedious embarrassment before cold altars."[20]

Unger and Kennedy promptly lit a fire under the altars of legal education and roasted the unsuspecting clergy. While Unger dissected legal thought with the instruments of critical social theory, Kennedy produced a series of writings that (like the works of legal economists) traced hidden patterns in the history, structure, and operation of the Anglo-American common law. But where economists saw a more or less purposeful groping for efficiency in a world of scarcity, Kennedy discerned a more or less sinister pursuit of class, gender, or other interests in a hegemonic struggle for power.

Kennedy's intelligence, charm, and energetic networking awakened academic neo-Marxism from its dogmatic slumber. His persona figured prominently in the growth of CLS into a "movement" complete with humorous underground broadsides and a "summer camp." He went on tour, captivating law school audiences with his bad-boy humor and winning converts with his New Age evangelistic style. His outrageous proposals shocked the grown-ups and amused students: law graduates should become "moles" in large firms, subverting hierarchy at every opportunity; professors, secretaries, and janitors should all receive the same pay and occasionally do each other's jobs. (Harvard Law School janitors, polled by a student journalist, liked the pay idea, but said Kennedy's plan couldn't work because most professors couldn't possibly handle a real job.[21]) While Madonna was still in her playpen, Duncan Kennedy had discovered that there is enormous entertainment value in turning conventional symbols on their heads, in trashing icons, and in celebrating polymorphous sexuality.

Unger's charisma, no less powerful, is of a different sort, more passionate, less playful, cooler, but more intense. To a lecture style of the type brought to perfection by continental European law professors, Unger adds the zest of political oratory—all the more effective for being carefully controlled. He and Kennedy, with legal historian Morton Horwitz, quickly became the intellectual leaders of a group of students and academics who saw mainstream legal scholarship as lacking intellectual challenge, suffocatingly dull, and slavishly dedicated to the perpetuation of the existing economic and political order. At last there was a field to engage the interest of students who were neither keen on traditional law nor attracted by the economic approach to legal analysis. Like law-and-economics, critical theory could be used to explain and reorder all the substantive areas of law. There were at least two decades' worth of critical analyses of various fields to be written by aspiring law professors. And math was not a prerequisite.

The energy of CLS adherents, however, was seldom directed toward any constructive legal or social changes. In the face of the laborious task of keeping legal institutions abreast of and responsive to human needs, the economic purist says, "If it's broke, government can't fix it." The purist crit, for his part, has a simple prescription for the unfairness and inefficiencies of the legal system: the wrecking ball. "Context smashing" is central to the program of transformative politics advocated by Unger, who criticizes eighteenth-century constitutional techniques like the system of separated powers and checks and balances for the drag they place on liberating change.[22]

Unger calls his program "superliberalism" because it "requires the abandonment of the forms of governmental, economic, and legal organization with which liberalism has traditionally been associated."[23] Where mere hyperliberals like Ronald Dworkin and Laurence Tribe were content to keep constitutional design in the background, superliberal Unger proposes dismantling it with the aim of ensuring that fundamental issues (except for "basic" rights) are continually "up for grabs." Once freed of the paralytic effect of checks and balances, Unger's reconstructed constitutional order would be kept from settling into routine by "destabilization rights" designed to ensure constant ferment and creative disarray.[24] One must be careful, Unger has occasionally noted in passing, not to let context smashing become one's sole preoccupation,[25] but that part of the message was lost on some of his excited followers.

The arrows aimed by the critical scholars at traditional American legal institutions often seem oddly off-target. What they have added to Holmes and the Realists is mainly borrowed from theorists in France, Italy, and Germany—countries that had never had experience with anything like the common law, where reason has often meant *raison d'état*, and which in the past have had difficulty establishing regimes in which the rule of law was respected. Like Holmes's attack on "logic," the crits' transplanted critiques are not especially illuminating when applied to the legal system of the United States. Like the playful Dadaists and grim Futurists who are their counterparts in the art world, the crits have added only marginally to the achievements of their "tradition-haunted" predecessors. Moreover, just as Dada's descendants now include a number of "artists" who never learned how to draw,[26] many legal avant-gardists have only a nodding acquaintance with craft techniques.

At its best, as represented by some of Unger's work, critical theory invites common-law lawyers to unite theoretical to practical reasoning and to correct for excessive individualism by recognizing the social dimension of human personhood. At its worst, critical theory shows an alarming readiness to dispense with hard-won political achievements and procedural safeguards.

Many commentators, including several critical scholars themselves, see the crits as the direct descendants of the Realists. It is a big step, however, from observing, as Holmes and Llewellyn did, that there are certain leeways inherent in fact finding and rule application to asserting that there is no such thing as a fact and that all rules are radically indeterminate and manipulable. It is another major leap from being realistic about the difficulties of fair and impartial decision making to a condemnation of the entire legal system as fatally corrupted by racism, sexism, and exploitation. And there is a world of difference between the lawyerly reformism of the New Dealers and the view that law is nothing more than concentrated politics—between Felix Frankfurter and the Frankfurt School. Holmes, that arch-debunker, enjoyed trashing legal traditions and conventional pieties as much as any modern crit. But he was aware that it was a high-stakes game. "Experimenting in negations," he wrote, is "an amusing sport if it is remembered that while it takes but a few minutes to cut down a tree it takes a century for a tree to grow."[27]

The contempt of some critical scholars for constitutionalism, together with their predilection for fancy theory, led to division within their own ranks. Some female and minority scholars, who had been attracted to the movement initially, began to complain that the crits, for all their talk of equality and liberation, had not paid much attention to the practical concerns of members of disadvantaged groups. Some began to wonder whether it was wise to junk the rule-of-law tradition which, with all its imperfections, had often been a bulwark against oppression for unpopular and powerless members of society. The original crits, for their part, were not very forthcoming about what sort of regime they would like to see in place of the ongoing American experiment. After the worldwide disenchantment with state socialism that dramatically erupted in

1989, it was the turn of many crits to stand in some discomfort before cold altars.

But they did not stand for long. Many of the crits' disciples had defected to women's and minority studies, and offered sanctuary to their chagrined former masters. Those fields have blossomed to the point where it seems fair to say that the CLS torch has passed to feminist jurisprudence and critical race theory. Feminist legal scholars like Catharine MacKinnon have already had a substantial impact on the legal treatment of rape and sexual harassment. And the perspectives on pornography put forth by feminists, together with the points of view of critical race theorists on speech, voting, and equality have cast new light into many dim corners of the legal system. Now that the insights of Marx's social theory have been absorbed into postmodern thought and his economic theories are no longer modish in the academy, many "old" crits are reinventing themselves as feminists, multiculturalists, champions of gay rights, and environmentalists.

"Diversity"

With assorted rivalries and internal divisions among academic camps, the atmosphere at some law schools occasionally has been compared by journalists to that of Beirut or Bosnia. But law school strife is more like *Revenge of the Nerds*, in which warring fraternities and sororities rush promising candidates, lob smelly missiles at each other, and caucus in the comfort of their clubhouses. Were it not for their spillover effects on the profession, the law school squabbles could be classed as harmless outlets for the excess energy of the sedentary class.

Intramural battles in the legal academy are waged with such fervor that it is easy for an outsider to overlook the relatively great ideological homogeneity of law school culture. The official line of most law school deans is that legal education has never been more alive with diversity, creativity, and spirited intellectual controversy. That's the administrators' story, and they're sticking to it. But the facts are otherwise. Most law faculties have actively sought and achieved a rainbow look where gender and minority status are concerned. But the outward appearance of heterogeneity conceals a surprising degree of consensus on many points of politics, on the practice of law, the primacy of theory, and on constitutional law.

Descriptions of law school strife as occurring between "right" and "left" wings are particularly misleading. In most law schools, the "right" is composed mainly of New Deal Democrats and libertarians, who are traditionalists with regard to scholarship and standards. The libertarian inclinations of most law-and-economics scholars place them to the right of most Americans on economic issues, but to the left on social questions. Cultural conservatives and Republicans of any stripe are a decided minority. One law school administrator who recently boasted of the diverse composition of his faculty admitted in the next breath that probably not one of his forty faculty members had voted for the winning candidate in the 1988 presidential election![28] At a law school dinner party shortly before that election, one of my colleagues asked those assembled for their guesses as to how many votes George Bush would receive from the sixty-five or so Harvard Law School faculty members. A relative newcomer at that time, I guessed five. No one else guessed more than three. Even more telling is a Chicago professor's recollection that the faculty at that "conservative" law school favored Mondale by a comfortable margin in 1984, and were narrowly divided in favor of McGovern in 1972!

It is voting behavior in faculty meetings, not at the polls, that differentiates the law school "right" from the "left." Fierce battles occur over what constitutes excellence in scholarship—whether a candidate's unorthodox work belongs to an important new genre or is merely, as Duke's former dean Paul Carrington (borrowing from Foucault) puts it, the sort of thing "that has given bullshit a bad name."[29] When such disputes involve the work of women and members of minority groups, charges of sexism and racism are often hurled in the heat of conflict. One side cries standards; the other diversity. But no one is quite sure what standards and diversity mean. "Let's be honest," says Alan Dershowitz, "the demand for diversity is at least in part a cover for a political power grab by the left. Most of those recruited to provide politically correct diversity—Afro-Americans, women, gays—are thought to be supporters of the left."[30]

Another commonality among contemporary law professors concerns their attitudes toward the practice of law, especially private practice. Even clinical instructors tend to look down on the many areas of legal work that do not meet their standards of social awareness. In this they are joined by eminent mainstream scholars like John Hart Ely, who, when dean of Stanford Law School, said, "Frankly, deep down, most of the faculty don't have a lot of respect for [corporate practice] as a career choice. I don't think that what corporate lawyers do is evil, but I myself would be uncomfortable working for a large firm. I wouldn't want to feel I was just a cog in a big machine."[31] The practitioner's life, as we have seen, might prove daunting even to a top-notch dean, but legal educators' aloofness from the world of practice is problematic, too.

Such attitudes not only have widened the separation between the academy and the bar; they have also created an unfortunate gap between the interests of professors and the concerns of students.[32] Professorial disdain or indifference toward the sorts of careers most of their students will follow manifests itself in myriad ways. Few would openly declare, as has Yale's Owen Fiss, that "law professors are not paid to train lawyers, but to study the law and to teach their students what they happen to discover."[33] But an overall shift toward that point of view is unmistakable. One reason is that appointments committees, impressed by honors and high grades, do not always attend closely to the courses in which these grades are obtained. Serving on the hiring committees at Boston College and Harvard law schools, I was struck by the number of candidates for teaching positions who had graduated with high honors from fine law schools while taking hardly any law courses at all after the obligatory first-year surveys. With no practical experience beyond a yearlong judicial clerkship, many of these skillful curricular navigators are now teaching basic courses in torts, contracts, property, criminal law, procedure, and constitutional law to people who will one day practice law.

It is commonly believed that second- and third-tier law schools are more profession-oriented than elite law schools, but the fact is that homogenizing forces are at work, with varying degrees of strength, throughout legal education. For one thing, a handful of schools have had a disproportionate influence on the formation of law teachers. Nearly a third of the 6,000 full-time law faculty members at the nation's 176 ABA-accredited law schools are products of just five law faculties: Chicago, Columbia, Harvard, Michigan, and Yale.[34] The proportion is far higher in those law schools that are regularly rated among the top twenty.

Another element of homogeneity is the widespread acceptance among legal academics of a constitutionalism from which many important features of the Constitution have been subtracted. The attitudes of law professors toward constitutional law have considerable political significance, for law school provides the only civics education that many lawyers possess. And lawyers, as we shall see, are the principal instructors in the year-round law school that all Americans willy-nilly attend.[35] Moreover, an intimate synergy links the appellate judiciary and the legal academy. Despite recent strains in the relationship, each is an important consumer of the other's output. Many professors strive mightily to influence the course of judicial decisions. Many judges reach out in their opinions to "constituents" in the professoriat. It is common for judges to rely on trusted professors to help select the clerks to whom they increasingly delegate important duties. Thus, the professors' ideas are cycled, via the clerks, into the opinions that will be later chosen by the professors for classroom study by future clerks.[36]

Unfortunately, the "Professors' Constitution" has long been

a partial Constitution. Prior to the 1960s, constitutional law courses lavished attention on some parts of the Constitution (federalism, the commerce clause) and neglected others (the Bill of Rights, the Fourteenth Amendment). In the Warren and Burger eras, the jurisprudence of individual and minority rights revitalized constitutional law, attracted many of the best minds, and made it one of the most popular elective courses.

But the new constitutional law was as lopsided as the old. Many instructors treated the Constitution only as a fountain of rights, barely introducing their students to federalism and the separation of powers. Today, constitutional law, in the typical course, is to the Constitution what the Elgin marbles are to the Parthenon. Course books and class discussions concentrate on a prized collection of fragments, but the well-proportioned structure in which each of these treasures once had its appropriate place is not on display. An interested student can, of course, turn to the course book's appendix and contemplate the Constitution: a wonder of another world, an ancient temple once used for activities that are no longer much practiced—deliberation, voting, legislation, local government.

To be sure, there are great differences of emphasis from one course to another. Some professors dwell on freedom of expression, some on privacy, some on economic liberties. Some subscribe to the view that original intent should control inter-pretation, while most defend more expansive approaches rang-ing from Cardozo's yin and yang of freedom and restraint to freewheeling judicial creativity. But a number of common features unite the constitutional views of a wide variety of law professors, in and out of the field of constitutional law. Utili-tarians and pragmatists who believe that government is mainly a matter of finding technical solutions to technical problems are as impatient with checks and balances and local self-determination as are visionaries who see themselves as the vanguard of the oppressed. Devotees of economic liberties are as mistrustful of majoritarian institutions as are their colleagues who exalt liberties of self-expression. Few professors can be found insisting on the fact that the Constitution is first and foremost a framework for a particular sort of political regime that remains, in a complicated way, democratic.

At its best, the rights-oriented constitutional law of the 1960s, 1970s, and 1980s has deepened understanding and appreciation of previously neglected parts of our constitutional tradition. But its failing has been to neglect the constitutional framework for a system of representative government where the freedom of individuals and groups is safeguarded not only by judicial enforcement of rights but by federalism, voting, and the separation of powers. Contemporary constitutional law teaching does an excellent job of reinforcing what everyone already knows about the dangers of unfettered majority rule, but tends to induce forgetfulness of the ways in which the Constitution was meant to prevent a more ancient and intractable evil in human history—capture of the reins of government by the powerful few. That central weakness in constitutional law instruction has aggravated other problems. The near-exclusive focus on court decisions promotes indifference or disdain toward the legislative process and ordinary electoral politics. By the time they graduate, many students can see no reason why social and economic policies should not regularly emerge from enlightened courts rather than from time-consuming democratic processes involving men and women who may not have had college educations.

The relatively homogeneous political science of the law school classroom does not proceed from any sinister antidemocratic plot. Much of it is simply a by-product of the traditionally court-centered nature of legal education and the fact that law professors feel a greater affinity with judges than with elected officials or the people they represent. For a short time, it was otherwise. Realists and New Dealers addressed much of their work in the 1940s and 1950s to legislators and administrators. But in the 1960s, with state and federal courts taking the initiative in law reform in many areas, and the Warren Court revolutionizing constitutional law, the professoriat resumed its old love affair with the judiciary.

That affair, always attended by bickering, has recently gone through an especially rough patch. Judge Harry Edwards caused something of a sensation with a 1992 polemic complaining that current legal scholarship is of little use to judges and practitioners.[37] No outsider to the academy, Edwards had taught at several leading law schools before his appointment to the federal bench. Thus his words had a special sting when he wrote: "Our law reviews are now full of mediocre interdisciplinary articles. Too many law professors are ivory tower dilettantes, pursuing whatever subject piques their interest, whether or not the subject merits scholarship, and whether or not *they* have the scholarly skills to master it."[38] But there is an even more damning charge to be leveled against legal education itself: neither the old doctrinal scholarship nor the new interdisciplinary varieties have done much thus far to prepare lawyers to deal with the most difficult challenges that face practitioners and judges in the modern regulatory state. Regarding the "litigation explosion," Judge Posner has written: "[N]othing in a conventional legal education . . . equips a person to notice, let alone to measure, explain, temper, and adjust to, an increase in the demand for judicial services."[39]

Law professors, for their part, became increasingly disenchanted with the courts in the Reagan-Bush years. Many judges seemed not to be paying any attention at all to what professors were telling them! A chorus of disappointment rose from several points on the limited political spectrum of the legal academy. The dean of the University of Michigan Law School wrote that changes in the judiciary have made it a "less appealing audience" for legal scholars.[40] Yale's former dean Guido Calabresi, a pioneer in law-and-economics, called the Rehnquist Court "disgusting."[41] A liberal Texas constitutional law professor lamented "the 'capture' of the judiciary, in the last decade especially, by a political party with which most legal academics do not identify."[42] Legal historian Robert Gordon noted the sense of legal academics ("mostly pretty liberal in politics") that they had little hope of influencing anyone in power.[43] A critical theorist from Colorado added that "there is the beginning of a question as to whether judges are particularly well suited or well situated to think critically or deeply about law."[44] Pow!

The Law School Without Law

Why did law schools stray so far from their original vocation to teach law? It is not as though the old academy had been merely a glorified trade school where students were drilled on rules and doctrines that could be swept away by tomorrow's legislation or decisions. Though the early treatises were heavily doctrinal, university law professors from the beginning had de-emphasized particular rules and outcomes in their classrooms, concentrating on fundamental techniques and concepts. The practitioners of Langdell's case method were out to teach law "in the grand manner." The best of them, like Harvard's Phillip Areeda, were very grand indeed. In a recent interview, Areeda described the aims of the method he continues to employ with virtuosity. Through critical discussion of problems and issues in the first-year Contracts course, Areeda said:

> I try to do several things. First is to lead the students to some understanding about how the institution known as Contracts relates to what people do in the real world.
>
> Second, I hope students will gain a deep understanding of substantive doctrine.
>
> Third, I hope to lead students to an understanding of how the law develops, the legal process, what judges do, what the common law means.
>
> Fourth, I teach students many skills in, for example, reading statutes and reconciling apparent conflict within a statute. As in the common law, the relevant principles often point in different directions.
>
> Fifth, I try to help students to refine their logic, their reasoning, their use of analogy, and those other things we talk about as legal reasoning.[45]

Why did dedicated law teachers, treatise writers, and erstwhile public servants like Areeda, Loss, Cox, and their counterparts in law schools across the nation hire so many young colleagues who had little desire to carry on that once-dominant style of teaching and scholarship? Initially, it seems to have been a healthy impulse for diversity that prompted the most lawyerly professors to welcome into their midst a variety of individuals whose interests were very different from their own. The old-fashioned liberals who were in power in the early 1960s often bent over backward to compensate for their own deficiencies. But with the changing of the guard, it appeared that the Young Turks and Turkettes were not prepared to be so tolerant. Just as Ingrid Beall discovered it was no longer enough merely to be a good lawyer in the fiercely competitive big firms of the 1980s, legal academics found it was no longer enough merely to teach and write about law in the new academy.

Persons whose main interests are in fields other than law now wield considerable influence on the hiring and promotions process, especially at elite schools. But they seem less interested than their predecessors in maintaining a mutually beneficial balance among fancy theory types, doctrinalists, and practice-oriented teachers. The dean of one leading school wrote Judge Edwards: "[S]tudents who are not interested in interdisciplinary work, but are merely extraordinarily talented lawyers, shy away from a career in the academy because they know that the kind of work that they would be interested in doing is not valued. As a consequence, virtually all of the applications law schools like ours receive . . . come from individuals with a strong interdisciplinary bent."[46] Then there was the visiting professor at a top law school who asked a group of colleagues at the lunch table whether they would hire a teaching prospect who was very smart but interested only in teaching and writing about law. "Certainly not," was the answer. "If she only wanted to do law, by definition she could not be very smart!"

As retirements and deaths take their toll, intellectual diversity on law faculties can only be expected to decrease. The dwindling number of professors with background or interest in practice is already having adverse effects. Since casebooks by definition are collections of pathological situations where things went spectacularly wrong, it is hard for students to grasp what a healthy functioning system looks like without help from an experienced teacher. If the professor does not ask how the problem might have been avoided by drafting, or the dispute settled through negotiation, neither will the student. If the professor does not point out how often cases are dropped, settled, or summarily dismissed, because, remarkably enough, the law or the facts are fairly clear, the student will tend to overestimate the leeways of facts and law.

Without guidance, the steady classroom diet of borderline cases inevitably fosters a litigator's mentality, a major complaint of former Harvard president Derek Bok in his widely publicized critique of the nation's law schools. According to Bok, a former law dean and law professor himself, legal educators train students "more for conflict than for the gentler arts of reconciliation and accommodation."[47] Without some practical experience, however, it is quite difficult for the instructor to lead the students' attention from the disaster on the printed page to such questions as how good planning might have averted the problem in the first place; whether and how alternative methods of dispute resolution might have yielded a better outcome than litigation; and whether law reform efforts are in order to deal with the general type of problem. As negotiation expert Robert Mnookin explains: "[O]ver 90 percent of all lawsuits that are filed end up getting resolved through negotiation. A key challenge is to try to figure out how that can happen sooner rather than later."[48]

The teachers and scholars who proclaim the radical indeterminacy and infinite manipulability of legal rules can have only the sketchiest notion of what goes on in a law office. When a client comes to a lawyer for planning advice—say, in connection with taxes, drafting a will or a long-term contract, or setting up a real estate transaction—the lawyer must, at his peril, take the relevant body of law very seriously indeed. It will be of no service to the client—and no defense to a malpractice action

—to maintain that any provision of the Internal Revenue Code can be imaginatively construed to mean the opposite of what the courts and informed professional opinion say it means. To be sure, a good counselor will advise the client where there seems to be some flexibility in the rules and where one might prudently take a risk, but that is a far cry from saying all bets are off.

A related problem arising from professors' lack of practical experience is the failure to distinguish in the classroom between the planner's and the litigator's perspective. As a former litigator assigned to teach first-year property, I found myself in a curious situation. Property has always been the planner's and drafter's field par excellence. Yet the dominance of the case method means that teaching materials for property, as in all other fields, consist primarily of opinions rendered in disputes. It was a constant struggle for me in the beginning to try to imagine how the transaction in each case could have been better designed, as well as to evaluate the quality of the lawyering that took place after everything went wrong. If I had never practiced law at all, I probably would not have understood how crucial it is for students to know that rules look very different for planning purposes from the way they appear in the context of a lawsuit. The same body of law that looks fairly well settled to a lawyer consulted in advance of a proposed action will often seem far more open to interpretation if the client comes in for advice *after* the IRS has challenged his tax deductions, *after* she learns she has been disinherited by her father, or *after* her tenant has repudiated a ten-year lease in the third year. Yet both perceptions will be appropriate for the circumstances. Students need to know, too, that the main source of uncertainty in litigation is not the leeways of the relevant law, but the vagaries of litigation itself—the availability of evidence, the credibility of witnesses, the quality of representation, the characteristics of the judge, the unpredictability of juries.

The legal academy's turn away from law has been a real misfortune for those students, still a large majority, who come to law schools for professional training. It is a misfortune, too, for their future clients, the legal system, and the community at large. Concerned especially about the effect on disadvantaged students, two prominent minority judges have spoken out. Federal Judge José A. Cabranes has strongly advised that the best education for one who aspires to public or private leadership roles in this country "is to be found in the courses which form the backbone of the mainstream law school curriculum," prudently combined with interdisciplinary courses.[49] Judge (then Professor) Edwards opposed the development of "alternatives" to standard courses in connection with affirmative action programs for the same reason.[50]

Since Cabranes and Edwards expressed those views, the situation has only deteriorated. An ignoble alliance between faculty interests and short-run student desires has created curricular disasters. In some schools, a hefty proportion of first-year introductory courses are taught by proselytizing legal economists, critical theorists, or representatives of the schools that grew out of critical theory. One of Judge Edwards's clerks recounted that, as a beginning student, "I was expected to *deconstruct* a body of law before I understood it!"[51] The devastating indictment once aimed by *New York Times* legal writer David Margolick against his alma mater, Stanford Law School, now applies to several law schools.

> By preparing their students for careers they openly disdain; by discussing legal problems in an arid, overly intellectualized setting in which ideals are often considered either irrelevant or insufficiently "hard-headed"; by spending three years reminding their classes that judicial opinions are frequently arbitrary, poorly crafted or intellectually dishonest, the professors make cynics, even nihilists of their students. Shorn of their ideals, students, not surprisingly, select the most lucrative jobs.[52]

Why are students not up in arms over the unresponsiveness of many professors to the eminently reasonable desire to obtain legal training in law school? Law faculties have finessed the issue of whether they are shortchanging their students by accommodating students' short-term interests in what may be called credentialing with comfort. Straight lecturing, practically unheard of in the old academy, has steadily advanced at the expense of the discussion method, so demanding of teacher and student alike. And much of the sting has been removed from the once-dreaded sorting process of examinations, grading, and ranking. Now, as in Garrison Keillor's Lake Wobegon, all the children are above average. In many schools, half or more of the class graduates with honors.

After grades had been inflated to near-bursting point, other means of rewarding especially talented or hardworking students had to be made more democratic, too. At one time, each law school typically had a single law review staffed by a small group of students who were selected on the basis of first-year grades. At the end of the second year, some of these students were elected officers after writing publishable notes or comments. Over the 1970s and 1980s, that system was radically revised. Staffs began to expand, and important-sounding titles multiplied. But so long as there was only one law review, that solution had limits. So law schools began to create new, specialized law journals, some organized like extracurricular activities with membership available to any interested student. During the eighteen years I taught at Boston College, I witnessed the birth of an environmental law journal, an international and comparative law journal, and a Third World law journal.

The proliferation of new legal periodicals made nearly everyone happy except spoilsports like Judge Edwards. Any law student could put "law review" on his or her résumé, and any professor's scholarly efforts could be crowned with publication. Still, there was the nagging problem that membership on the most prestigious law reviews was available only on the basis of grades. In the 1970s, therefore, many law reviews decided to extend membership to students who showed exceptional promise in a writing competition. That was still too meritocratic for some schools, so they arranged to incorporate affirmative action preferences into their writing competitions. On the *Harvard Law Review*, for example, only about half of the forty positions filled each year are still allocated on the basis of grades.[53]

In the classroom, the crusty, demanding law teacher satirized in *The Paper Chase* has by and large been supplanted by "sensitive," "supportive" paragons of political correctness. The sensitivity of some professors can be truly exquisite when students disagree with their political views. At least that was the disturbing finding of a survey conducted for the American Bar Association's Section on General Practice by the associate dean of the University of Montana Law School, Steven C. Bahls.[54] Among the 449 student members of that section, a majority reported that some professors at their law schools were intolerant of political beliefs that differed from their own and that students often did not feel free to disagree with the political perspectives of their professors in class discussions, exams, or papers. Bahls could not say whether these student fears of politically biased grading were well founded. It does not seem unreasonable, though, for a student to wonder whether professors who deride impartiality in judging would strive to act impartially themselves when evaluating student work. If romantic judges are fine, why not romantic law professors?

Most students, if you ask them how intrafaculty disputes affect them, will say, "Not at all." Their preoccupations are different from those of their professors. Yet anyone who speaks with recent law graduates knows, too, how many upon reaching the end of their studies have felt the same vague disappointment that sometimes came over us, their predecessors in the good-old, bad-old days. It is like the feeling Socrates had one morning after arguing all night about justice with a group of friends and companions.

That was a fascinating conversation, Socrates says to Thrasymachus at the end of the first book of *The Republic*. It was like a splendid banquet for the mind to speak for hours about this or that aspect of the just and the unjust. Still, in the lonely hours before dawn, the old philosopher confesses to pangs of spiritual hunger. The banquet was for him "a feast without satisfaction." The discussion was lively enough, but the participants had rambled from one topic to another, like ill-mannered guests who grab at whatever is on the table. They made no progress at all with the question they had meant to discuss when the evening began: What is justice?

The new academy, like the old, provided much food for thought, but both academies offered students salt water for their deepest thirst. This was so even though refreshing springs were always near at hand. Fortunately, those ever-present sources of renewal are now beginning to be tapped.

11

The Mighty Princess and the Woman by the Wayside

When I think of the Law [as an anthropologist or philosopher would], I see a princess mightier than she who once wrought at Bayeux, eternally weaving into her web dim figures of the ever-lengthening past—figures too dim to be noticed by the idle, too symbolic to be interpreted except by her pupils, but to the discerning eye disclosing every painful step and every world-shaking contest by which mankind has worked and fought its way from savage isolation to organic social life. . . .

When I think of the Law as we know her in the courthouse and the market, she seems to me a woman sitting by the wayside, beneath whose overshadowing hood every man shall see the countenance of his deserts or needs. —OLIVER WENDELL HOLMES (1885)[1]

How did we get from the old academy devoted to the law of courthouse and market to the new academy where law is often barely distinguishable from anthropology or philosophy? Why were the suitors of the woman by the wayside put to rout by the chevaliers of the mighty princess?

There can be no doubt that legal education in the 1950s and early 1960s had real deficiencies—remoteness from hands-on experience, insularity regarding other disciplines and nations, an underdeveloped empirical as well as theoretical side, and a near-paralysis in the face of moral arguments. Addressing those problems, however, did not require discarding proved sources of strength—practical reason, mastery of craft, and attentiveness to the concrete details of social and economic relations. Why did neither the old guard nor the avant-garde accept that one cannot find the princess without passing by the way of the hooded woman and that the face of the hooded woman will always be partially hidden to those who do not seek the princess?

The stumbling block was that teachers and scholars of law had never consciously appropriated the foundations and dynamics of their own discipline. They could "do" law very well, but they were tongue-tied when it came to explaining and defending their ingrained, habitual doings. The fact is, as the critical legal scholars saw more clearly than most, that lawyers *do* need big theory, especially in times of crisis and challenge. Again, Holmes had left large footprints in the sand. "Theory," he wrote in 1897, "is the most important part of the dogma of the law. . . . It is not to be feared as unpractical, for, to the competent, it simply means going to the bottom of the subject."[2]

The instinct of common law lawyers, nevertheless, has always been to oppose theory with common sense. Most lawyers, when they think of the common law, regard it as a pragmatic tradition to which highfalutin philosophical speculation is unnecessary or useless. But once legal education moved into the university setting, that stance could not be indefinitely maintained. Research conducted without regard to immediate applications is as much an adjunct to training lawyers as basic science is to the formation of physicians and engineers. Academic lawyers sooner or later had to come to terms with the fact that practical reason and speculative reason are complementary—they are the two blades of the scissors, the handles of a two-handled jug.

When Roberto Unger described the eminent law professors of the late 1960s as embarrassed, he was on to something. But what? The professors he encountered were masters of their subjects, yet like common law lawyers from time immemorial they were not much given to big theory. Most of them, if asked point-blank, "What is your philosophy?" would have replied as Louis Loss once did: "I don't have a good philosophy other than use good judgment."[3] What Unger took for a loss of faith was actually the legal equivalent of the lag between everyday pastoral theology and the cutting-edge theology of the universities. Neither fish nor fowl, law professors were the amphibians of the legal world, with some of the limitations as well as some of the strengths of practicing lawyers and university scholars. Uncomfortable with metaphysics and epistemology, old-guard law professors were nonplussed by the kinds of questions that began to be posed in the 1970s by younger colleagues fresh from history, literature, and philosophy departments.

Unger was perceptive in noting the consternation of the elders, but wrong in guessing its cause. The professors were not like a priesthood that had lost its faith. They were like a priesthood that had long been preaching to the already, or almost, converted; a priesthood wholly unaccustomed to dealing with sophisticated unbelievers. Nothing in their training, moreover, had equipped them to deal with late-twentieth-century philosophical controversies. But, being lawyers, they hated being caught without a response to challenges from smart-alecky juniors. A common reaction was to adopt an aggressively anti-intellectual tough-guy stance: "That's a question for airy-fairy philosophers." The bespectacled Bogarts could not hide their vulnerability, however, from critical colleagues who, heartened by success, kicked more sand in the faces of their opponents.

The law-and-economics scholars were relatively immune to CLS avant-gardism. They had already emancipated themselves from legal tradition and had staked their own camps on high intellectual terrain. "It takes a theory to beat a theory," said Chicago's Richard Epstein, confident that the theories coming out of the law-and-economics movement could best any and all competitors. But most doctrinalists, traditionally antitheoretical (and proud of it), resisted what they saw as the dogmas of legal economists almost as stubbornly as the sallies of the crits. The feigned bravado of old-school professors, the rational science of the economists, and the tradition trashing of the crits made for a strange atmosphere in the academy. Cornell's former dean Roger Cramton spoke for many traditionalists when he worried aloud in a much-discussed 1978 article that law schools had come to the brink of "a moral relativism tending toward nihilism, a pragmatism tending toward an amoral instrumentalism, a realism tending toward cynicism."[4]

Why couldn't intelligent traditional scholars defend themselves? The problem was that they had long been in the university without really being of the university. The legal academics' unique combination of middling theory, savoir-faire, practical judgment, and worldly experience enabled them to produce work that was valued and respected by judges and practitioners. That was enough for the great majority of law teachers, who were content to leave the quest of knowledge for its own sake to colleagues in other departments. Eventually, however, that middle road took law professors far away from scholars in the other human sciences.

With hindsight, it was a hint of trouble to come that teachers of law had never found it easy to explain to outsiders what was going on in their endless classroom discussions of the facts and reasoning of particular court decisions. "We're teaching them how to think like lawyers," they said. But what did that mean? To persons without a sense of the praxis, it was no answer at all. It was a mantra, a tautology. To someone like Unger who had not been socialized in the common law tradition, the vaunted case method of teaching looked like "a game of easy analogies" and elementary rhetorical stunts.[5]

Part and parcel of the legal academy's traditional indifference to high theory was the pretense that law could be taught in a "value-free" manner. On the first day of the Equity course I took in 1960, Sheldon Tefft asked the students what they thought "equity" was. Some of us walked right into the trap. Fairness? Justice? Giving everyone his due? Treating like cases alike? "No, no, no!" shouted Tefft, waving his arms like a scarecrow. "If that's what you want, you'd better go across the Midway to the theological seminary." Equity, we learned, was just a technical term for the set of rules and remedies developed in the English Chancery Courts, parallel to the rules and remedies available "at common law."

Professors like Tefft were not uncommon. They turned the "Socratic" method into a sophist's toy or tool, using it only to

show off or to expose the weaknesses in a student's argument
or a court's decision. When the performance was finished, the
professor would go on to the next case, leaving mental confusion and moral shambles behind. Tefft was very popular with
some students, for, like many skilled sophists, he was a good
entertainer. He was less admired by the women in our class,
for we were often chosen as straight persons for his brand of
entertainment. The teaching style at which he excelled is at
the basis of the common complaint that "the traditional classroom fosters adversariness, argumentativeness, and zealotry,
along with the view that lawyers are only the means through
which clients accomplish their ends."[6]

That style of teaching has little in common with the Socrates
of the Platonic dialogues, who (most of the time) searched for
what was sound, as well as for what was false, in the opinions
of his conversational partners. Plato portrays Socrates with the
gift of discerning in any position not only the slippery slope of
its errors but the rocky ascending path to its highest potential.
Some law teachers stumble onto that technique; many do not.

Beginning in the 1940s, a few speculative law teachers began
to reflect systematically on the commonsense tradition of Anglo-
American lawyers. Harvard's Lon Fuller, who understood law
as an activity or process rather than a collection of rules and
predictions, was one pioneer.[7] Langdell's legal "science" by
then had been thoroughly discredited by the Realists, but even
the Realists found the "case method" of teaching an excellent
means for developing a broad range of legal skills—even
though no one could say exactly why it worked. Fuller saw that
one reason for the success of the case method was that at its
heart it was a "problem method." The study of judicial opinions
rendered in particular human situations permitted students to
enter imaginatively into the dispute as well as the legal process.[8]
In this way, students begin (as law teachers are fond of saying)
to "think like lawyers." Chicago's Edward Levi, analyzing the
law's use of analogy and distinction, elucidated the mechanisms
through which litigation and court decisions keep the law
abreast of social and economic change.[9] He showed with great

elegance and precision how analogical reasoning in law creates a "moving classification system" in which categories change in the course of being applied.

Karl Llewellyn, too, set out to uncover the latent methodology of the common law. Characteristically, he proceeded with great energy. Like Tycho Brahe recording the movements of heavenly bodies, Llewellyn gathered masses of data. He charted the courses of judicial decisions in a large group of states over long stretches of time: New York and Ohio in the 1840s; New York in 1939; Pennsylvania in 1944; Massachusetts, New York, North Carolina, Ohio, Pennsylvania, Mississippi, Alabama, Washington, Kansas, Oregon, Illinois, California, Indiana, Missouri, and New Mexico in the 1950s. He read *all* the decisions of certain courts in selected periods, volume after volume, cover to cover, painstakingly tracking shifts and trajectories of doctrine, noting the traits of individual judges and the styles of each panel of judges, seeking to discern what had most strongly moved each court into deciding cases the way it did.[10] That had been the method of some Realist authors dealing with particular topics, but no one had ever carried out such an investigation on so vast a scale. Llewellyn summed up his findings in a book published two years before his death, *The Common Law Tradition*.

That book, described by Anthony Kronman as "the best account of common-law adjudication that any American has ever offered,"[11] remains important for its description and analysis of "period styles" in American judicial decision making. But Llewellyn did not fully succeed in decoding the mysteries of the dynamic common law tradition. He courted his lady in the environs of courthouses and markets, but did not follow her into the castle. He mainly wanted to be useful to students, practitioners, and judges; and he was satisfied when he felt able to demonstrate that appellate judging in his day was reasonably predictable—as reckonable as a good business risk —despite the well-known leeways in the materials of legal reasoning.[12] The task of further explaining the common law to itself awaited legal scholars with a more philosophical bent.

Edgar Bodenheimer: the gentle immigrant who enlisted the service of the mighty princess *(Courtesy Rosemarie Bodenheimer)*

Edgar Bodenheimer's Discovery

One such person was Edgar Bodenheimer, an émigré legal philosopher from Hitler's Germany. He came to the American legal academy in the 1930s as an outsider, but with a practiced eye and a buoyant willingness to immerse himself in a new way of seeing the legal world. Like Roberto Unger, he was puzzled at first by what he saw. To one who had cut his teeth on the German Civil Code of 1900, the American case law system appeared chaotic, disorderly, shot through with irrationality. American law professors, compared to their classically educated European counterparts, were more like engineers than scientists. But Bodenheimer, making the best of the fate that had deposited him on such strange shores, was determined to understand his new environment from the inside out. With enormous effort, this man who had already earned his doctorate at Heidelberg, began all over again, taking courses at night and working in a law firm's library by day. Eventually, he became a member of the bar and found employment, first with the Department of Labor and later with the Alien Property Custodian's Office. After the war, he served on Chief Prosecutor Robert Jackson's staff during the Nuremberg trials. With those experiences behind him, Bodenheimer returned at last to his first love, scholarship.

Once he had mastered the peculiar habits and practices of common law lawyers, Bodenheimer had a stunning insight: the Anglo-American legal tradition was an operating model of a form of reasoning that had long been neglected by philosophers.[13] He was in the presence of a living, breathing example of the type of reasoning that is dramatized in the Platonic dialogues and discussed in Aristotle's *Ethics*. That form of reasoning was embodied not so much in notionally Socratic classroom discussions as in the incremental development of the common law itself. Bodenheimer had trailed the princess to her residence and discovered the source of her power—in the dynamic structure of human knowing.

Dialectical reasoning is not a single form of reasoning, but an integrated set of related mental operations. It builds on practical reason, but subjects common sense to a process of critical examination and evaluation in which logic has its appropriate but auxiliary role. Similar to scientific method, dialectic method attends to available data and experience, forms hypotheses, tests them against concrete particulars, weighs competing hypotheses, and stands ready to repeat the process in the light of new data, experience, or insight. But unlike the method of the natural sciences, dialectical reasoning begins with premises that are doubtful or in dispute. It ends, not with certainty, but with determining which of opposing positions is supported by stronger evidence and more convincing reasons. That is what has made dialectical reasoning so unsatisfying to the many professional philosophers who have chosen to take their bearings from the natural sciences.

Dialectical reasoning's weakness, then, is that it can never yield the satisfaction of a mathematical proof. But, as Aristotle pointed out long ago, no other form of reasoning is of much use in "the realm of human affairs."[14] In law and politics, premises *are* uncertain and one *can't* be sure of being right, but it is crucial to keep trying to reach better rather than worse outcomes. Dialectical reasoning is a leaky vessel. But it's what we've got. The life of the law is not logic, but neither is it raw experience. What animates the law is the habit of critical, ongoing, reasoned reflection on the contents of common sense.

Dialectical reasoning, with its constant, recursive self-scrutiny, also provides the common law tradition with a limited capacity to resist, and correct for, bias and arbitrariness. Modest though it may be, that capacity is no small thing. We must concede to Holmes, the Realists, and the crits that the open texture of the evolving common law does permit bias to creep in, and that its reliance on precedent can preserve not only the wisdom but also the sins and ignorance and power relations of the past. We must admit as well that the conclusions we reach are apt to be flawed, due to our own shortcomings and the limitations of those upon whose accomplishments we build. Over time, though, the recurrent, cumulative, and potentially self-correcting processes of experiencing, understanding, and judging enable us to spot and to overcome some of our own errors and biases, the errors and biases of our culture, and the errors and biases embedded in the data we received from those who have gone before us. The wheel of dialectical reasoning not only turns but also rolls along.[15]

Bodenheimer, a quiet, unassuming person who did not live to see his ideas appreciated, examined the relation between legal and dialectical reasoning in a book titled *Jurisprudence*.[16] In a way, he anticipated and confirmed the claim of critical theorists like Unger[17] and legal economists like Posner[18] that there is no such thing as legal reasoning. Bodenheimer convincingly demonstrated that what lawyers have called "legal" reasoning is an especially interesting concrete instance of dialectical reasoning. That contribution made by a grateful refugee to his adopted legal system has been almost completely ignored by American lawyers and legal philosophers.

The fate of Bodenheimer's ideas is part of the sad story of how, unlike their counterparts in the scientific world, American legal scholars denied themselves many of the benefits they might have derived from the brilliant legal theorists from Germany and Austria who came to our shores in the 1930s.[19] But for the rise of National Socialism, Bodenheimer would have been a respected member of the faculty of a great German university. In the United States, after mastering a new legal system and a new language, he slowly made his way from a post as a law librarian to full-time teaching and scholarship, first at the University of Utah and after 1966 at the University of California at Davis. From time to time, he published clear, intelligent, unpretentious analyses of legal theory. His insights lay there in legal journals, like messages in a bottle. But sadly for the gentle man whose passion was dialectic, they elicited little comment or reply.

The Rediscovery of Character

Bodenheimer's work helps us to better understand what lawyers are doing when they say they are thinking like lawyers. James Boyd White and Anthony Kronman in recent years have insisted on the importance of who is doing the thinking. Firmly resisting the disjunction of theory and practice, White and Kronman also reject the idea that the activity of law can be understood apart from the character of the persons engaged in that activity. In the search for law, it seems, as in folkloric tales of other sorts of quest, prowess is not enough. What the searcher discovers may depend as well on how he or she has lived. Some of those who looked beneath the hood of the woman by the wayside, Holmes warned in one of his bracing after-dinner speeches, would behold only "the inexorable face of death."[20]

White, literary and intuitive, and Kronman, philosophically trained and analytical, took two paths to similar insights. Those insights are that by engaging in the activity of law one makes oneself into a certain kind of person and that lawyers in the aggregate constitute a certain kind of community.[21] Or, as philosophers put it, our choices and activities have a "constitutive" effect on our character: we become what we do.

In a sense, Holmes and other reflective common law lawyers had understood all along about the way in which legal habits and attitudes leave their stamp for better or worse on individual lawyers. That must have been what Holmes meant when he said that the practice of law "tends to make good citizens and good men."[22] That is surely what Llewellyn was driving at when he proclaimed that reckonability in law was provided mainly by a number of "steadying factors."[23] With hindsight, it is plain that most of the factors on which he relied were elements of a common legal culture, habits and practices that were widely shared until the close of the "golden age." A critical theorist like Duncan Kennedy grasps one end of the rope when he says of the law to his students: "You think you ate it, but it ate you." A commonsensical practitioner grasps the other end when she says that the quality of justice in our society depends on what kind of men and women administer it. White and Kronman braid the rope into a spiral—a never-ending process that shapes its participants even as it is shaped by them.

Most academic lawyers have regarded character (or its lack) as something that students bring with them when they come to law school. A typical attitude is that law professors do not form character—that is the job of families and religious or ethical traditions. The critical theorists, to their credit, saw clearly that law professors could not fail to have some influence on the unformed professional attitudes of future lawyers. But they did little with that knowledge except to describe how legal training *de*forms character by treating the ends of legal activity as matters of indifference. In the face of that challenge, most traditionalists stood mute.

Kronman, however, undertook to provide an explanation of how participation in the common law craft tradition promotes the formation not only of good lawyers but of good citizens and good human beings. Taking yet another look at the now thoroughly scrutinized "case method," Kronman asked what habits of mind and traits of character it fosters. What is likely to be the effect on a young person of regular participation in an exercise where nothing that appears in a judicial opinion is accepted at face value; where one learns to present the competing positions of the disputants in the most attractive way possible; and where one is required to concentrate on the unsettled gray areas at the boundaries of doctrine—the "hard cases" where policies and principles of great weight compete for priority? Kronman's answer is that such a regimen strengthens one's capacity for sympathetic understanding while cultivating moral detachment.[24] The knack of combining empathy with detachment is somewhat unusual; it does not come easily to most people. When achieved, it promotes a cast of mind which, though not exclusive to lawyers, is so prevalent among them as to give legal culture a distinctive spirit.[25]

So far, nothing distinguishes that view of the lawyer's cultivated moral imagination from, say, Keats's "negative capability" of holding opposed ideas together in one's mind. Unlike poets, philosophers, and academics, however, practicing lawyers and judges cannot remain suspended in that lofty state. They must give advice, make decisions, and bear responsibility for the consequences. Thanks to the Realists and critical theorists, judges and legal strategists today are more vividly aware than ever that their decisions are made on the basis of imperfect information and often with but sketchy guidance from precedents and enacted law. Llewellyn showed how professional traditions and habits could serve to maintain an impressive degree of reckonability in the law in spite of those difficult conditions. Kronman went a step further, maintaining that the more fully one is immersed in the traditions of the common law and legal statesmanship, the *better* his or her judgments will be: "[T]he person who values an activity and cares about it will tend, in the long run and on average, to form more solid and reliable opinions regarding the good of the activity, where this is a matter of controversy, than the person who studies it but places no value on the activity or its ends."[26]

In other words, so long as there are enough judges who care for the good of the legal order and for the constitutional regime it supports, and the polity it serves, even Holmes's "bad man" will have to enter imaginatively into the mental world of such people if he wishes to predict accurately "where the axe will fall." The better the would-be predictor does his job, the more likely it is that his own character and habits will be affected. As Kronman neatly puts it, someone who begins to exercise only for the sake of appearance will often come to an appreciation of the good of health.[27] Similarly, in law, those who imaginatively place themselves in the shoes of one who cares for the legal order, the regime, and the polity may come to care about those goods, too.[28] Through their choices and actions they, too, may constitute themselves not only as skilled practitioners of preventive law and canny predictors of outcomes but as men and women with a certain set of habits and attitudes. They think they ate it, but it ate them.

At this point, a critical friend might inquire: Does not empathic immersion in your prized common law tradition constitute you as mainly a lubricator of the market and involve you in racism and patriarchy? Does not detachment constitute you as a mere hired gun? The traditionalist must frankly admit that empathy and detachment carry those risks and more. We lawyers may be dull, but the least among us lives on the moral edge. More than most other professionals, we are daily forced to face up to the plurality of human goods, the inevitability of conflict among them, and the necessity for tragic choices. That puts us only a hairline away from relativism, quietism, and moral compromise. What keeps the scholar true to the quest for knowledge, the judge striving for impartiality, and the practitioner faithful to client and court? Only a set of ingrained habits and attitudes that are shored up, sustained, nourished, and animated by a vital ongoing community—in other words, a tradition.

Does the common law tradition retain enough vitality to sustain the profession in years to come? Can contemporary lawyers hold up their end of a vigorous conversation across generations about the goods embodied in our legal and political order? As we have seen, that tradition is precisely what is at risk in the new academy. Of law professors with a serious interest in the common law as such, Kronman says, "Their numbers are declining and the authority of their position weakens year by year. The future lies with their adversaries, with those who want to make law teaching an adjunct of legal scholarship and to define its goals in similar terms."[29]

If Kronman is right, it would be a misfortune for lawyers, clients, and the legal system. It would be as though medical faculties decided to devote themselves entirely to basic research in chemistry, biology, and genetics, but continued to send their graduates out to treat patients and to design systems for the delivery of health services. The more law professors give themselves over to high theory, the closer we come in a full circle to a stripped-down version of the old apprenticeship system. Law school provides advanced general education on top of a liberal arts degree, and new graduates, it is assumed, will pick up what they need to know on the job as they go along. The flaw in that assumption, however, is that students are being sent from law schools without law into law firms where senior lawyers are too busy to provide much supervision.

But is Kronman right? If one looked only at a handful of elite law schools, the situation might appear grim. A student in such an environment, trying to update Unger's description of a quarter-century ago, might say, "When we came, most professors had ceased pretending that law was anything other than power and preference. Their legal apostasy often coexisted, however, with a fervent devotion to this or that cause or dogma. Disdaining their predecessors, they did not hesitate to live off the inheritance amassed by the labor of others. Turning their backs on the laity (who still naively looked to law for justice), they decked their altars with mirrors—into which they gazed long and attentively, self-made men worshipping their creators."[30]

Still, Kronman's prognosis seems too gloomy. In the first place, there remain significant numbers of men and women in the nation's law schools who are pleased to profess law and proud to train practicing lawyers. Many of these nonconformists are active, as Llewellyn was, in the exacting, unglamorous, but vitally important work of the American Law Institute and the National Conference of Commissioners on State Laws. Kronman's longtime colleague Geoffrey Hazard, for instance, serves with distinction as executive director of the American Law Institute and is one of the nation's leading experts on the legal profession. Moreover, the current period, for all its alarums and excursions, has witnessed an extraordinary flowering of serious scholarship, with the most important advances attributable to collaborative interdisciplinary and empirical work. Public law studies have been enriched through insights from history and political science, and business law has benefited from economic and sociological studies.

There are many signs, too, that the difficult cohabitation between theory and practice, forced on the profession a century ago when universities took over the training of lawyers, is finally maturing into a fruitful relationship. At Kronman's home institution, Yale Law School, there is much evidence of a springtime for legal studies. For one thing, Kronman himself was named dean of that influential institution in 1994. Only a decade earlier, George Priest, then a newcomer to Yale, had enthusiastically hailed the advent of the law school without law: "The Enlightenment is coming. . . . The ambitious scholars on law-school faculties will insist on teaching subjects of increasingly narrow scope. The law-school curriculum will come to consist of graduate courses in applied economics, social theory, and political science."[31] Revisiting the subject in 1993, an older and wiser Priest conceded that his evaluation of the importance of legal studies had been "a severe underestimate."[32] "To emphasize disjunction or division" between theory and practice, he wrote, "substantially distorts what is more accurately described as a functionally cooperative relationship."[33] In a footnote, Priest acknowledged the influence on his thinking of a recent addition to the Yale faculty, John Langbein, a veritable one-man band of creative theory and practice.

Langbein does not write about the two blades of the scissors. He is too busy using them. The author of several distinguished works in comparative law and legal history, Langbein is also preeminent in three substantive fields, each of immense practical importance: procedure, pension law, and the law of trusts and estates. As Louis Loss had done a generation earlier, Langbein created an academic subject out of a complex regulatory field that did not even exist when he graduated from law school in 1968. Langbein did not disdain to put some of the fruits of his research on pensions and employee benefits into a course book—a genre that is even less esteemed than the treatise among the avant-garde. Thanks to his collaborative efforts with other members of the Uniform Law Commission and the American Law Institute, millions of people will be rescued from intent-defeating rules, as well as unnecessary expense and delay in connection with property distribution on death. His comparative studies of procedure have illuminated the deep causes of malfunction in our litigation system.

The work of dynamic traditionalists like Langbein is living testimony to the fruits of interdisciplinary cooperation; team-

work among judges, practitioners, and scholars; and the happy
union of theory and practice. Such efforts have the potential
to consolidate and build on the contributions of clinical education, law-and-economics, and critical theory. They have the
power as well to unite the two halves of the divided soul of
constitutionalism, rights, and structure. Whether that potential
will ever be realized, no one can say, but it is just barely possible
that dynamic traditionalists are still a significant presence
among the nation's 6,000 or so law professors. If so, it is not
unrealistic to think in terms of a counter-reformation in legal
education. Some such movement must take place if law teachers
are to successfully cultivate the skills and habits that an increasingly legalistic, complex, pluralistic republic requires in its lawyers. But what are the prospects?

Counter-reformation

In 1945, the dean of the Harvard Law School wrote, "We
must train men to handle the combination of law and government. We can't go on teaching law in the old-fashioned way."[34]
Dean Landis was wrong. His generation could and did go on
teaching law in the old-fashioned way for another twenty years.
Not only did legal education fail to keep pace with the growth
of the regulatory state; it did not prepare young men and
women nearly as well as it might have for private practice in
an increasingly complex economy or for public service in an
ever more pluralistic society.

Today, we no longer teach law in the old-fashioned way. In
fact, many professors hardly teach law at all. And the problem
Landis flagged is still shamefully neglected. Most nonlawyers
would probably be astonished to know how little systematic
attention is devoted in law schools to the drafting or interpretation of statutes, to the functioning and relationships among
legal institutions, or to the study of how various regulatory

arrangements work out in practice. In the spring of 1992, a committee appointed to review the curriculum at Harvard Law School reported that Harvard, like most other law schools, was still teaching the basic first-year required program "almost without regard to the coming of the regulatory state, and without recognition that its characteristic legal modes—statutes and regulations—have become the predominant legal sources of our time." This does not mean that legal studies are especially retarded. Consider that Darwin's *On the Origin of Species* was published in 1859, but it was not until the 1940s that the classification systems used in the life sciences were adjusted to reflect the changes brought about by his theories.[35]

At present, a number of wholesome transformative developments seem to be gathering momentum. One area of the curriculum has always been a stronghold of lawyers' law while providing ample scope for creative academic work. Year in, year out, whatever fads and fancies took hold of legal education, courses in procedure have provided a steady anchor to the practice, while stimulating theorists and law reformers. The prestige of procedure only grew with the rights revolution and the litigation explosion. Few students escape its discipline and challenges, for procedure is universally part of the compulsory first-year curriculum and it is difficult (though not impossible) to turn procedure courses into vehicles for legal space voyages. Furthermore, though procedure can be taught and apprehended as a bag of tricks, the very idea of process is profoundly subversive of antitraditionalism. Procedure implies structures and rules that endure beyond the controversies of the moment, that permit men and women to make reliable plans, that keep arbitrary discretion at bay.

And procedure teaching and scholarship have never been in better condition. Procedure specialists are beginning to extend their horizons beyond litigation to alternative modes of dispute resolution (ADR). Within and alongside procedure courses, and in law clinics, many law schools now require students to assess the relative merits of litigation, negotiation, arbitration, and mediation. Teamwork is opening up new frontiers between evidence and probability theory, as well as between cognitive science and fact investigation.

While procedure continues to thrive, counter-reformation is brewing in the field of constitutional law. The twenty-year dominance of constitutional lawyers of the left and right who neglected the structure of government in order to concentrate on their favorite rights is currently being challenged by a diverse group of scholars who are reuniting constitutional law with democratic theory. They are approaching the Constitution, not as a collection of separate and independent starting points for freewheeling judicial creativity, but as a design for government whose parts must be understood in relation to one another and to the whole, against the background of history. Akhil Amar, John Hart Ely, Michael McConnell, Geoffrey Miller, and others are setting the constitutional law agenda for the next century by insisting on the relationship between our system of limited government and the system of rights that has been at the forefront of constitutional theory for the past twenty-five years. Their holistic approach to constitutional language, design, and tradition offers the surest path toward consolidating the achievements of the rights era while restoring separation of powers, federalism, and constitutional text and structure to an appropriate place in constitutional law.

As for "handl[ing] the combination of law and government," however, nearly everything remains to be done. But the task at least is beginning—fifty years after Dean Landis said it must. Many fine scholars have created teaching materials for courses in new areas of regulatory law—dealing with the workplace, the environment, pensions, welfare, provision of health care, and so on. Over the past decade, there has also been a spurt of impressive scholarly writing on statutory interpretation. Many law schools are beginning to offer courses on legislation, and finding, to their surprise, that the subject is popular with students. Some of the teachers now working with statutes have taken the next step to institutional analysis, carrying forward the unfinished work of Hart and Sacks on the functions and interrelationships of courts, legislatures, the executive, and administrative agencies.

In the foreseeable future, if only in response to students facing an increasingly competitive job market, the pendulum in the legal academy may well swing back toward law, carrying along all the benefits that philosophy, history, politics, economics, sociology, and cross-national comparisons can offer to legal analysis. If we are hopeful, we may anticipate, too, that insights from those disciplines will aid law professors in preparing their students for roles in a society that urgently needs specialists in long-range planning, imaginative problem solving, legislation, regulation, and institutions.

It does not seem fanciful to imagine that the academy is waking up from Llewellyn's nightmare of ideals without technique and technique without ideals. Today's law students are responding better to demanding teachers than their recent predecessors did—at least when they sense that the professor's rigor arises from a desire to prepare them well for their chosen profession. Harvard law students in Visiting Professor Elizabeth Warren's bankruptcy class in 1992 were at first dismayed when they realized she was not going to be indifferent to class preparation and attendance. Early in the course, Warren called on a student who was unprepared. The student responded with a request to be excused from reciting: "Can I pass?" "That depends," said Warren, deliberately misunderstanding the question. "Whether you can pass depends entirely on whether you do the work in this course." Once they recovered from their initial shock, Warren's students apparently appreciated being treated like adults. They clamored for Harvard to offer her a permanent position (we did), and were keenly disappointed when she declined.[36]

Like Warren, Yale's Langbein does not belong to the laissez-aller school of legal pedagogy. Yet his classes in difficult subjects are among the most popular at that citadel of high theory. After emergency surgery forced him to cancel his classes in the spring of 1993, third-year students celebrated his return by asking him to be their commencement speaker. In 1994, his trusts and estates course, which includes a heavy drafting requirement in addition to a final examination, had the largest enrollment of any course in the Yale Law School. That same year, Phillip Areeda, who has taught rigorous contracts and antitrust courses in and out of season since 1963, was voted best teacher at Harvard Law School by the graduating class.

It is unlikely that the revived interest in law on the part of students is prompted entirely by nervous contemplation of the job market. The current atmosphere in law schools reflects, as the legal academy always has, the prevailing ethos of under-graduate liberal arts education. In one of his last public appearances before his untimely death, historian and social critic Christopher Lasch observed that undergraduates in re-cent years have shown declining interest in "big theoretical nondebates about the nonissues of structuralism and post-structuralism and postmodernism and Marx and Lacan and Foucault." Speaking to the graduating class at the University of Rochester in 1993, Lasch maintained that "it's not that they're interested only in jobs, though in view of the state of the economy they could easily be excused for thinking exclu-sively about jobs." Rather, said Lasch, "it's just that they want to hear some plain words of truth. . . . They want to grow up."[37] That new postideological mood is already discernible in the law schools. It suggests the possibility that tomorrow's law students will be rebellious enough to debunk the debunkers, intelligent enough to rediscover the joys of craftsmanship, and bold enough to harness the latent energies of the common law tradition.

As for the other half of Llewellyn's nightmare, technique without ideals, the problem is a persistent one, the gimpy leg of the legal profession. Still, one cannot discount the influence on students of extraordinary teachers like Karl Llewellyn, Clark Byse, Elizabeth Warren, and many others less well known who unabashedly love the law and the experiment in ordered liberty it serves. That sort of law professor will always be rare, but, after all, it only takes one great teacher to change a person's life forever. The great ones influence students not so much by their eloquence and wit as by their way of being in the world. The eros of the mind is contagious.

Law professors cannot cure society's ills, no matter how firmly they believe they know just what to do. But they *can* cure the ills of legal education. One way to begin would be to make our students aware of the rich web of habits and understandings surrounding the stories of the extraordinarily diverse individuals who are part of the common law tradition. That is their rightful inheritance by which they can begin to make sense of their professional environment and to understand themselves as lawyers. We owe our students not only professional training and theoretical sophistication but the deep sustenance afforded by a tradition with great latent energies for self-correction. Only when we succeed at that threefold task will legal education cease to be a "feast without satisfaction."

It has been the fashion in recent years to dwell on the failings of our forebears—on the way *Brown* v. *Board of Education,* for example, was a stumbling block, for different reasons, for John W. Davis and Learned Hand. A generation of legal scholars has dined out on the shortcomings of great, deceased judges and lawyers. But "unmasking" heroic figures may reveal more about the debunkers than the objects of their attacks.[38] The limitations of the law's flawed giants are indeed admonitory, yet their flaws should not be permitted to obscure the way their greatness inspired others to build on their strengths. Will our own blind spots, when we are weighed in the balance, appear less grave?

One recent morning, looking out of my office window, I saw Archibald Cox climb out of his shiny gray pickup truck and head for his office. His crew cut and the bow tie looked the same as they had in the famous photographs from the Watergate era, but his tall lean frame is now slightly bent. The expressions on students' faces as they watched him cross the parking lot lifted my spirits. For many of them, a man like Cox still embodies the highest ideals of the legal profession—

in private practice, in government service, in community life, and in the classroom. Best of all, they can imagine that just possibly, with a lot of effort, they might become a little bit like him—as he in certain ways resembles the lawyers who inspired him.

Cox was a product of what many now consider to be the bad old days. But recalling his mentors Austin Scott, Warren Seavey, Felix Frankfurter, Erwin Griswold, and Learned Hand, Cox recently said, "They taught, instilled, exemplified a love of the law and the role of law."[39] In words that many of his colleagues would apply to Cox himself, he added:

> And they taught that there is for each time and place (but also therefore, by implication, at all times and all places but always different) an ideal fitness of things that corresponds to those beliefs, and that we ought to do what we can to make that fitness prevail.
>
> I think they had, too, the deep belief that judges and academic scholars had an obligation to pursue that goal, putting aside all private predilections, commitments, self-interest, and using only the most disinterested and detached reason they could bring to bear.

As for the debunkers of such traditional sentiments, Cox's response is as simple as it is profound:

> It was said then, of course, and it is said far more often now, "Aw come on! That's not the real world. That's not the way it works. It's not true." I think the answer is: pursuing an ideal—that ideal—is a fact; people engage in the pursuit seriously, persistently, perseveringly; it's just as much a reality as earth and water.[40]

Watching Archibald Cox disappear into Langdell Hall on a fine spring day, I almost thought I could hear Karl Llewellyn's gravelly voice singing:

Some say our Law's in a sorry plight, and folly its fruition.

The answer to that is to set it right, in the Common Law Tradition.

Rowdy dowdy doodle-ee-o

PART IV

LAWYERS AND
THE DEMOCRATIC
EXPERIMENT

What made the United States the most legalistic society the world has ever known? Why do Americans, who bridle at regulation, seek legal cures for virtually every social ill?

Does the turbulent state of the legal profession merely mirror our complex, heterogeneous American society, or do law and lawyers aggravate social discord?

What are the implications for the American version of the democratic experiment of a rising proportion of iconoclasts in a profession that has traditionally wedded order to freedom, responsibilities to rights?

Could the profession's creative energies be harnessed more effectively to the country's needs for peacemakers, planners, and problem solvers?

12

One Vast School of Law

The spirit of the law, born within schools and courts, spreads little by little beyond them; it infiltrates through society right down to the lowest ranks, till finally the whole people have contracted some of the ways and tastes of a magistrate. —ALEXIS DE TOCQUEVILLE[1]

One fine evening in the early spring of 1978, Tom Horsley, a San Jose accountant, was looking forward to a date with Alyn Chesslet, a San Francisco waitress. That night, countless young men the world over must have been in a similar frame of mind, sprucing themselves up for the initial step in age-old minuets of courtship. Some set out on foot, some on bikes, some on horseback or mule, and many, like Tom, in automobiles. Some had no further to travel than the house next door; for others, like Tom, the meeting place was many miles away. Many had no definite program in mind; some, like Tom, had made more or less elaborate arrangements. In his case, the plan was for a classic American date: he would take Alyn to dinner and a show. Most of the evening's swains, we may assume, rendezvoused successfully with the women they had arranged to meet. But some, like Tom, found no one at the appointed spot. In many of these situations, the problem was a simple mistake concerning day, time, or place. But some unlucky suitors, like Tom, were well and truly stood up.

One may imagine various reactions to such a setback. Some men would have shrugged, made a date with another girl, and chalked the disenchanted evening up to life's inevitable disappointments. Others must have felt the need to protest to the woman herself, and perhaps even to complain to her friends and family. Some might have spread the word of her inconsiderate behavior. Most would probably have resolved to have no further dealings with her. What seems almost inconceivable is that any of these young men would have taken their grievance to court—except, that is, in the United States of America. In May 1978, Tom Horsley filed an action against the heartless Alyn, claiming compensation for the time and expense involved in his futile trip to and from San Francisco.[2]

Suits like Tom's, less of a novelty now than in the 1970s, are a bizarre contemporary offshoot of the legalism that has long been a hallmark of our national identity. In no other country has "the spirit of the law" penetrated so deeply into popular culture. Today, as in Tocqueville's times, to live in the United States is to be a pupil, willing or not, in a vast, bustling school of law.[3] The curriculum of that institution, however, has undergone some startling changes, and the students are displaying some odd behavior.

The legalistic spirit today has taken far different forms from the sober legalism that our nineteenth-century visitor regarded as one of the sturdiest bulwarks of the democratic experiment. Where Tocqueville saw a people with "the ways and tastes of a magistrate," one is now more likely to encounter popular imitations of the language and attitudes of adversarial advocates. In American workplaces, schools, shops, streets, playgrounds, and homes one finds men, women, and even children caricaturing the behavior of hardball litigators. Consider what happened when a lower school principal recently punished a third-grade "riot" by requiring all members of the class to write statements of apology. The pupils who had not participated in the disorder were understandably offended, but their complaints had a strange sound. As one mother recounts the incident, one pint-sized prosecutor asked his parents, "Should we sue her?"[4] "Isn't it illegal for her to punish those of us who did nothing?" demanded another pre-pubescent pettifogger. Where do eight-year-olds learn to talk this way?

Law is the silver chain that links contemporary Americans of all ages and origins to eighteenth-century revolutionaries

and seventeenth-century colonists. Much of America's unique-
ness, in fact, lies in the degree to which law figures in the
standard accounts of where we came from, who we are, and
where we are going. Unlike those of older nations, our origins
are not shrouded in myth or legend. Our country's birthday
commemorates the formal signing of a real document—a bill
of grievances in which rebellious but fussily legalistic colonists
recited their complaints, claimed that they had been denied
"the rights of Englishmen," and officially pronounced the
severance of their ties with the mother country.[5] Tocqueville
marveled at the contrast between the American struggle for
independence and the French Revolution: "No disorderly
passions drove it on; on the contrary, it proceeded hand in
hand with a love of order and legality."[6] Eventually, those
lawstruck rebels opted for a single-document constitution,
rejecting the English model of an "unwritten" charter resting
on customary understandings. The design for government that
emerged from the convention held in the summer of 1787 was
a masterpiece not only of statesmanship but of juridical art.
And no wonder, for thirty-one of the fifty-five delegates were
lawyers.

A singular role for courts in the new regime was assured
with Chief Justice Marshall's landmark decisions filling out the
contours of federalism and his fateful assertion of judicial
authority to review governmental action for conformity to the
Constitution. No other country's judiciary had ever possessed
such independence or exerted such power. Over the years, as
in no other liberal democracy, lawyers garnered the lion's share
of starring roles in the national drama. Among the marble
busts in the French Pantheon or Germany's Walhalla, a tourist
finds only a scattering of jurists. The National Portrait Gallery
in Washington, by contrast, is crowded with men of law—John
and Samuel Adams, Patrick Henry, Thomas Jefferson, Alexander Hamilton, John Jay, John Quincy Adams, John Marshall,
Joseph Story, Abraham Lincoln, Daniel Webster, William Jen-
nings Bryan, Clarence Darrow, Oliver Wendell Holmes, and
Franklin Delano Roosevelt, to mention but some of the cele-

brated names. In the darkest days of the Civil War, at a little crossroads town in Pennsylvania, one of those great lawyers provided us with what many still regard as the definitive expression of our national aspirations: the idea of "a new nation, conceived in liberty and dedicated to the proposition that all men are created equal," and the hope "that this nation, under God, shall have a new birth of freedom, and that government of the people, by the people, for the people, shall not perish from the earth."

As for the citizenry, there was something peculiar about us from the beginning. Even when lawyers were scarce, historians say, the early settlers possessed a turn of mind that was decidedly legalistic.[7] To Tocqueville, that odd trait seemed to augur well. It not only promoted the aptitude for self-government but fostered the reverence for the Constitution and laws on which, according to the authors of *The Federalist*, the freedom of a democratic people depends.[8] During the French uprisings of 1848, Tocqueville's troubled thoughts turned back to the continent he had visited in his youth: "The principles on which the constitutions of the American states rest, the principles of order, balance of powers, true liberty, and sincere and deep respect for law, are indispensable for all republics; they should be common to them all; and it is safe to forecast that where they are not found the republic will soon have ceased to exist."[9]

The legalistic spirit that Tocqueville admired has shown itself at many crucial junctures when the mighty and the lowly alike abided by legal rulings that seemed to them disadvantageous, wrong, or even dangerous. Lincoln's defiance of the Supreme Court by suspending the writ of habeas corpus during the Civil War is a rare exception. During the Korean War, President Truman relinquished control of the steel industry when the Supreme Court told him to—even though he feared the impending strike would interfere with the flow of supplies to the front. President Nixon complied with the Court's command to turn over his "smoking gun" tapes to the Watergate special prosecutor, although it was far from clear how the Court would have been able to enforce its order had he chosen to defy it.

And countless black and white parents nervously submitted to having their young children transported to schools in distant neighborhoods when federal courts ordered busing in an attempt to achieve school desegregation.

What keeps a measure of hardy legalism alive in our turbulent country? Tocqueville speculated that the mere presence of great numbers of lawyers in the population had a significant influence on the habits and attitudes of their fellow citizens. The courthouse in every county seat was like a "free school" where "every juror is given practical lessons in the law."[10] Local government was a sort of lab school with a variety of opportunities for active participation, ranging from the town meeting to numerous elective offices from fence viewer to selectman. By taking an active role in local affairs, he wrote, an American "gets to know those formalities without which freedom can advance only through revolutions, and becoming imbued with their spirit, develops a taste for order, understands the harmony of powers, and in the end accumulates clear, practical ideas about the nature of his duties and the extent of his rights."[11]

Today, the good news is that those free schools are open to all adults, including many who could not have voted, held office, or served on juries in Jacksonian America. The bad news, however, is that top-down regulation of various sorts reaches deeply into every town and hamlet, drastically reducing opportunities for citizens to participate in making the decisions that affect their own families and communities. With more law came still more lawyers, their influence magnified by newspapers, magazines, television shows, and films that report on and dramatize their doings. Bureaucrats grew plump with power and briefcase-toting litigators replaced Western gunslingers as popular heroes and villains. The country's legal education shifted to different sorts of classrooms. Alongside the old teachings, a new curriculum emerged with a more ambiguous relationship to the democratic enterprise. The legal teachings of the jury room and town hall were eclipsed by lessons absorbed passively from the communications and entertainment industries.

A contemporary citizen's direct contacts with the legal system are apt to be passive, too. Americans learn more about law and government in the toils of the tax, welfare, or social security system than in the jury room, town meeting, or party precinct organization. Such experiences tend to engender feelings of frustration and helplessness, rather than a sense of empowerment. Any parent who has dealt with the educational bureaucracy knows firsthand what it is to be treated like a subject rather than a citizen. We are encountering law more, but participating less in its creation and administration. Frustration with normal politics has fueled resort to a poor substitute: litigation aimed at bringing about social change.

Curiously, widespread popular discontent with law's daily operation coexists with an exaggerated confidence in its power to cure social and economic ills. The same citizens who want to get annoying regulations out of their own lives often believe that the way to deal with a broad range of social problems is to bring a lawsuit, to criminalize unwanted activity, or to augment the power of police and prosecutors.

One of the most striking elements of the new legalism is its adversarial nature. Filmmakers, journalists, novelists, and television programmers are fascinated with the activities of the minority of lawyers who are engaged in courtroom work. Don't look soon for a TV sitcom on "Eleanor the Estate Planner," or an action-adventure series titled "This Is Your IRS," or real-life episodes from "Judge Wapner's Conciliation Clinic." Ratings thrive on crime, conflict, and courtroom drama. As a legal adviser to the popular *L.A. Law* show puts it, to depict what most lawyers do most of the time would violate media "rules" against complexity and detail: "Transactional work is intellectually fascinating, but dramatically deadly."[12] Of the forces that are contending for the soul of the legal profession, only a select few will be seen on prime time.

The overdramatized antics of lawyers in perpetual attack mode, though, are unfortunate models for the handling of routine disputes and disappointments, whether in the capillaries of the social system or in its political and commercial arteries. The fact is that everyone usually loses when rigid positions are taken too quickly, harms exaggerated, and claims made in all-or-nothing terms. Consider the escalation of the argument that developed between twelve-year-old Kimberly Broussard and her homeroom teacher when Kimberly wore a T-shirt reading "Drugs Suck" to the Blair Middle School in Norfolk, Virginia. The teacher was adamant that the shirt not be worn in the school. Kimberly was equally insistent on her right to express herself. The teacher held to the view that displaying vulgar language violated the decorum necessary for the educational enterprise. Kimberly was suspended. Backed by the American Civil Liberties Union, she sued the school district, claiming a First Amendment right to wear the shirt to school. Eventually, a federal district judge ruled in a twenty-six-page opinion that school officials had acted reasonably in barring her display of an offensive word.[13] The dispute was resolved, but not without serious cost to the school district, to the taxpayers, to other litigants in the crowded federal courts, and to human relations in the Blair Middle School.

Miss Manners Makes a Point

Inevitably, as systems of informal social regulation lose their effectiveness, new and greater demands are made on a judicial system that was designed primarily to be a last-ditch resort for the settlement of disputes. Americans are learning, painfully, that law is not well suited for all the tasks it is now being asked to perform. In 1978, when Tom Horsley's courtship wound up in court, the story was so unusual that it was prominently featured in the national press.

The suit over a broken date was, in fact, a law professor's farfetched hypothetical come to life. For generations, beginning students of contract law had cut their teeth on versions of an imaginary "invitation to dinner" case where a guest reneges on a promise to attend a friend's dinner party even though he knew his host was counting heavily on his presence to help close a business deal, and was well aware that certain expenses had been incurred in reliance on his agreement.[14] In the classroom exercise, students are expected to see why there are some promises that the law will not enforce even though all the elements of a legally binding contract are technically present. The exercise provides a kind of reality check for first-year law students lest, in entering the house of law, they close the door on everything they once knew about life. It affords one of those all too rare occasions in the legal academy for teachers and students to remind themselves that law has limits; that there are aspects of life which the state wisely refrains from regulating; that not every injustice can or should be adjudicated; and that few people would enjoy living in a society where every insult or injury gave rise to legal remedies. The San Francisco judge said as much when he threw out Tom's claim. This type of suit, according to Judge Richard Figone, "should never have been in court."

In the 1980s and 1990s, however, suits over the disappointments of everyday life have become more common and judges somewhat more receptive. No one suggests that these freakish lawsuits are statistically significant or a major cause of congestion in our overcrowded courts. They are extreme, cartoonlike manifestations of a growing problem—the breakdown of nonlegal constraints on behavior and of informal methods of handling disputes. When Albert Spremo, a night watchman who had brought more than fifty legal actions on his own behalf, was rebuked by the New York courts, he complained to a reporter: "You know, you're taught in school to seek justice. You can't go around hitting people, so the only thing you can do is sue."[15] Spremo (whose litigation spree included a suit against his mother for accidentally slamming a door on his finger) grasped correctly that law, in its most basic sense, is civilization's attempt to provide a substitute for violent self-help. But an even greater human achievement was the development of an elaborate range of alternatives to hitting that do not involve going to court. What has happened to the apparatus of custom, convention, etiquette, religion, and ethics?

In 1978, the same year that Tom Horsley sued Alyn Chesslet, journalist Judith Martin began to address herself to the poor condition of American manners and mores. Since then, as "Miss Manners," Martin has waged a spirited crusade to regenerate a workable ethics of everyday life. Her task has been an arduous one, for many men and women in our individualistic, mobile society have had little practice in the skills of associating. We are not born with those skills, she points out. We learn them, beginning in the family, where we first learn to consider the feelings and needs of others, to accommodate differences and to assume responsibilities. "No one has yet come up with a satisfactory substitute for family training in the earliest years of life," Martin has written, "to foster the development of such principles as consideration, cooperation, loyalty, respect, and to teach the child such etiquette techniques as settling disputes through face-saving compromise."[16] But families and their surrounding support systems are not in peak condition.

It cannot be coincidence that over the same thirty years that saw the legal profession shedding many traditional constraints, families and other communities of memory and mutual aid have been undergoing upheavals, too. As Daniel Yankelovich sums up changes in our culture since the 1960s: "The quest for greater individual choice clashed directly with the obligations and social norms that held families and communities together in earlier years. People came to feel that questions of how to live . . . were a matter of individual choice not to be governed by restrictive norms. As a nation, we came to experience the bonds to marriage, family, children, job, community, and country as constraints that were no longer necessary. Commitments were loosened."[17]

In other words, the very mobility, opportunity, and diversity that make American society so exciting and attractive render us prone to fragmentation and anomie. It is our national version of the Midas touch. Our social controls are relatively weak and shared understandings about proper behavior relatively thin. And as Miss Manners points out, this state of affairs fosters unhealthy forms of legalism: "A declining belief in etiquette as a legitimate force in regulating social conduct has prompted American society to try to get along without it. People who find rude but legally permitted behavior intolerable have attempted to expand the law to outlaw rudeness."[18] When he was asked by reporters why he bothered to sue over a broken date, Tom Horsley's plaintive explanation was: "There's too much of this sort of thing . . . [P]eople are not sincere." But the attempt to "legalize" areas once regulated by informal understandings is not only ineffective at restoring civility; it is itself a symptom of disorder in the body social.

A certain amount of strife is unavoidable between people who do not grasp each other's expectations concerning right conduct—between country folk and city folk, knowledge class and working class, newcomers and established residents, as well as among members of differing ethnic and religious groups. Consider the squabbles that provide the daily grist of *The People's Court*. This popular television program, which first appeared in 1981, closely resembles the actual proceedings of a small claims court. A huge audience watches in fascination as retired Judge Joseph A. Wapner, in his shrewd, no-nonsense way, sifts fact from opinion, winnows truth from falsehood, and dispenses rough justice in disputes of a kind that everyone has experienced at one time or another.

The men and women who come before him are parties to real lawsuits, who, for a fee, have agreed to dismiss their claims and accept Judge Wapner's rulings. They wrangle over what Mr. Washington must pay when his mongrel mutt jumps over the fence and assaults Ms. Madison's pedigreed poodle, or whether the ring John gave Abigail was a gift or on loan, or whose fault it was that the toilet in Samuel's apartment overflowed, wrecking the work laid out on Benjamin's desk in the apartment below. Day after day, landladies and lodgers, shopkeepers and customers, hairdressers and unhappy clients, former boyfriends and girlfriends, present their claims, counterclaims, and defenses before the gruff, grandfatherly judge-turned-celebrity.

Look closely, though, and you will observe that, in a hefty proportion of the cases, the parties appear to be from different generations or different ethnic and social backgrounds. The elderly landlady has an Italian surname; her youthful lodger wears a turban. The black shopkeeper speaks standard English; his irate customer's speech is halting and heavily accented—he has brought a friend along to help. The hairdresser is Asian; his client Puerto Rican. The quarreling ex-lovers come in all assortments. Listen to them carefully, and you will notice how often the source of the difficulty seems to have been a misunderstanding—how frequently both parties seem to have placed entirely different interpretations on the same words and events. The landlady finds it incredible that her lodger assumed he could cook aromatic meals on a hot plate in his room; the roomer is outraged that he is not allowed to prepare his food where he lives.

Judge Wapner's court is a microcosm of a land of strangers; an America where opportunity lies just around the corner, but next-door neighbors do not know each other; where disputing parties often recognize no common source of authority (other than the law) and have no mutually respected umpire to consult (other than a judge); where people pack up their belongings and move to a new home over and over again in the course of a lifetime, often spending most of their lives far away from the communities in which they were raised; and where many parents are trying to hold full-time jobs while raising children without the support, interference, advice, criticism, nosiness, care or concern of relatives, friends, and neighbors.

The spreading erosion of unofficial social controls is also apparent in American business and economic life. A classic study of commercial disputes in the early 1960s documented the existence of a well-established and extensive pattern of reliance on informal norms and sanctions to deal with problems that arose among competitors, suppliers, and buyers.[19] Like many useful sociological studies, that one delivered no great surprises. It served, rather, to confirm what anyone familiar with the role of custom in the history of commerce would have expected. Over the past thirty years, however, there has been a marked turn in the commercial world from social methods of dispute resolution to law and the courts. Corporations that once shunned litigation are now regular and aggressive users of the legal system.[20] Many are going to court as an early, rather than a last, resort. Some, abetted as we have seen by changes in the legal profession, deliberately use lawsuits for harassment and coercion, rather than to pursue legitimate claims. Though big business has been the source of many of the loudest complaints about growing litigiousness, recent research reveals that contract suits brought by companies against one another compose the largest single category of federal cases.[21]

In sum, the heavy machinery of law is being wheeled out to deal with a growing array of personal, economic, and political matters to which it is poorly suited. As *Boston Globe* economic reporter Robert J. Samuelson has written, the law's all-or-nothing approach to right and wrong virtually guarantees unhappy results in the vast numbers of conflicts where there are gradations of blameworthy conduct on both sides. "We . . . are gradually turning every bad judgment, indiscretion or even honest mistake into a potential suit or crime."[22] The result of such overuse, needless to say, is to undermine the respect for law that the Founders rightly saw as a vital pillar of the democratic experiment.

Law has begun to extend its cultural empire beyond customs and manners to popular speech. Law talk has become part of the lingua franca that we use to make ourselves understood, or at least heard, across a great variety of generational, linguistic, social, and ethnic divides. The language of rights is the most obvious example.[23] On the benign side, concepts like individual liberty, privacy, evenhandedness, egalitarianism, and fair procedures probably have exerted a salutary unifying influence in our heterogeneous society. But legalese can also have a corrupting effect on everyday discourse in a country where many people take their moral bearings to some extent from law.

When "no fault" divorce was proposed in the 1960s, for example, law reformers did not mean to imply that no one is ever to blame when a marriage breaks up. But they failed to reckon with the common American propensity to equate legality with morality. The "no fault" tag thus came in handy for those who were using divorce, not to escape physically and mentally injurious situations, but to pursue dreams and upgrade choices. Blending all too readily with the no-guilt language of psychotherapy, legal "no fault" provided a shield against moral evaluation and helped to justify decisions that might otherwise be viewed as self-indulgence at the financial and emotional expense of others. One began to hear parents of young children discussing their divorces in terms that would have aroused considerable skepticism a generation earlier. The breakup was "no one's fault"; like a natural disaster, it "just happened"; the spouses "grew apart"; their needs changed, etc. (Rarely do both ex-spouses, or children of divorced couples, talk this way.)

The mannerisms of adversarial advocates, as portrayed in films and television, can also exert an unwholesome influence on everyday human relations. Outside the courtroom, few causes are advanced by selective and self-serving presentation of facts and issues, by the artful use of epithet and innuendo, by avoiding the slightest concession that the other person might be partly right, or by the strident assertion of rights. Many laypeople do not realize what all real-life litigators know: adversarial tactics in court are rigorously policed by a system of formal pleadings and answers, the supervision of a judge, canons of relevance, burdens of proof, the existence of a written record, the law of evidence, and so on. Liberated from such constraints and transplanted to homes, schoolrooms, and workplaces, the advocate's winning ways are apt to leave a fair amount of social wreckage in their wake.

The Crazy Curriculum

The compulsory legal schooling to which Americans currently are subjected is a bewildering welter of contradictory impressions and experiences. Sometimes law appears to us as a powerful tool for social change; yet just as frequently it seems to pose irrational obstacles to commonsense approaches to concrete problems. Bar leaders like to portray lawyers as champions of liberty, equality, and justice for all. Yet few Americans can have such a champion unless they are very poor or very rich. One day we complain of suffocating in a regulatory miasma; on the next we ransack the legal cupboard for nostrums to rectify every wrong, to ward off every risk, and to cure every social and economic ill.

Much of the responsibility for promoting exaggerated and simplistic notions of the saving power of law lies with the legal profession itself. Lawyers, to be sure, have good reason to take pride in their contributions to protecting political and civil rights. They can justly claim to have made some modest contributions to improving the quality of our social, economic, and political life. When the nation made discernible progress in race relations, it was understandable that lawyers would place greater emphasis on the role of celebrated court cases like *Brown* v. *Board of Education* than on the gradual alteration of American sentiments or on legislative achievements like the Civil Rights Act and the Voting Rights Act. That natural professional pride became dangerous hubris, though, when reform-minded lawyers ignored the important openings to political participation afforded by the landmark civil rights decisions and turned them into launching pads for a series of ever more audacious flights from ordinary politics.

Premature and excessive resort to the courts, however, has been a disaster for the political health of the country. By politics here I mean the nearly forgotten activity now being revived and put into practice by men and women like Texas community organizer Ernesto Cortes. Cortes's multiracial, multidenominational Industrial Areas Foundation is dedicated to training citizens to organize their community groups, to initiate action about matters that are important to them, and, in general, to renew their interest in public life.[24] "Politics, properly understood," says Cortes, "is about collective action which is initiated by people who have engaged in public discourse. Politics is about relationships which enable people to disagree, argue, interrupt one another, clarify, confront and negotiate, and, through this process . . . forge a compromise and a consensus which enables them to act . . . In politics, it is not enough to be right . . . one also has to be reasonable, that is one has to be willing to make concessions and exercise judgment in forging a deal." To regain the ability to engage in politics in that sense, Cortes rightly insists, Americans must also regenerate the decaying civic, religious, and cultural organizations where people can learn how to constructively engage others in argument, to reflect upon their actions, and to make informed judgments. Sadly, court decisions have gone beyond addressing failures of politics to displacing politics altogether—and, often, to undermining the groups where political skills are acquired and nurtured.

Ironically, these unintended effects have often outweighed the courts' power to achieve specific results, particularly when judges have aimed beyond settling the dispute at hand. Gerald Rosenberg's study of the aftermaths of Supreme Court rulings reveals that even spectacular courtroom successes have had only a limited capacity to bring about broad changes sought by the winning side.[25]

Ten years after the historic 1954 *Brown* v. *Board of Education* ruling, for example, the proportion of African-American children who attended integrated schools in the South had hardly budged; it was a mere 1.2 percent.[26] The southern officials who had simply ignored *Brown* and its sequels did not stop dragging their feet until faced with congressional withdrawal of federal funding for their schools. But with passage of the Civil Rights Act of 1964, the proportion of southern black children attending schools with whites increased rapidly and impressively—jumping to 16.9 percent by the end of 1967 and to 85.9 percent in 1971.[27] It was legislative rather than judicial action, Rosenberg concludes, that prompted concrete and substantial steps toward desegregation. Rosenberg may have underestimated the long-term influence of *Brown* in the many-stranded process of shaping attitudes that led to the Civil Rights Act and other advances, but his research casts serious doubt on the power of litigation and court decisions to effect significant social change.

While some lawyers were touting litigation as a quick fix for social ills, others were teaching that for nearly every injury suffered by a private individual there is someone with deep pockets, the government or a large corporation, who can be sued and made to pay. Several unusual features of American law—the use of juries in civil cases, the wild card of damages for emotional distress, the legality of arrangements under which the lawyer agrees to be paid only if successful—helped to foster the impression that litigation could be a profitable gamble. As Lawrence Friedman has observed, a "total justice" mentality emerged: "If a person feels wronged or injured, she feels that there must be a remedy, somewhere in the system."[28]

In the wake of a national frenzy of blaming and claiming, however, it is far from clear that the benefits (to persons other than lawyers) have outweighed the costs. While spellbinding lecturers on national platforms extol the lawsuit as a potion for social change or a passkey to corporate and governmental treasuries, many Americans are learning different, and harder, lessons in one-to-one tutorials with their own lawyers.[29] There is little talk of "total justice" in these private sessions with the meter running. Even rough justice is elusive, especially when one is neither in the lowest nor in the highest income brackets. That lesson has been learned the hard way by countless homemakers in divorce cases.

Many small businesspeople, too, have been dunked in the legal reality tank. What would the owners of a Brooklyn sports bar have done, for example, if a lawyer customer had not donated his services when they were sued by the mighty Los

Angeles Dodgers? In 1988, when Richard Picardi, Kevin Boyle, and David Senatore opened the Brooklyn Dodger, the L.A. team's owner wished them good luck in their new venture. Shortly thereafter, though, someone in the Los Angeles organization had a change of heart. Their next communication to the tavern owners was transmitted by a Wall Street law firm: change the name or face a trademark infringement suit. Picardi said, "They thought they would just grind us down. They figured we were little guys in Brooklyn."[30]

After four years of litigation, Federal District Judge Constance Baker Motley held that the big guys' suit was without merit. The former Brooklyn Dodgers gave up their name long ago, she ruled, when they left for the West Coast in "one of the most notorious abandonments in the history of sports."[31] The California organization, she said, was free to use the Brooklyn Dodgers name in marketing sports paraphernalia, but the bar owners were at liberty to continue their use of it in the restaurant business. That David and Goliath story would almost certainly have had a different outcome were it not for Ronald Russo, a former criminal defense lawyer who represented the tavern owners free of charge for the entire four years.

Middle-class men and women are no less vulnerable when they need to file suits themselves than when they are on the receiving end of a complaint. Ask any small-time landlord who has been up against a tenants' advocacy organization or a zealous rent control board—say, one of the thousands of taxi drivers, schoolteachers, or retirees who own a three-decker and rent out two units. Or ask Rose Pucci, a twenty-four-year-old Boston secretary, who thought it was her lucky day when she found a three-room Beacon Hill condo she could afford on her $23,000-a-year salary.[32] True, the cut-rate price of $45,000 reflected the fact that the premises were occupied by a tenant who was reluctant to leave. But the response to Pucci's preliminary query to the Boston Rent Equity Board led her to believe that Boston's rent control law posed no obstacle to repossession by an owner who intended to personally occupy the premises. It was only when she took title and proceeded to file for eviction that Pucci found out the real reason for the markdown. As she put it to a *Boston Globe* reporter, the condo was in the possession of a "tenant from hell," a lawyer who was determined not only to remain on the premises but to avoid paying rent, apparently in hopes of forcing a sale to himself.

With condo fees and mortgage installments consuming her paycheck, Pucci was unable to afford either shelter or a lawyer of her own. She took refuge in her brother's apartment and contacted legal assistance agencies. But to no avail. She made too much money to be eligible for ordinary legal aid. Public interest groups that specialize in landlord-tenant law only help tenants. Nor could she find a lawyer who would accept installment payments.

With such a crazy curriculum in our vast law school, it is small wonder that Americans lash out at lawyers, bridle under laws that seem to make no sense, and deplore the "litigation explosion"—even as they demand legal remedies for virtually every type of personal or social problem. Common sense suggests, however, that what is disrupting the vast law school is not "too much law," "too many lawyers," or too much litigation. As a society becomes larger and more complex, its needs for law and lawyers will inevitably increase. What is problematic is not the amount so much as the quality of the new law that is being produced; not the number of lawyers so much as the way they imagine their roles; not the rise in litigation so much as the peculiar uses to which the courts are being put.

A Place for Law and Law in Its Place

Law, as Tocqueville taught, is not the most important of "the causes that tend to maintain a democratic republic."[33] But it is second only to what he called the "mores," by which he meant the "whole moral and intellectual state of a people."[34] One prominent member of the legal profession who did not hesitate to admit the priority of culture over law was Judge Learned Hand. Hand's sober warning against expecting law to substitute for active citizenship was delivered in New York City at a celebration of I Am an American Day during World War II. To a large audience in Central Park, including 150,000 newly naturalized citizens, he said, "I often wonder whether we do not rest our hopes too much upon constitutions, upon laws, and upon courts. These are false hopes; believe me, these are false hopes. Liberty lies in the hearts of men and women; when it dies there, no constitution, no law, no court can save it; no constitution, no law, no court can even do much to help it. While it lies there it needs no constitution, no law, no court to save it."[35]

The country's mood was receptive to straight talk about civic responsibilities. The radio broadcast of Hand's address prompted so many requests for the text that it was printed, reprinted, and anthologized many times under the title "The Spirit of Liberty." Hand's message is incomplete, however, without the recognition that law has a certain power to affect "the hearts of men and women," especially in a country like the United States. It is true that law is unsteady if not supported by habits and beliefs. But it is also the case that habits and beliefs can benefit from legal reinforcement; and that the seedbeds of civic virtues can be trampled by clumsy governmental feet. That's one reason why law is too important to be left entirely up to lawyers.

The moment is long overdue for a realistic appraisal of what a democratic republic should and should not expect of law and lawyers, of what courts and legally trained individuals can do especially well, and of what tasks are better left to other institutions and actors. With every passing day, the limits of law loom larger, and new adverse side effects of well-intentioned measures come to light. Problems that cannot be whisked away by judicial fiat or resolved by the invention of new rights and crimes continue to fester. In peddling an idea of law that promised too much, legal opinion leaders for the past thirty years set the stage for disappointment, disillusion, and disrespect. Consider Judge Posner's dispiriting litany of recent reforms that have proved ineffective or counterproductive:

> [A] bankruptcy code that has led to a large and unanticipated increase in the number of filings coupled with the disappointing results (and lethal side effects) of the no-fault automobile compensation movement; a no-fault divorce movement that has boomeranged against the women's movement that urged its adoption; the creation of a system of environmental regulation at once incredibly complex and either perverse or ineffective in much of its operation; . . . the rather hapless blundering of the federal courts into immensely contentious, analytically insoluble ethical-political questions such as capital punishment, prison conditions (how comfortable must they be?), sex and the family, and political patronage; the accidental growth of the class action lawsuit . . . into what many observers believe is an engine for coercing the settlement of cases that have no real merit yet expose defendants to astronomical potential liabilities; the flood of one-way attorney's fee-shifting statutes, which overencourage litigation; and the creation of an intricate code of federal criminal procedure . . . in the name of the Constitution, and the wholesale imposition of the code on state criminal proceedings.[36]

Some of Posner's examples would merit a legal Inspector Clouseau award. Take, for instance, the high-minded family law reforms of the 1960s. In a country where the majority of divorces occur between couples with minor children, how can one explain that reformers took childless couples as the norm and treated couples with children as exceptions?[37] Or that, in utter disregard of the economic realities of single parenthood, they constructed the marital property and support law around an image of spousal "self-sufficiency" after divorce?

In many of the instances cited by Posner, lawmakers could

have made more constructive contributions if they had tested their ideas in pilot programs before embarking on wholesale reforms. It is nothing short of tragic that the United States has not exploited the full potential (pointed out long ago by Louis Brandeis) of our federal system to serve as a network of laboratories for trying out novel approaches to intractable problems. There are few other ways to increase our limited store of knowledge concerning such matters as: What are the actual effects of legal measures? How can law help to maintain a beneficial balance in the constantly shifting ecology of state, market economy, mediating structures of civil society, and individual rights? How can government regulate without co-opting or destroying what it touches? How can one foresee and avoid unintended consequences or harmful side effects of regulation? How can lawmakers determine the optimal proportion between fixed rules and individualizing discretion in various concrete situations?

It is disheartening that in such a legalistic country we know so little about how law works, what it can do well, and what it cannot accomplish at all. In the vast law school we all attend, there is a growing sense that something has gone deeply wrong. As in the nation's primary and secondary schools, that realization is attended by much finger pointing and recrimination. Just as teachers blame parental irresponsibility for disorderly classrooms, it is common for lawyers to blame professional ills on client demands and conditions in the general culture. And just as parents complain that the schools are undercutting their efforts to instill good habits at home, Americans have the sense that the legal system often operates against the general welfare.

To some extent, popular discontent with the law and its minions seems to be a case of the mirror despising its own reflection. Lawyers, after all, *represent* their fellow citizens. But it is also the case, in our legalistic country, that the ways of lawyers exert a powerful effect on culture, as well as on political and economic life. At one time, Americans formed their impressions of law and lawyers mainly through direct experience and observation. Now those impressions are increasingly gained from images presented through news and entertainment. Through the filters of the media, the rise in adversarial legalism within the profession is magnified manyfold to the outside world. The lawyer as peacemaker and problem solver is rarely newsworthy, rarely entertaining, and rarely glimpsed. A troubling synergy is set in motion between the most visible segment of the profession and a diverse popular culture short on unifying influences. Small wonder that increasingly adversarial forms of legalism have cropped up alongside the old magisterial spirit that Tocqueville admired. What does it mean, though, for our experiment in ordered liberty when legalism, instead of helping to harness the passions, is increasingly pressed into their service?

What does it mean for our vast law school when the instructors leave their customary posts? When practitioners forsake the business of representation to become operators on their own account—pursuing the rewards of the marketplace, but evading the market constraints to which most other businessmen are subject? When office lawyers behave like litigators— without the discipline of procedural rules and courtroom protocol? When judges mimic executives and legislators— without the accountability or checks by which those officials are restrained? When law professors begin to profess everything but law—without peer review or advanced training in other fields? Socrates, in *The Republic*, took a dim view of craftsmen who did not perfect their own arts and stick to them. It's not so terrible, he said, if a cobbler tries to be a carpenter, or a carpenter tries to make shoes, but "men who are not guardians of the laws and the city but only seem to be, utterly destroy a city."[38] Injustice is certain to run rampant in a polity where the guardians of the laws seek forms of happiness that "will turn them into everything except guardians."

While it may be excessive to claim that the very survival of the republic is at stake, it seems clear that the internal struggles currently roiling the American legal profession have far-reaching political implications. Although these struggles are taking place largely out of public view, every citizen has a stake in the accommodations that are being struck among the many competing claims on the allegiance of individual lawyers and among the order-affirming and order-challenging activities of the profession as a whole. The arrangements that are emerging will not represent the total victory of one set of ideals and habits over others. Rather, it will be a matter of proportion and emphasis.

Several nice issues of balance, then, confront the profession and the citizenry it serves: balance between liberty and order; balance among the branches of government; balance among federal, state, and local authority; balance between public and private spheres; balance among the conflicting loyalties that tug at every individual lawyer; balance between traditionalism and iconoclasm in the law; balance between artisans of order and connoisseurs of conflict in the profession as a whole. How will those delicate accommodations be made?

13

In the Balance

Some harmonious skeptic soon in a skeptical music
Will unite these figures of men and their shapes
Will glisten again with motion, the music
Will be motion and full of shadows.

—WALLACE STEVENS[1]

It took a foreign visitor to point out that no one can fully understand the American version of democracy without inquiring into the habits and opinions of the nation's lawyers. Not only do they apply their legal ways to the conduct of public affairs, but their pervasive presence lends a juridical tinge to everyday life. As Tocqueville saw it, the contagious legal spirit provided a useful antidote to popular government's tendencies toward present-mindedness, disorder, and majoritarian oppression. Far from causing concern, the numbers, prestige, and influence of the legal profession seemed to him to be "the strongest barriers" the United States possessed against the innate weaknesses of democratic regimes.[2] He likened the effect of a large lawyer class scattered throughout our society to that of deposed but still cohesive European aristocracies. "If you ask me where the American aristocracy is found, I have no hesitation in answering that it is not among the rich, who have no common link uniting them. It is at the bar or the bench that the American aristocracy is found."[3]

Tocqueville's analogy rested on a quasi-ecological notion: that a healthy regime requires social, as well as political, checks, supports, flywheels, and countervailing forces. If liberty was not to drift into license, and if government "by the people" was neither to breed despotism nor to degenerate into mob rule, the world's emerging republics would need the kinds of social institutions that promote responsibility, moderation, and long-range thinking, such as strong families, religious groups, and local communities. The infant democracies would also need to cultivate an appreciation of orderly proceedings. In Europe, he believed, that might grow from the diffusion of aristocratic manners. But in the United States, the best source seemed to be the legal profession: "Men who have made a special study of the laws . . . have derived therefrom habits of order, something of a taste for formalities, and an instinctive love for the regular concatenation of ideas."[4]

Tocqueville's famous comparison of American judges and lawyers to hereditary aristocrats is often misunderstood. He was not referring to their power and standing (though that was of interest to him), but to their potentially civilizing effect on manners and opinions. He knew that lawyers were a diverse and motley crew, but saw that their shared training and experiences gave them a "common link." Their tastes and habits were slightly different from those of other citizens. For that reason, he expected them to be a force for moderation as they circulated through a volatile society inclined toward impulsiveness and excesses. They would be like the dash of tartar that helps to stiffen the egg whites in a soufflé.

The subject of formalities, Tocqueville maintained, merited more serious attention than it had ever received from students of politics. Not only did forms and procedures promote the responsible exercise of freedom and self-rule; they also sheltered the weak from the strong while disciplining the power of the state. Their importance increased, moreover, in proportion to the power of the sovereign. The problem for aspiring democratic republics, unfortunately, was that popular governments "need formalities more than other peoples, [but] by nature have less respect for them."[5] Americans, in particular, seemed to have a positive aversion to custom and ceremony. Precisely for that reason, the country needed a reliable supply of what we now call role models who marched to a different, and steadier, drum.

The young Abraham Lincoln, in those years, was thinking

along similar lines. In an 1838 address, he warned his contemporaries against popular disregard for law and against public figures whose ambitions resembled those of the Founders and revolutionaries. The leaders of a settled constitutional order, he said, cannot be those who belong "to the family of the lion, or the tribe of the eagle."[6] The passions that served the nation well at the Founding, he continued, "will in future be our enemy." The lasting pillars of liberty must be "hewn from the solid quarry of sober reason. . . . Reason, cold, calculating, unimpassioned reason, must furnish all the materials for our future support and defense."

As Tocqueville surveyed the American social landscape of the 1830s for sources of reason and sobriety, lawyers seemed to him to offer the most promise. True, the rough-and-ready American legal profession bore no resemblance to a hereditary nobility. Chief Justice John Marshall's dress and table manners would have raised eyebrows even in the servant hall at Versailles. But with their pretensions to learning, picky habits, archaic rites, attention to protocol, attachment to procedure, orientation to precedent, and alertness to long-term effects, lawyers and judges provided social ballast. "The more one reflects on what happens in the United States, the more one feels convinced that the legal body forms the most powerful and, so today, the only counterbalance to democracy in that country."[7]

Tocqueville understood that many lawyers shared their countrymen's aversion to formality and tradition. But their common training, craft habits, inherited lore, and need for predictability made the group in the aggregate a steadying force. It was of no importance to his theory that American lawyers had never envisioned themselves in such a role. To Tocqueville, it was enough that they filled a niche in the political ecology of a fledgling nation embarked on a brave but risky experiment.

As we have seen, the habits and attitudes Tocqueville considered most essential to a democratic republic can no longer be said with certainty to prevail among American judges and lawyers. They are rivaled by the habits and attitudes of judges with grandiose visions of judicial authority, practitioners eager to blaze new trails to the nation's crowded courthouses, and legal scholars yearning to be philosopher-kings and -queens. Thus, an important segment of the profession has become a counterforce, not to democracy's excesses, but to popular government itself. That self-appointed vanguard of an aspiring oligarchy is united, not by any ancient attachment to order and formality, but by knowledge-class disdain for bourgeois values and ordinary politics.

It seems likely that most judges still try to decide disputes impartially, striving to achieve justice for the parties while promoting coherence in the legal order. And that most practitioners still endeavor to pursue their livelihood in the spirit of public service. But it has never been easy for a judge to construe generously the statute he would have opposed as a legislator; for a practitioner to place his duty to client and court above personal gain or popular approval; or for a legal scholar to pursue the research that confounds his cherished hypotheses. But those "ordinary" virtues have become more difficult to practice now that the old, austere preoccupations of lawyers have increasingly yielded to yearnings for self-expression, a zest for novelty, a growing impatience with the needlepoint of law.

These longings are not new, nor is their recent outbreak without parallel in other professions and other fields of knowledge. Tocqueville himself noted that, as there have never been enough positions of power and influence to satisfy all the legally trained individuals who aspire to them, there would always be many lawyers who direct their energies against the arrangements on which other attorneys thrive.[8] What is novel is the rise in visibility, power, and prestige of lawyers, judges, and scholars who are in open revolt against traditional conceptions of their roles.

It is of interest, but of less immediate political concern, that other professions are experiencing similar upheavals. In the first place, Americans have not packed their legislatures, courts, agencies, corporations, and city halls with doctors, dentists, accountants, literary critics, historians, and philosophers. For better or worse, it is lawyers who are stationed at all the pulse points and switches of our vast legalistic republic. And a legal profession increasingly liberated from its customary internalized constraints while wielding power on a vaster scale than anyone could have imagined in the nineteenth century must certainly give pause to friends of popular government.

Law, moreover, plays a much more central role in American society than in most other liberal democracies. Our nation is rich in diversity, but relatively poor in shared memories, sufferings, triumphs, religious beliefs, poems, songs, heroes, and legends. Yet we do have a remarkable, and widely shared, faith in constitutionalism and law. For better or worse, law is a principal carrier of the handful of values that command broad allegiance among Americans of varied religions, ethnic backgrounds, and economic levels: freedom, equality, fair procedures, and the rule of law. (In what other country would a filmmaker, with a straight face, portray a fallen woman's progress to self-respect and upright living through her study of the Declaration of Independence, the Constitution, and the Gettysburg Address, as in the classic *Born Yesterday*?)

The defection of an influential proportion of lawyers from their own traditions thus strikes at the heart of our particular version of the democratic experiment. Yet it is reasonable to ask: Why should lawyers as a group be different from other members of the country's knowledge class? How could a profession so intimately connected with (literally, representing) every aspect of culture remain so much apart from that culture as to constitute a significant counterweight? What would really be surprising would be to find the profession developing according to a genetic code of its own, even as it adapts to new conditions. Nevertheless, something of that sort may be occurring. Law is neither a world unto itself nor a simple reflection of the world around it. The legal profession is open to every sort of influence, but processes everything in its own peculiar way. That is why, beneath the surface of recent developments in the most prominent and visible sectors of the profession, it is difficult to discern what movements may be taking shape.

How much is passing fad and fashion? How much is genuine transformation? What happens when a complex adaptive system like law enters the interesting state that scientists call "the edge of chaos"?

The Edge of Chaos

The history of the legal profession, no less than the course of the law itself, has been a ceaseless process of discord and discovery, of gathering order here and deepening commotion there, of patterns emerging and dissolving as new ideas and practices nibble at the edges of old arrangements. It could hardly be otherwise. Law is the most permeable of disciplines, highly sensitive to shifts in behavior and ideas, intimately connected with every human activity. For most of their history, though, Anglo-American lawyers have been accustomed to experiencing those movements at a relatively leisurely pace. Despite having had nearly a century to get used to accelerating rates of social and economic change, we are still playing catch-up.

To some anxious observers, the legal profession appears to be in a shambles, its recent history a sorry tale of lost consensus, of missed and botched opportunities, of a birthright abandoned for a pot of message or sold for cash on the barrelhead. Others, more sanguine, discern an encouraging trajectory of emancipation from constraints, repudiation of exclusionary practices, progress in vindicating human rights, and new frontiers in scholarship. Almost anyone's hopes and fears can be aroused by pondering this or that uncertain line of development. By all indications, the normally staid legal profession is in the interesting state that students of systems as diverse as the weather, the economy, fluid dynamics, and biological evolution call "the edge of chaos." That metaphor describes the point at which a relatively orderly process erupts into turbulence; where new developments invade the most entrenched settlements;

where familiar arrangements come apart, their components flying off in all directions; where equilibrium is punctuated with variation; where the system seems from one angle to be collapsing, yet from another to be a crucible of new arrangements too formless to be named.[9]

That transient and intensely busy state is not so alarming as it sounds, for it is full of potency as well as contingency. Complex adaptive systems, it seems, are never more spontaneous and creative than when they are teetering between stagnation and anarchy. The fact that the possible paths away from the edge of chaos are practically unlimited, however, is daunting. Few lawyers are comfortable with the realization that our familiar political and legal arrangements are more flawed and open to revision than we previously admitted. It is even more daunting to realize that in law, unlike, say, in natural selection, the course of events can be affected to some extent by human intelligence, cooperation, determination, and good-will. As in the founding period, the stately evolution of Anglo-American legal traditions is once again being profoundly disrupted and infused with new content. For lawyers, it is a time of risk and promise, responsibility and testing. In a more immediate fashion than most other citizens, they are stewards of the Founders' project to establish good government by "reflection and choice," rather than merely being subject to "accident and force."[10]

Does the profession contain a critical mass of men and women with the right stuff to seize the opportunities and avoid the pitfalls in the current situation? The history of ideas tells us something about the stuff, or, more precisely, the combination of stuffs, that is conducive to making the most of a time of turbulence. Paradoxically, the most successful and path-breaking work in all fields of human knowledge has emerged, time and again, from mastery of, and deep immersion in, the very traditions that will be transformed by the most creative workers.[11] What Thomas Kuhn gleaned from his study of major scientific accomplishments is also true of great and small achievements in other fields of specialized knowledge, including law: important breakthroughs are most likely to be produced by men and women who are rigorously grounded in the theory and practice of the normal science of their times, yet who possess the boldness to make a break with the reigning paradigm within which that normal science takes place.[12] Sometimes paradigm shifts are accomplished by a single exceptional individual who combines the traits of the traditionalist and the iconoclast (Holmes, Darwin), but more often they are the collective achievement of a group whose members include a goodly mix of traditionalists and iconoclasts (the American Founding, quantum mechanics).[13]

As in other fields, so with the legal profession. It has always been the case that some individuals are more tradition-bound, while others are more inclined to challenge the tradition. Much of a lawyer's work is order-affirming: the endless rhythm of planning and drafting; the imposition of procedures on the dicey business of fact finding and adjudication; the preference for gradualism over abrupt change; the weight accorded to precedent. But lawyers regularly shatter order, too, as they probe the limits of, and directly attack, established procedures and institutional settlements. The lawyer-poet of the "Blessed rage for order" was also the "Connoisseur of Chaos."[14] When both sets of qualities are well represented in the professional mix, and both kinds of worker are well grounded in normal science, the resulting tension tends to benefit the entire group by pulling all of its members in both directions.[15] The stage is set for creativity. Thus, it is cause for some concern that our highly permeable legal culture has been so deeply penetrated —in the academy at least—by disdain for normal science.

No one knows how to gauge when order-affirming and order-shattering activities fall fatally out of proportion. We do know that the world's legal professions have generally provided more grain than yeast to the legal order. As Max Weber pointed out long ago, the profession has always been a reservoir of both conservative forces and revolutionaries, of defenders and challengers of the status quo, of stewards of hard-won experience and agents of change, but with the former typically predominating everywhere.[16] What is anomalous about the United States, beginning in the 1960s, is the remarkable rise in the influence of legal innovators and iconoclasts with shallow roots in legal traditions and poor grounding in normal legal science. Over the past thirty years, a heady New Age spirit has wafted from high courts, celebrated practitioners, and elite law schools into every nook and cranny of the profession. Even lawyers who were old enough to know better cast off a host of little habits and restraints, like an Edwardian matron shedding her corsets at the seashore.

It would be premature, however, to forecast an endless holiday. Thirty years is a short span in the life of traditions that have been evolving since the thirteenth century, when lawyers began to congregate in inns near the King's Courts at Westminster. In the United States, as the spirit of Philadelphia has yielded to the spirit of Palm Beach, the mood in the profession has been uneasiness rather than relief, a sense of being in the wrong place and not knowing quite how we got there, of feeling bad when we expected to feel good. The grandiose expectations fostered by bold judicial opinions, novel lawsuits, record profits in some quarters, and high-voltage theory have clashed in everyday life with experiences of official arbitrariness, clogged courts, declining civility, numbing routine, and a sense of the irrelevance of much legal education to pressing social problems in which law, for better or worse, is implicated. The rank and file are anxious and restless.

In the midst of the confusion, there are scattered signs that the extended orgy of legal hubris is winding down. To the disappointment of journalists, Supreme Court decisions are becoming more difficult to sensationalize. The boom years in the world of practice appear to have peaked; firms are tightening their belts. The heyday of judges who recognize few constraints on their powers, of practitioners who acknowledge few limits on the uses of litigation, and of academics who look down their noses at constitutionalism and craft traditions may be drawing to a close.

Consider the frame of mind with which the country's newest lawyers are facing the future. Few expect to find a pot of gold awaiting them at the end of the rainbow curriculum. Even in leading law schools, most students can no longer count on degrees alone to open doors to desirable jobs. Law students seem to be studying harder than in the fat years, though of course pretending not to. The "cold-eyed realism" that Christopher Lasch detected among undergraduate students has begun to trickle up to law schools. The current generation of college men and women, according to Lasch, are equally disillusioned with the revolutionary dreams of the 1960s and 1970s and the self-indulgence and greed of the 1980s. And a good thing, too, he added, for both sets of aspirations involved "superficially different but fundamentally similar fantasies of glamor and power." The students of the 1990s, Lasch predicted, will look for "decent, honorable work, the kind of work that confers self-respect and a sense of being useful."[17]

If so, many will find in law the special opportunities for "usefulness to your fellow-men" of which Louis Brandeis spoke many years ago.[18] As postideological young men and women enter the legal profession, who is to say they will not be drawn to the nonconformist professors who, year in, year out, have stubbornly preached the hard practices of a demanding discipline? Or find heroes among the great, flawed individuals who built upon the best of their predecessors—the politically savvy Emancipator who stood on the shoulders of a freedom-loving slave owner, the Llewellyn who worshipped the common law even as he replaced large chunks of it with codifications, the chauvinist civil rights lawyer who modeled himself on a segregationist who was the greatest appellate advocate of his time, the Learned Hand who brought forward the finest in Holmes but could not quite see the constitutional authority for *Brown* v. *Board of Education*, the Archibald Cox who learned from Felix Frankfurter and Learned Hand that ideals are "as real as earth and water." Who is to say tomorrow's legal profession will not play a constructive role as American society confronts

the three great challenges of an increasingly heterogeneous
society, a complex, internationalized economy, and a polity that
still aspires to be a republic?

To a doubtful reader who wonders what on earth might
induce today's pragmatic students to strike off in new and
difficult directions, I would cite the magnetic force of the
Anglo-American legal tradition itself, its power to captivate
many of the best minds of any generation. Like the ancient
fertility goddesses winking out from the eyes of the *Demoiselles
of Avignon*, law's eternal impulses toward renewal resurface in
surprising forms and places. Few of the young men and women
who pass through the nation's law schools entirely escape its
spell. The law is the most human of the human sciences, as
fallible yet filled with potency as men and women themselves.
That is the source of its lasting fascination for the curious and
sociable.

As "cold-eyed" young men and women take their places in
a profession where judicial Caesars, courtroom Rambos, and
classroom Rimbauds have temporarily held the center of the
stage, it would be a mistake to look for a new consensus.
Lawyers, as Weber taught us, have never been of one mind
about what is the good life for a lawyer and how to live it. The
glory of Anglo-American lawyers is that they *have* had a dynamic tradition of rational argument about the most important
questions. Long central to that tradition were notions of evenhandedness in judging, public-spiritedness in practice, and
open-mindedness in pursuit of knowledge. But the tradition
did not exclude lively controversy over the precise nature and
meaning of judicial impartiality, practitioners' duties to client
and court, and academic integrity. For the past three decades,
with the rise to prominence of lawyers, judges, and teachers
who openly flouted those ideals, individual lapses from probity
have been more readily rationalized and excused; judicial bias
and arrogance have paraded as compassion and sensitivity;
abuse of the courts as improved access to justice; shoddy scholarship as a new "genre." The ongoing argument that is the
sign of a living tradition has faltered, yielding to mere clashes

of preferences, tests of strength, or agreements to disagree.

But one should not underestimate the resilience of the dynamic legal traditions of craft professionalism, constitutionalism, and practical reasoning. If we are hopeful, why should we not believe that the energies of those fertile traditions can be harnessed to the needs of a modern, diverse democratic republic? That task will not be accomplished by the sort of traditionalist who wishes to live in a world that no longer exists, or by the sort of innovator who begins with a clean slate and an empty head. What will count are sufficient numbers of lawyers who are knowledgeable enough to be at home in the law's normal science, imaginative enough to grasp the possibilities in the current situation, bold enough to explore them, and painstaking enough to work out the transitions a step at a time.[19]

Are there such men and women in this nation under lawyers? Are they numerous enough to make a difference? As we have seen, there are currently at large in the land legions of law-trained individuals whose powers exceed their self-control and whose ambitions for law outrun its capacity. But like long-legged water striders playing on the surface of a woodland pond, they are only the most visible and acrobatic inhabitants of a complicated world. To a passerby who stops to watch their feats on a summer day, the slow, deep movements of life below remain invisible. So it is with the late-twentieth-century legal profession. Among the nearly 800,000 lawyers in America's towns and cities, the profession's future is taking shape, bodying forth from the restlessness of countless practitioners, from the realism of the youngest arrivals, from a proud tradition known for men and women who are skeptical but not cynical, self-disciplined but not timid, detached but sympathetic, tradition-haunted yet innovative.

The Rage for Order

Oliver Wendell Holmes once likened the law to a magic mirror in which a properly trained eye could see all the triumphs and tragedies, struggles and routines of the human race.[20] Someday, no doubt, that mirror will reveal clear directions and patterns in the maelstrom of interests, beliefs, and hopes that now swirl about us, vying for recognition and competing for followers. But for today's judges, practitioners, and educators there is only the fact of exceptional turbulence in our formerly staid traditions and the unsettling knowledge that even now those traditions are being reshaped by what we have done and what we have failed to do. Will future lawyers murmur their appreciation of the documents, decisions, statutes, and essays we leave behind? Or will some third-millennium finger scrawl across the pages of our legacy: "Mene, Mene, Tekel, Upharsin: You have been weighed in the balance and found wanting"?

Let those who are able to do so take comfort in the notion that what constitutes an advance or an accomplishment in law will always be more contestable than in the natural sciences. The fact is that the day of reckoning cannot be indefinitely postponed. For lawyers, like architects and builders, create structures in which human beings must live, love, and work. It's plain soon enough if the materials are cheap, the work shoddy, the dwelling unsuited for habitation.

At any given point on its journey, the law's caravan is laden with the accumulated accidents and inventions of our predecessors—a cargo of useful ideas and practices that await development, and a jumble of outworn artifacts that might well be left behind. Today's lawyers, judges, teachers, and scholars are in the process of adding their own contributions. Future lawyers one day will form opinions concerning whether we burdened or enriched their inheritance. Citizens in times to come will judge whether we advanced or hindered the project of establishing good government by reflection and choice.

Long ago, in another great nation where republican government flourished for a time, a legal system was created that remains one of the wonders of the world. Later, as republic shaded into empire, lawyers were more numerous than ever, but the spirit of the law slept. Gibbon's judgment was harsh:

> After a regular course of education, which lasted five years, the students dispersed themselves through the provinces in search of fortune and honors; nor could they want an inexhaustible supply of business in a great empire already corrupted by the multiplicity of laws, of arts, and of vices. . . . The noble art, which had once been preserved as the sacred inheritance of the patricians, was fallen into the hands of freedmen and plebeians, who, with cunning rather than with skill, exercised a sordid and pernicious trade.[21]

The American legal profession, at century's close, shows signs of drifting toward a future where there would be no shortage of law and lawyers, but where constitutionalism and craft professionalism would be but ghostly memories, a glittering in the veins of whatever form of government succeeds the republic we did not try hard enough to keep. But the die is not cast. The shades of our ancestors whisper that law is a means of taming as well as serving power; an instrument for the orderly pursuit of dignified living; a sturdy framework for democracy's hurly-burly; a witness to the ability of fallible men and women to give themselves rules, to abide by them, and to fashion them anew when need arises.

Legal traditions speak in many voices, but their deepest impulse is more ancient than speech. In the struggle with our old enemy chaos, we mortals can never win more than a skirmish here, a delaying action there. He lurks in our very flesh, he mocks our plans, he taunts us from our natural surroundings, and, tragically, he insinuates himself into our relations with our fellow human beings. But we put up a gallant fight. We defy him with jokes, and make laws to hold him at bay. Wallace Stevens celebrated, as perhaps only an office lawyer could, our brave stratagems—the twinkling lights of settlements along a darkened shore; the melody of a woman's song rising above the meaningless din of wind and sea:

> It may be that in all her phrases stirred
> The grinding water and the gasping wind;
> But it was she and not the sea we heard.
> For she was the maker of the song she sang.
> The ever-hooded, tragic gestured sea
> Was merely a place by which she walked to sing.
> . . . . .
> Oh! Blessed rage for order, pale Ramon,
> The maker's rage to order words of the sea,
> Words of the fragrant portals, dimly starred,
> And of ourselves and of our origins,
> In ghostlier demarcations, keener sounds.[22]

How to wrest the strands of freedom and order from the chaos of history? How to assure that neither will overwhelm the other? How to weave those wavering cords into sturdy fabrics that our successors will admire even as they fashion them anew? "Reason," say the ancient voices. "Reason, now and always, the life of the law."

NOTES

The author acknowledges with gratitude the able and dedicated research assistance of Jennifer A. Cabranes and Michael R. Pompeo, members of the Harvard Law School class of 1994.

CHAPTER 1

1. Steve France, "Did the Lawyers Win?" *American Bar Association Journal*, February 1993, p. 102.
2. Alexis de Tocqueville, *Democracy in America*, George Lawrence trans., J. P. Mayer ed. (New York: Doubleday Anchor, 1969), p. 264.
3. Grant Gilmore, *The Ages of American Law* (New Haven: Yale University Press, 1978), pp. 105–6. (The 1974 Storrs Lectures at the Yale Law School.)
4. *Planned Parenthood of Southeastern Pennsylvania* v. *Casey*, 112 S.Ct. 2791, 2816 (1992). The case is discussed in Chapter 6 below.
5. Terry Carter, "Crossing the Rubicon," *California Lawyer*, October 1992, pp. 39, 40, 104.
6. Calabresi's statement, aimed at the conservative wing of the Court, appeared in an Op-Ed piece endorsing the nomination of Yale alumnus Clarence Thomas, "What Clarence Thomas Knows," *New York Times*, July 28, 1991, Section 4, p. 15. In 1994, Calabresi himself was nominated to the Second Circuit Court of Appeals.
7. "Quotes," *American Bar Association Journal*, November 1989, p. 39. On the benefits of certain forms of legal advertising, see the discussion in Chapter 3, at note 51.
8. Louis Auchincloss, "The Tender Offer," in *Legal Fictions*, Jay Wishingrad ed. (Woodstock, N.Y.: Overlook Press, 1992), p. 3.
9. "One-Man Law" (editorial), *New York Times*, October 22, 1973, p. 30.
10. Quoted in Alexander Haig, *Inner Circles* (New York: Warner Books, 1992), p. 385.
11. James Jones, *From Here to Eternity* (New York: Scribner's, 1951), p. 209.
12. Gilmore treated procedural due process and related ideas as elements of a version of the rule of law espoused by naive academics, *Ages of American Law*, pp. 105–6. For a discussion of the rule of law as an eminently *practical* ideal, see Stephen Macedo, "The Rule of Law, Justice, and the Politics of Moderation," in *NOMOS XXXVI: The Rule of Law*, Ian Shapiro ed. (New York: New York University Press, 1994), pp. 148–77.
13. Tocqueville, *Democracy in America*, p. 270.

CHAPTER 2

1. Roscoe Pound, *The Lawyer from Antiquity to Modern Times* (St. Paul: West, 1953), p. 5.
2. Marc Galanter and Thomas Palay, *Tournament of Lawyers: The Transformation of the Big Law Firm* (Chicago: University of Chicago Press, 1991), p. 10.
3. Ibid., p. 36.
4. For a description of the process of promotion to partnership, see ibid., pp. 26–31.
5. Charles E. Wyzanski, Jr., "My Years with Ropes & Gray" (unpublished manuscript dated January 25, 1984, Harvard Law Library).
6. Galanter and Palay, *Tournament of Lawyers*, p. 28.
7. Don J. DeBenedictis, "Firings to Continue," *American Bar Association Journal*, March 1992, p. 24.
8. "Survey Finds Retrenching in Law Firms," *New York Times*, September 20, 1993, p. D2.
9. Mark Hansen, "Partner in Name Only," *American Bar Association Journal*, January 1992, p. 26.
10. See Galanter and Palay, *Tournament of Lawyers*, p. 53 (describing increased pressures on partners to generate business), and Ronald J. Gilson and Robert H. Mnookin, "Sharing Among the Human Capitalists: An Economic Inquiry into the Corporate Law Firm and How Partners Split Profits," 37 *Stanford Law Review* 313 (1985) (describing the organizational benefits of the lockstep sharing model and the pressures that led to its modification).
11. Michael Abramowitz, "One Woman v. Her Law Firm," *Washington Post*, October 14, 1991, p. D1.
12. John Heinz and Edward Laumann, *Chicago Lawyers: The Social Structure of the Bar* (New York and Chicago: Russell Sage Foundation and American Bar Foundation, 1982), pp. 90–134.
13. Robert M. Swaine, *The Cravath Firm and Its Predecessors, 1819–1947* (New York: Ad Press, 1948), p. 11.
14. See Lincoln Caplan, *Skadden: Power, Money and the Rise of a Legal Empire* (New York: Farrar, Straus and Giroux, 1993), pp. 184–85.
15. DeBenedictis, "Firings to Continue," p. 24.
16. For studies of the changes in the culture of large firms in this period, see generally Galanter and Palay, *Tournament of Lawyers*; and Robert L. Nelson, *Partners with Power: The Social Transformation of the Large Law Firm* (Berkeley: University of California Press, 1988).
17. Galanter and Palay, *Tournament of Lawyers*, p. 46.
18. See Ronald J. Gilson and Robert H. Mnookin, "Coming of Age in a Corporate Law Firm: The Economics of Associate Career Patterns," 41 *Stanford Law Review* 567 (1989).
19. DeBenedictis, "Firings to Continue," p. 24.
20. William H. Harbaugh, *Lawyer's Lawyer: The Life of John W. Davis* (New York: Oxford University Press, 1973), p. 258.

21. Alan Desoff and Jodi Cleesattle, "Hanging by a Thread," *The National Jurist*, October/November 1992, pp. 14, 21.
22. James E. Brill, "The Secret of Success," *American Bar Association Journal*, October 1992, p. 100.
23. Marcia Chambers, "Sua Sponte," *National Law Journal*, February 1, 1993, pp. 17, 18.
24. Lawrence Lederman, *Tombstones: A Lawyer's Tales from the Takeover Decades* (New York: Farrar, Straus and Giroux, 1992), pp. 14, 28–29.
25. Leo Herzel, "The Future of Corporate Law," *University of Chicago Law School Record*, Spring 1992, pp. 19, 20.
26. Stephanie B. Goldberg, "Then and Now: 75 Years of Change," *American Bar Association Journal*, January 1990, pp. 56, 60.
27. Ibid.
28. Harry T. Edwards, "The Growing Disjunction Between Legal Education and the Legal Profession," 91 *Michigan Law Review* 34, 72–73 (1992).
29. Timothy May, quoted in Edward Frost and Margaret Cronin Fisk, "The Profession After 15 Years," *National Law Journal*, August 9, 1993, pp. 1, 40.
30. See Nancy D. Holt, "Are Longer Hours Here to Stay?" *American Bar Association Journal*, February 1993, p. 62; James E. Brill, "The Secret of Success," *American Bar Association Journal*, October 1992, p. 100.
31. That average probably does not reflect a mean: many lawyers do no pro bono work at all, while many others devote far more than fifteen hours a year to public service of various sorts. The fifty-hour recommendation was added to the ABA's *Model Rules of Professional Conduct*, Rule 6.1, by amendment in 1993. The fifteen-hour figure is from Robert L. Nelson's *Partners with Power*, p. 260.
32. Barry Reed, *The Choice* (New York: Crown, 1991), p. 5.
33. Goldberg, "Then and Now," p. 60.
34. William Ross, "The Ethics of Hourly Billing by Attorneys," 44 *Rutgers Law Review* 1, 16 (1991).
35. Lederman, *Tombstones*, p. 112.
36. Junda Woo, "Lawyers Argue over Impact of Survey That Ranks Nation's Top Law Firms," *Wall Street Journal*, June 19, 1993, p. B5.
37. Quoted in Desoff and Cleesattle, "Hanging by a Thread."
38. Harbaugh, *Lawyer's Lawyer*, p. 110.
39. Potter Stewart, "Professional Ethics for the Business Lawyer," 31 *The Business Lawyer* 463, 464 (1975).
40. Jerome Carlin, *Lawyers' Ethics: A Survey of the New York City Bar* (New York: Russell Sage Foundation, 1966), pp. 168–69.
41. Mark Stevens, *Power of Attorney: The Rise of the Giant Law Firms* (New York: McGraw-Hill, 1987), pp. 8–9.
42. Nelson, *Partners with Power*, pp. 54, 58, 84.
43. Gary Hengstler, "News," *American Bar Association Journal*, April 1989, p. 36.

44. Rita H. Jensen, "Where Were the Lincoln Lawyers?" *National Law Journal*, May 6, 1991, p. 26.

45. See Robert W. Gordon, "The Independence of Lawyers," 68 *Boston University Law Review* 1, 40 (1988). See also Robert L. Nelson and David M. Trubek, "Arenas of Professionalism: The Professional Ideologies of Lawyers in Context," in *Lawyers' Ideal/Lawyers' Practices: Transformations in the American Legal Profession*, Robert Nelson, David Trubek, and Rayman L. Solomon eds. (Ithaca: Cornell University Press, 1992), pp. 177, 178.

46. Discussions of the hortatory rhetoric of early bar leaders can be found in Robert Gordon, " 'The Ideal and the Actual in Law': Fantasies and Practices of New York City Lawyers, 1870–1910," in *The New High Priests: Lawyers in Post-Civil War America*, Gerard Gawalt ed. (Westport, Conn.: Greenwood Press, 1984), p. 51; and Rayman L. Solomon, "Five Crises or One: The Concept of Legal Professionalism, 1925–1960," in *Lawyers' Ideals/Lawyers' Practices*, p. 144.

47. For an eloquent plea for reviving the "lawyer-statesman" and "wise counselor" roles, see Anthony Kronman, *The Lost Lawyer: Failing Ideals of the Legal Profession* (Cambridge: Harvard University Press, 1993).

48. Gordon, "The Independence of Lawyers," pp. 32–33.

49. Gerard W. Gawalt, "Introduction," in *The New High Priests*, p. 4.

50. Rayman Solomon analyzed 729 articles and speeches that appeared in law reviews and state and local bar journals from 1925 to 1960. "Five Crises or One," pp. 145, 150–51, 168.

51. For a leading legal ethicist's discussion of this point, see Deborah L. Rhode, "Ethical Perspectives on Legal Practice," 37 *Stanford Law Review* 589 (1985).

52. Randall Samborn, "Anti-Lawyer Attitudes Up," *National Law Journal*, August 9, 1993, pp. 1, 22.

53. In Judge Posner's economic analysis, heightened competition is unlikely to have significant effects on lawyers' ethical obligations to their clients ("competitive markets are not notable for disserving their customers"), but can be expected to undermine ethical duties to court and community ("competition implies the subordination of other interests to those of the consumer"). Richard A. Posner, *Overcoming Law* (Cambridge: Harvard University Press, 1995), Ch. 2.

54. Randall Samborn, "Who's Most Admired Lawyer?" *National Law Journal*, August 9, 1993, p. 24.

CHAPTER 3

1. Quoted in Charles Fried, "The Lawyer as Friend: The Moral Foundations of the Lawyer-Client Relation," 85 *Yale Law Journal* 1060, n. 1 (1976). Lord Brougham made this famous statement in connection with his defense of Queen Caroline in her 1820 trial before the House of Lords. For a comparison of its original context with what it has come to mean to lawyers today, see Deborah L. Rhode, "An Adversarial

Exchange on Adversarial Ethics," 41 *Journal of Legal Education* 29 (1991).

2. Anthony Chase, "Lawyers and Popular Culture: A Review of Mass Media Portrayals of American Attorneys," 1986 *American Bar Foundation Research Journal* 281, 282.

3. Large firms responding to a 1993 survey typically reported that litigation accounted for a hefty percentage of their legal work, but well below half, e.g., Cravath, Swaine & Moore (38 percent); Davis Polk & Wardwell (30 percent); Fulbright & Jaworski (35 percent); Gibson, Dunn & Crutcher (44 percent); Mayer, Brown & Platt (29 percent); Pillsbury, Madison & Sutro (42 percent); Shearman & Sterling (22 percent); Skadden, Arps, Slate, Meagher & Flom (25 percent); "Annual Survey of the Nation's Largest Law Firms," *National Law Journal*, September 27, 1993, pp. S29, S30. See also Robert C. Clark, "Why So Many Lawyers? Are They Good or Bad?" 41 *Fordham Law Review* 275, 281 (1992), citing a more broad-based study that found fewer than 12 percent of practitioners reporting that their primary practice was in litigation.

4. Robert M. Swaine, *The Cravath Firm and Its Predecessors, 1819–1947* (New York: Ad Press, 1948), p. 371.

5. Ibid., pp. 554–55.

6. Charles E. Wyzanski, Jr., "My Years with Ropes & Gray" (unpublished manuscript dated January 25, 1984, Harvard Law Library).

7. Marc Galanter and Thomas Palay, "The Transformation of the Big Law Firm," in *Lawyers' Ideals/Lawyers' Practices: Transformations in the American Legal Profession*, Robert P. Nelson, David M. Trubek, and Rayman L. Solomon eds. (Ithaca: Cornell University Press, 1992), pp. 31, 43.

8. Jerold Auerbach, *Unequal Justice: Lawyers and Social Change in Modern America* (New York: Oxford University Press, 1976), pp. 17–18.

9. For most of the information about Davis in this chapter I am indebted to William H. Harbaugh's superb biography, *Lawyer's Lawyer: The Life of John W. Davis* (New York: Oxford University Press, 1973).

10. The voting case, *Guinn and Beal* v. *United States*, 238 U.S. 347 (1915), provided an early and important beachhead in civil rights law. For a discussion of its significance and of Davis's advocacy, see Richard Kluger, *Simple Justice* (New York: Vintage, 1977), pp. 104, 527.

11. Harbaugh, *Lawyer's Lawyer*, p. 90.

12. Ibid., p. 128.

13. Ibid., p. 181.

14. 260 U.S. 393 (1922). In 1987, the Court substantially retreated from, but did not overrule, *Pennsylvania Coal* in *Keystone Bituminous Coal Assn.* v. *DeBenedictis*, 480 U.S. 478 (1987).

15. Harbaugh, *Lawyer's Lawyer*, p. 406.

16. Ibid., p. 404.

17. Ibid., p. 400.

18. Ibid., p. 405.

19. Ibid., p. 202.

20. Ibid., p. 262.
21. *United States* v. *McIntosh*, 283 U.S. 605 (1931).
22. *Girouard* v. *United States*, 328, U.S. 61 (1946).
23. Harbaugh, *Lawyer's Lawyer*, p. 299. Also noting Davis's interest in civil liberties cases but claiming they consumed "relatively little of his time" is Kluger, *Simple Justice*, p. 528.
24. Lord Eldon, quoted in Harbaugh, *Lawyer's Lawyer*, p. 298.
25. Ibid., p. 482.
26. *United States* v. *Nixon*, 418 U.S. 683 (1974).
27. *Plessy* v. *Ferguson*, 163 U.S. 537 (1896).
28. *Brown* v. *Board of Education of Topeka, Kansas*, 347 U.S. 483 (1954).
29. Harbaugh, *Lawyer's Lawyer*, p. 503.
30. "Third Person Singular," *The New Yorker*, February 8, 1993, pp. 4, 6 (unsigned).
31. Harbaugh, *Lawyer's Lawyer*, pp. 502, 503.
32. Constance Baker Motley, "In Memory of Thurgood Marshall," 68 *New York University Law Review* 205, 210 (1993).
33. Harbaugh, *Lawyer's Lawyer*, p. 503.
34. Ibid., p. 492.
35. Ibid., p. 516.
36. Ibid., p. 514.
37. Kluger, *Simple Justice*, p. 656.
38. Harbaugh, *Lawyer's Lawyer*, p. 519.
39. Ibid., p. 404.
40. Ibid., p. 482.
41. John J. Curtin, Jr., "Civil Matters," *American Bar Association Journal*, August 1991, p. 8.
42. David Margolick, "At the Bar," *New York Times*, April 16, 1993, p. B7. The lawyer was censured.
43. Harbaugh, *Lawyer's Lawyer*, pp. 263–64.
44. Milo Geyelin, "Suits by Firms Exceed Those by Individuals," *Wall Street Journal*, December 3, 1993, p. B1.
45. Marc Galanter, "The Life and Times of the Big Six; Or, The Federal Courts Since the Good Old Days," 1988 *Wisconsin Law Review* 921.
46. Marc Galanter, "The Day After the Litigation Explosion," 46 *Maryland Law Review* 3, 38 (1986).
47. Walter K. Olson, *The Litigation Explosion: What Happened When America Unleashed the Lawsuit* (New York: Dutton, 1991), p. 3.
48. L. Gordon Crovitz, "Rule of Law," *Wall Street Journal*, August 21, 1991, p. A13.
49. The typical arrangement for a contingent fee of a third to a half of the recovery is particularly susceptible to abuse in the growing proportion of personal injury cases where liability is fairly clear and little effort by the attorney is needed, therefore, to achieve a favorable early settlement for the client. See Lester Brickman, Michael Horowitz, and Jeffrey O'Connell, *Rethinking Contingency Fees* (Washington, D.C.: Manhattan Institute, 1994).

50. See Basil S. Markesinis, "Litigation-Mania in England, Germany, and the USA: Are We So Very Different?" 49 *Cambridge Law Journal* 233 (1990).

51. *Bates* v. *State Bar of Arizona*, 433 U.S. 350 (1977); see also *Zauderer* v. *Office of Disciplinary Counsel*, 471 U.S. 626 (1985). By striking down blanket bans on advertising, the Court did not rule out all regulation of legal marketing. In fact, a number of states have enacted laws that regulate the types of advertising in which lawyers may engage.

52. Robert Nelson and David Trubek, "New Problems and New Paradigms in Studies of the Legal Profession," in *Lawyers' Ideals/Lawyers' Practices*, p. 25.

53. Abraham Lincoln, "Notes for a Law Lecture," in *Selected Speeches, Messages, and Letters*, T. Harry Williams ed. (New York: Holt, Rinehart, 1957), p. 33.

54. Quoted in "Those #*X!!! Lawyers," *Time*, April 10, 1978, pp. 56, 59.

55. Quoted in Nick Armstrong, "Discovery Abuse and Judicial Management," *New Law Journal*, July 3, 1992, p. 927.

56. Edward Gibbon, *The Decline and Fall of the Roman Empire*, D. M. Low ed. (New York: Harcourt, Brace, 1960), p. 259.

57. *Lincoln Savings & Loan Assn.* v. *Wall*, 743 F. Supp. 901, 920 (D.D.C. 1990).

58. Robert W. Gordon, " 'The Ideal and the Actual in the Law': Fantasies and Practices of New York City Lawyers, 1870–1910," in *The New High Priests: Lawyers in Post-Civil War America*, Gerard Gawalt ed. (Westport, Conn.: Greenwood Press, 1984), p. 51.

59. Geoffrey C. Hazard, "Ethics," *National Law Journal*, July 12, 1993, pp. 15, 16.

60. Robert L. Nelson, *Partners with Power: The Social Transformation of the Large Law Firm* (Berkeley: University of California Press, 1988), pp. 271–72.

CHAPTER 4

1. American Bar Association, *Model Rules of Professional Conduct* (1983), Preamble.

2. Ray Patterson, "Legal Ethics and the Lawyer's Duty of Loyalty," 29 *Emory Law Review* 909, 918 (1980).

3. Steven Lubet, "Professionalism Revisited," 42 *Emory Law Journal* 197, 205 (1993).

4. Ibid., p. 206.

5. Ibid.

6. The social stratification of the Chicago bar is the subject of John Heinz and Edward Laumann, *Chicago Lawyers: The Social Structure of the Bar* (New York and Chicago: Russell Sage Foundation and American Bar Foundation, 1982).

7. Jane Jacobs, *Systems of Survival: A Dialogue on the Moral Foundations of Commerce and Politics* (New York: Random House, 1992), pp. xi, 130.

8. For the following summary, I have drawn on Jacobs's 1992 book, *Systems of Survival*, and on the proceedings of the 1987 Jane Jacobs Conference at Boston College, *Ethics in Making a Living*, Fred Lawrence ed. (Atlanta: Scholars Press, 1989).

9. Lincoln's legal career is currently being reconstructed from 50,000 documents retrieved from 71 county courthouses in central Illinois. Herbert Mitgang, "Documents Search Shows Lincoln the Railsplitter as a Polished Lawyer," *New York Times*, February 15, 1993, p. A12.

10. See, generally, Heinz and Laumann, *Chicago Lawyers*, pp. 109–18.

11. Jerold Auerbach, *Unequal Justice: Lawyers and Social Change in Modern America* (New York: Oxford University Press, 1976), p. 42.

12. Thomas L. Shaffer, "The Legal Profession's Rule Against Vouching for Clients: Advocacy and 'The Manner That Is the Man Himself,' " 7 *Notre Dame Journal of Law, Ethics & Public Policy* 145 (1993).

13. Karl N. Llewellyn, "On Warranty of Quality, and Society," 36 *Columbia Law Review* 699, 720–21 (1936).

14. Ibid.

15. Thomas L. Shaffer (with Mary M. Shaffer), *American Lawyers and Their Communities* (Notre Dame: University of Notre Dame Press, 1991).

16. Ibid., pp. 30–47, 96–97.

17. Robert W. Gordon, "The Independence of Lawyers," 68 *Boston University Law Review* 1, 20 (1988).

18. Thomas L. Shaffer, "Beyond the Rules: The Responsibility and Role of Continuing Legal Education to Teach Alternative Ethical Considerations," in A L I - A B A, *CLE and the Lawyer's Responsibilities in an Evolving Profession* (Report on the Arden House III Conference, November 13–16, 1987) (1988), pp. 493, 505–6.

19. Typical in a long series of laments is Justice Harlan Stone's in 1932, that lawyers were becoming "tainted . . . with the morals and manners of the market place in its most antisocial manifestations." "The Public Influence of the Bar," 48 *Harvard Law Review* 1, 6–7 (1932).

20. See Abraham Lincoln, "Notes for a Law Lecture," in *Selected Speeches, Messages, and Letters*, T. Harry Williams ed. (New York: Holt, Rinehart, 1957), p. 33.

21. Brandeis's speech, "The Opportunity in the Law," criticizing "the leading lawyers" for their alliance with business and neglect of the public interest, appears in *Business—a Profession* (Boston: Hale, Cushman & Flint, 1933), p. 329.

22. Erwin N. Griswold, *Ould Fields, New Corne: The Personal Memoirs of a 20th Century Lawyer* (St. Paul: West, 1992), p. 399.

23. Quoted in Karen Dillon, "Jenner & Block Tries a Little Management," *The American Lawyer*, May 1989, p. 106.

24. There is a vast literature on this subject. See, for example, Robert C. Soloman, *Ethics and Excellence: Cooperation and Integrity in Business* (New York: Oxford University Press, 1992); *Business Ethics: The State of the Art*, R. Edward Freeman ed. (New York: Oxford University Press,

1991); and periodicals such as *Business Ethics Quarterly, Business and Society Review,* and *Business Horizons.*

25. The U.S. Supreme Court delivered a mortal wound to the claim that the practice of law is not a business when it held in *Goldfarb* v. *Virginia State Bar,* 421 U.S. 773 (1975), that the law business is in "trade or commerce" as that expression is used in the antitrust laws.

26. Stephen Volk, quoted in Lincoln Caplan, *Skadden: Power, Money and the Rise of a Legal Empire* (New York: Farrar, Straus and Giroux, 1993), p. 52.

27. Quoted in Stephanie B. Goldberg, "Then and Now: 75 Years of Change," *American Bar Association Journal,* January 1990, pp. 60–61.

28. Lawrence Lederman, *Tombstones: A Lawyer's Tales from the Takeover Decades* (New York: Farrar, Straus and Giroux, 1992), p. 106.

29. Ibid., p. 108.

30. Ibid., p. 109.

31. See David B. Wilkins, "Making Context Count: Regulating Lawyers After Kaye, Scholer," 66 *Southern California Law Review* 1145, 1160–81 (1993).

32. Marianne Lavelle, "Proposed Limits on Asset Freezes Called Inadequate," *National Law Journal,* November 8, 1993, pp. 17, 22.

33. Erwin Smigel, *The Wall Street Lawyer: Professional Organization Man?* (Bloomington: Indiana University Press, 1969), p. 342. Smigel did not try to determine, however, how often lawyers actually exercised that independence.

34. Robert L. Nelson, *Partners with Power: The Social Transformation of the Large Law Firm* (Berkeley: University of California Press, 1988), p. 5.

35. Ibid., p. 282.

36. Quoted in Ted Schneyer, "Some Sympathy for the Hired Gun," 41 *Journal of Legal Education* 11, 14 (1991).

37. Caplan, *Skadden,* p. 314.

38. Nancy Zeldis, "Curtain Drops on Shea & Gould," *National Law Journal,* February 7, 1994, p. 3.

39. Jan Hoffman, "An End to a Law Firm That Defined a Type," *New York Times,* February 7, 1994, p. 1.

40. Ibid., p. B4.

41. Deborah L. Rhode, "Ethical Perspectives on Legal Practice," 37 *Stanford Law Review* 589, 641 (1985).

42. *Model Rules of Professional Conduct* (1983), Preamble.

43. See the Shaffers' discussion in *American Lawyers and Their Communities,* p. 8.

44. American Bar Association, *Code of Professional Responsibility* (1969), Preamble.

45. American Bar Association, *Canons of Professional Ethics* (1908), Canon 32.

46. *Code of Professional Responsibility* (1969), Ethical Consideration 7–8.

47. *Model Rules of Professional Conduct* (1983), Rule 2.1.

48. Wilkins, "Making Context Count," pp. 1216–18.

49. A number of state bar groups, however, have rejected the ABA's resolution of this issue.
50. Lisa Belkin, "Woman Behind the Symbols in Abortion Debate," *New York Times*, May 9, 1989, p. A18.
51. Alan R. Marks, "Where Is the *Real* Conflict of Interest?" *American Bar Association Journal*, February 1993, p. 112.
52. Walter K. Olson, *The Litigation Explosion* (New York: Dutton, 1991), p. 5.
53. Shepard Remis, quoted in Nick King, "The Law Gets Down to Business," *Boston Globe*, May 17, 1983, pp. 37, 42.
54. Archibald Cox, "Ethics in Government: The Cornerstone of Public Trust," 94 *West Virginia Law Review* 281, 300 (1991–92).
55. As a perceptive observer of the legal profession, Roger Cramton, puts it: "[O]ur materialistic culture, with its extraordinary emphasis on individual self-realization (frequently forgetting that our individual identity is shaped by the community of which we are part), does push selfish advantage to the fore and erode communal values." "The Trouble with Lawyers (and Law Schools)," 35 *Journal of Legal Education* 359, 361 (1985).

CHAPTER 5

1. Andrea Sachs, "From Prisoner to Preacher: Watergate 'Hatchet Man' Colson Wins Religion Award," *American Bar Association Journal*, May 1993, p. 38.
2. Robert Sayler and Anna Engh, "Litigators to Examine Lack of Funding, Access," *National Law Journal*, August 9, 1993, p. S3.
3. Nancy D. Holt, "Are Longer Hours Here to Stay?" *American Bar Association Journal*, February 1993, p. 62.
4. Ibid.
5. Oliver Wendell Holmes, "The Profession of the Law," in *The Occasional Speeches of Justice Oliver Wendell Holmes*, Mark DeWolfe Howe ed. (Cambridge: Belknap Press, 1962), p. 28.
6. "Speech" (Boston Bar Association, March 7, 1900), *Occasional Speeches*, p. 126.
7. Ibid.
8. Ibid., p. 123.
9. "The Profession of the Law," *Occasional Speeches*, p. 30.
10. "Despondency and Hope," *Occasional Speeches*, pp. 146, 147.
11. The data in this paragraph are taken from the survey reports in ABA Young Lawyers Division, *The State of the Legal Profession 1990* (Chicago: American Bar Association, 1991).
12. Lynne Pregenzer, "Substance Abuse Within the Legal Profession: A Symptom of a Greater Malaise," 7 *Notre Dame Journal of Law, Ethics, and Public Policy* 305, 306 (1993).
13. Ibid., p. 51.

14. See the discussion of *karoshi* by Tatsuo Inoue, "The Poverty of Rights-Blind Communality: Looking Through the Window of Japan," 1993 *Brigham Young University Law Review* 517, 532–38.

15. Julie Shoop, "Going It Alone Is Less Fun, Survey Says," *Trial*, September 1990, pp. 91–92.

16. See Steven Keeva, "Unequal Partners," *American Bar Association Journal*, February 1993, p. 50; Robert L. Nelson, *Partners with Power: The Social Transformation of the Large Law Firm* (Berkeley: University of California Press, 1988), p. 139.

17. Jill Abramson, "For Women Lawyers, an Uphill Struggle," *The New York Times Magazine*, March 6, 1988, p. 36.

18. Ibid.

19. Thomas Geoghegan, "Warren Court Children," *The New Republic*, May 19, 1986, p. 17.

20. Edward Frost and Margaret Fisk, "The Profession After 15 Years," *National Law Journal*, August 9, 1993, pp. 1, 40.

21. Ibid.; Junda Woo, "Law School Applications Show Decline," *Wall Street Journal*, March 8, 1994, p. B7.

22. Richard A. Posner, "The Material Basis of Jurisprudence," 69 *Indiana Law Journal* 1 (1993). The article appears in revised form in *Overcoming Law* (Cambridge: Harvard University Press, 1995).

23. Posner, *Overcoming Law*.

24. See Posner, "The Material Basis of Jurisprudence," p. 1.

25. "The Law," *Occasional Speeches*, pp. 20, 21.

26. "Daniel S. Richardson," *Occasional Speeches*, p. 57.

27. "Sidney Bartlett," *Occasional Speeches*, p. 54.

28. Charles E. Wyzanski, Jr., "The Living Streams of Value," in *Whereas— A Judge's Premises* (Boston: Atlantic Monthly Press, 1965), pp. 284, 289–90.

29. *The State of the Legal Profession 1990*, p. 52.

30. Learned Hand, "Mr. Justice Holmes," *The Spirit of Liberty: Papers and Addresses of Learned Hand*, Irving Dilliard ed. (New York: Knopf, 1952), pp. 57, 62. On this occasion, Holmes is supposed to have looked long at the painting (p. 121) and said, "Rather an imposing old bugger, isn't he?"

31. Lord Shawcross, "Robert H. Jackson's Contributions During the Nuremberg Trial," in *Mr. Justice Jackson* (New York: Columbia University Press, 1969), pp. 87, 90.

32. "Death by Midnight," *48 Hours*, CBS-TV December 2, 1991 (transcript from Burrelle's Information Services, Livingston, N.J.).

33. Geoghegan, "Warren Court Children," pp. 17, 23.

34. David Margolick, "At the Bar," *New York Times*, February 19, 1993, p. B7. Margolick's practice of occasionally devoting his regular legal column to verbal portraits or vignettes affords fascinating glimpses into the lives of lawyers outside the large firms to which legal sociologists have devoted most of their attention.

35. David Margolick, "At the Bar," *New York Times*, April 10, 1992, p. B10.

36. Richard L. Fricker, "Conversations with Seven Lawyers," *American Bar Association Journal*, December 1992, pp. 69, 71.

37. Ted Schneyer, "Some Sympathy for the Hired Gun," 41 *Journal of Legal Education* 11, 16 (1991).

38. John J. Curtin, Jr., "Civil Matters," *American Bar Association Journal*, August 1991, p. 8.

39. "George Otis Shattuck," *Occasional Speeches*, p. 93.

40. William H. Harbaugh, *Lawyer's Lawyer: The Life of John W. Davis* (New York: Oxford University Press, 1973), p. 399.

41. Walker Percy, *The Message in the Bottle* (New York: Farrar, Straus and Giroux, 1980), p. 7.

42. Paul Freund, *The Supreme Court of the United States* (Gloucester, Mass.: Peter Smith, 1972), p. 75.

43. Anthony Kronman, *The Lost Lawyer: Failing Ideals of the Legal Profession* (Cambridge: Harvard University Press, 1993), p. 362.

44. Charles Fried, "The Artificial Reason of the Law or: What Lawyers Know," 60 *Texas Law Review* 35, 57 (1981).

45. Karen Donovan, "Searching for ADR Stars," *National Law Journal*, March 14, 1994, pp. A1, A20.

46. Paul Freund, "The Legal Profession," *Daedalus*, Fall 1963, pp. 689, 693.

47. This is a central thesis of Anthony Kronman in *The Lost Lawyer*; see, especially, pp. 66–74.

48. Learned Hand, "The Contribution of an Independent Judiciary to Civilization," *The Spirit of Liberty*, pp. 155, 164.

49. Edmund Burke, *Reflections on the Revolution in France* (New York: Doubleday Anchor, 1973), p. 33.

50. Kronman, *The Lost Lawyer*, p. 217.

CHAPTER 6

1. Alexis de Tocqueville, *Democracy in America*, George Lawrence trans., J. P. Mayer ed. (New York: Doubleday Anchor, 1969), p. 276.

2. Terry Carter, "Crossing the Rubicon," *California Lawyer*, October 1992, pp. 39, 40.

3. David G. Savage, *Turning Right: The Making of the Rehnquist Supreme Court* (New York: Wiley, 1992), pp. 170–72.

4. Ibid., pp. 174–82.

5. *Planned Parenthood of Southeastern Pennsylvania* v. *Casey*, 112 S.Ct. 2791 (1992).

6. Carter, "Crossing the Rubicon," p. 103.

7. *Planned Parenthood of Southeastern Pennsylvania* v. *Casey*, 112 S.Ct. 2791, 2814 (1992).

8. Ibid., p. 2816: "Their belief in themselves as such a people is not readily separable from their understanding of the Court invested with the authority to decide their constitutional cases and speak before all others for their constitutional ideals."

9. Ibid., p. 2815: "To all those who will be so tested by following [the

decision], the Court implicitly undertakes to remain steadfast, lest in the end a price be paid for nothing."

10. Carter, "Crossing the Rubicon," p. 104.
11. *Marbury* v. *Madison*, 5 U.S. 137, 177 (1803).
12. *Planned Parenthood of Southeastern Pennsylvania* v. *Casey*, 112 S.Ct. 2791, 2815 (1992).
13. *Dred Scott* v. *Sandford*, 60 U.S. (19 How.) 393 (1856).
14. *Hammer* v. *Dagenhart*, 247 U.S. 251, 276 (1918).
15. *Brown* v. *Board of Education*, 347 U.S. 483 (1954).
16. *Federalist* No. 78.
17. Dennis J. Hutchinson, "Unanimity and Desegregation: Decisionmaking in the Supreme Court, 1948–1958," 68 *Georgetown Law Review* 1 (1979).
18. Justices Blackmun and Stevens, who went along with *Casey*'s result, filed separate opinions. Justices Scalia, Thomas, White, and Chief Justice Rehnquist dissented.
19. "Supreme Court Report," *American Bar Association Journal*, March 1990, pp. 44, 45.
20. *Texas* v. *Johnson*, 491 U.S. 397, 399 (1989).
21. For a candid insider's guide (by one of the country's most scholarly judges) to the earmarks of delegated opinion-drafting, as well as a discussion of the extent to which judges now delegate responsibility to clerks and staff, see Richard A. Posner, *The Federal Courts: Crisis and Reform* (Cambridge: Harvard University Press, 1985), pp. 102–19.
22. *Brown* v. *Board of Education*, 74 S.Ct. 686 (1954).
23. See, e.g., *Marbury* v. *Madison*, 5 U.S. (1 Cranch) 137 (1803).
24. Lawrence M. Friedman, *History of American Law*, 2nd ed. (New York: Touchstone, 1985), p. 132.
25. See, generally, Robert K. Faulkner, *The Jurisprudence of John Marshall* (Princeton: Princeton University Press, 1968).
26. See the engaging verbal portrait of Marshall in Edward G. White's informative book on American judges, *The American Judicial Tradition* (New York: Oxford University Press, 1988), pp. 10–12.
27. James Q. Wilson, *American Government: Institutions and Policies*, 5th ed. (Lexington, Mass.: D. C. Heath, 1992), p. 398.
28. *Pollock* v. *Farmers' Loan & Trust Co.*, 157 U.S. 429 (1895). An earlier income tax imposed during the Civil War went unchallenged and was repealed in 1872.
29. E.g., *Adkins* v. *Children's Hospital*, 261 U.S. 238 (1936) (minimum wage for female workers unconstitutional); *Hammer* v. *Dagenhart*, 247 U.S. 251, 276 (1918) (ban on commerce in products of child labor unconstitutional); *Coppage* v. *Kansas*, 236 U.S. 1 (1915) (state ban on "yellow dog" contracts forbidding employees to join labor unions unconstitutional).
30. *Holmes-Pollock Letters*, Vol. I, Mark DeWolfe Howe ed. (Cambridge: Harvard University Press, 1941), p. 101.
31. *Lochner* v. *New York*, 198 U.S. 45 (1905).
32. Ibid., pp. 75–76.

33. See, e.g., *Abrams* v. *United States*, 250 U.S. 616, 624 (1919). (Holmes, J., dissenting).

34. White, *The American Judicial Tradition*, p. 122.

35. See Clyde W. Summers, "Frankfurter, Labor Law and the Judge's Functioning," 67 *Yale Law Journal* 266 (1957), for a discussion of Frankfurter's committed efforts on behalf of labor for twenty years preceding his appointment to the Supreme Court, and his determination as a judge not to substitute his own opinions for the judgments of legislatures in labor and other matters.

36. See the account of Marshall's courtship of the NAACP secretary who became his second wife, in Carl T. Rowan, *Dream Makers, Dream Breakers: The World of Justice Thurgood Marshall* (Boston: Little, Brown, 1993), p. 234. ("Chauvinist, sexist Marshall watched the black aide relay his proposition to Suyat, who looked at him with irritation and dismissed him with a no-deal wave of her hand.")

37. *Of Law and Men: Papers and Addresses of Felix Frankfurter* (New York: Harcourt, Brace, 1956), p. 138.

38. Ibid., p. 33.

39. See, generally, Joseph P. Lash, *From the Diaries of Felix Frankfurter* (New York: Norton, 1975).

40. On Hand's progressivism, see Kathryn Griffith, "Learned Hand," in *The Remarkable Hands: An Affectionate Portrait*, Marcia Nelson ed. (New York: Federal Bar Council, 1983), pp. 11, 13, 18. On his anti-McCarthyism, see Gerald Gunther, *Learned Hand: The Man and the Judge* (New York: Knopf, 1994), pp. 579–91.

41. See Richard A. Posner, *Cardozo: A Study in Reputation* (Chicago: University of Chicago Press, 1990), pp. 1–2; Andrew L. Kaufman, "Benjamin Cardozo," in *Justices of the United States Supreme Court 1789–1969*, Leon Friedman and Fred Israel eds. (New York: Chelsea House, 1969), pp. 2287, 2288.

42. Learned Hand, "Mr. Justice Cardozo," 52 *Harvard Law Review* 361, 362–63 (1939).

43. Quoted in Linda Greenhouse, "The Thomas Hearings: In Trying to Clarify What He Is Not, Thomas Opens Question of What He Is," *New York Times*, September 13, 1991, p. A19.

44. Benjamin N. Cardozo, *The Nature of the Judicial Process* (New Haven: Yale University Press, 1921), p. 13.

45. Frankfurter, *Of Law and Men*, p. 40.

46. *Public Utilities Commission* v. *Pollak*, 343 U.S. 451, 467 (1952).

47. Oliver Wendell Holmes, *The Common Law* (Boston: Little, Brown, 1881), p. 1.

48. Clifford Geertz, *The Interpretation of Cultures* (New York: Basic Books, 1973), p. 30.

49. Frankfurter, *Of Law and Men*, pp. 40–41.

50. *The Spirit of Liberty: Papers and Addresses of Learned Hand*, Irving Dilliard ed. (New York: Knopf, 1953), pp. xxiv–xxv.

CHAPTER 7

1. "The Decline of Law as an Autonomous Discipline: 1962–1967," 100 *Harvard Law Review* 761, 771 (1987).

2. *Federalist* No. 17 (Alexander Hamilton).

3. See, generally, Mary Ann Glendon, Michael W. Gordon, and Christopher Osakwe, *Comparative Legal Traditions*, 2nd ed. (St. Paul: West, 1994).

4. *Southern Pacific Company* v. *Jensen*, 244 U.S. 205, 221 (1917) (Holmes, J., dissenting).

5. Benjamin N. Cardozo, *The Nature of the Judicial Process* (New Haven: Yale University Press, 1921), p. 166.

6. Charles E. Wyzanski, Jr., "Introduction," in Learned Hand, *The Bill of Rights* (Forge Village, Mass.: Atheneum, 1963), p. v.

7. Ibid.

8. Kathryn Griffith, "Learned Hand," in *The Remarkable Hands: An Affectionate Portrait*, Marcia Nelson ed. (New York: Federal Bar Council, 1983), pp. 11, 12.

9. "Augustus Noble Hand," in Charles E. Wyzanski, Jr., *Whereas—A Judge's Premises* (Boston: Little, Brown, 1965), pp. 65, 71.

10. Ibid., p, 75.

11. Samuel Eliot Morison, *The Oxford History of the American People* (New York: Oxford University Press, 1965), p. 569.

12. Henry M. Hart, Jr., and Albert M. Sacks, *The Legal Process: Basic Problems in the Making and Application of Law* (Cambridge, Mass.: Tentative Edition, 1958), pp. 781–86.

13. Edward G. White, *The American Judicial Tradition* (New York: Oxford University Press, 1988), p. 294.

14. The question of when particular types of legal changes ought to be made by a legislature rather than a court is the subject of considerable discussion in legal literature. See, for example, Robert E. Keeton, "Creative Continuity in the Law of Torts," 75 *Harvard Law Review* 463 (1962).

15. For a discussion of Traynor's constitutional decisions, see White, *The American Judicial Tradition*, pp. 310–11.

16. Ruth Bader Ginsburg, "Speaking in a Judicial Voice," 67 *New York University Law Review* 1185, 1205 (1992).

17. Hand, *The Bill of Rights*, p. 55.

18. Wyzanski, "Introduction," p. viii.

19. Ibid., p. xiv.

20. Nathan Glazer, "Towards an Imperial Judiciary?" 41 *Public Interest* 104, 123 (1975).

21. *Missouri* v. *Jenkins*, 495 U.S. 33 (1990).

22. David O. Stewart, "No Exit," *American Bar Association Journal*, June 1992, p. 49.

23. Judge Milton Shadur, quoted in Jon R. Waltz, "Uncle Sam in the Dock," *Washington Post*, June 26, 1983, Book Section, p. 6.

24. David S. Clark, "Adjudication to Administration: A Statistical Analysis of Federal District Courts in the Twentieth Century," 55 *Southern California Law Review* 65 (1981).

25. Henry J. Reske, "Molding the Courts," *American Bar Association Journal*, January 1993, p. 20; Bruce Fein, "A Court of Mediocrity," *American Bar Association Journal*, October 1991, pp. 75, 76.

26. *Annual Report of the Director of the Administrative Office of the United States Courts* (Washington, D.C.: U.S. Government Printing Office, 1981), p. 151.

27. *Annual Report of the Director of the Administrative Office of the United States Courts* (Washington, D.C.: U.S. Government Printing Office, 1991), p. 117.

28. Richard A. Posner, *The Federal Courts: Crisis and Reform* (Cambridge: Harvard University Press, 1985), pp. 97–98.

29. Wade H. McCree, Jr., "Bureaucratic Justice: An Early Warning," 129 *University of Pennsylvania Law Review* 777 (1981).

30. Posner, *The Federal Courts*, pp. 59–93.

31. Stephen Reinhardt, "Too Few Judges, Too Many Cases," *American Bar Association Journal*, January 1993, p. 52.

32. Harold Baer, Jr., "Why I Quit the New York Bench," *New York Times*, October 1, 1992, p. A25. In 1994, Baer was nominated to the federal bench in the Southern District of New York.

33. Richard A. Posner, "The Material Basis of Jurisprudence," 69 *Indiana Law Journal* 1, 21 (1993).

34. Posner, *The Federal Courts*, p. 102.

35. Ibid.

36. Ibid., p. 108.

37. Reinhardt, "Too Few Judges, Too Many Cases," p. 52.

38. Robert E. Keeton, "Times Are Changing for Trials in Court," 21 *Florida State University Law Review* 1, 15 (1993).

39. Joseph Vining, "Justice, Bureaucracy, and Legal Method," 80 *Michigan Law Review* 248–53 (1981).

40. Joseph Vining, *The Authoritative and the Authoritarian* (Chicago: University of Chicago Press, 1986).

41. Charles E. Wyzanski, Jr., "The Law of Change," 1968 *New Mexico Quarterly* 5, 18–19.

42. Nat Hentoff, "The Constitutionalist," *The New Yorker*, March 12, 1990, pp. 45, 60.

43. Posner, *The Federal Courts*, p. 20.

44. Kenneth Starr, "Supreme Court Needs a Management Revolt," *Wall Street Journal*, October 12, 1993, p. A23.

45. Ibid.

46. Kenneth W. Starr, "The Supreme Court and the Federal Judicial System," 42 *Case Western Reserve Law Review* 1209, 1212–14 (1992).

47. William H. Rehnquist, "Remarks on the Process of Judging," 49 *Washington and Lee Law Review* 263, 269–70 (1992).

48. McCree, "Bureaucratic Justice: An Early Warning," pp. 783–84.

49. Diana G. Culp, "Fixing the Federal Courts," *American Bar Association Journal*, June 1990, p. 63.
50. Martha Middleton, "Another First," *National Law Journal*, August 17, 1987, p. 2.
51. Culp, "Fixing the Federal Courts," p. 63; Reinhardt, "Too Few Judges, Too Many Cases," p. 52.
52. John J. Curtin, Jr., "The Crisis in the Justice System," *American Bar Association Journal*, February 1991, p. 8.
53. American Bar Association, *Code of Judicial Conduct* (1972), Canon 3A (6): "A judge should abstain from public comment about a pending or impending proceeding in any court. . . ."
54. Andrew J. Kleinfeld, "Politicization: From the Law Schools to the Courts," *Academic Questions*, Winter 1993, pp. 9, 18.
55. *National Law Journal*, December 28, 1992, p. 14.
56. Stanley Mosk, "Should Judges Speak Out? Yes," *The Judges' Journal*, Summer 1985, p. 42.
57. Quoted in *Modern Judicial Ethics* (National Judicial College, 1992), p. ix.
58. "Attacking Activism, Judge Names Names," *Legal Times*, June 22, 1992, pp. 14, 17.
59. Tony Mauro, "Does the Court Play to the Press Gallery?" *Legal Times*, June 22, 1992, p. 8.

CHAPTER 8

1. Quoted in Philip Hager, " 'Judicial Activism' Seen Threatening Democratic Process," *Boston Globe*, December 31, 1976, p. 1. Judge Bacon served twenty-one years on the District of Columbia Superior Court, retiring in 1991.
2. Laurence H. Silberman, "The American Bar Association and Judicial Nominations," 59 *George Washington Law Review* 1092, 1095 (1991).
3. Edward G. White, *The American Judicial Tradition* (New York: Oxford University Press, 1988), p. 336.
4. Ibid.
5. Fred Rodell, "It Is the Earl Warren Court," *The New York Times Magazine*, March 13, 1966, p. 92.
6. John Hart Ely, *Democracy and Distrust: A Theory of Judicial Review* (Cambridge: Harvard University Press, 1980), pp. 73–74.
7. *United States* v. *Carolene Products*, 304 U.S. 144, 152 n. 4 (1938).
8. Here, I speculate. Gerald N. Rosenberg in *The Hollow Hope: Can the Courts Bring About Social Change?* (Chicago: University of Chicago Press, 1991) points to the absence of concrete evidence that *Brown* had significant positive effects on racial attitudes (pp. 107–55). But the instruments of social science are not well geared to measuring the strength of each current in a long-term multi-causal phenomenon.
9. Melissa Fay Greene, *Praying for Sheetrock* (Reading, Mass.: Addison-Wesley, 1991), p. 335.
10. Kim Isaac Eisler, *A Justice for All: William J. Brennan, Jr., and the Decisions*

That Transformed America (New York: Simon & Schuster, 1993), p. 22.

11. Ellen L. Rosen, "The View from the Bench," *National Law Journal*, August 11, 1987, pp. S–17.

12. Eisler, *A Justice for All*, p. 15.

13. "Talk of the Town," *The New Yorker*, August 6, 1990, p. 27.

14. Lee's observation was made in a roundtable discussion, "The Brennan Legacy," *American Bar Association Journal*, February 1991, p. 52.

15. Bob Woodward and Scott Armstrong, *The Brethren: Inside the Supreme Court* (New York: Avon, 1981), p. 48.

16. Ibid., p. 49. See *The Brethren*, too, for an account, through the eyes of Supreme Court clerks, of how Brennan and William O. Douglas flattered and manipulated the insecure Harry Blackmun (pp. 266–84, 428–29).

17. Thurgood Marshall, "A Tribute to Justice Brennan," 104 *Harvard Law Review* 1, 5 (1990).

18. William J. Brennan, "State Constitutions and the Protection of Individual Rights," 90 *Harvard Law Review* 489, 491 (1977).

19. Robert A. Burt, *The Constitution in Conflict* (Cambridge: Harvard University Press, 1992), p. 353.

20. William J. Brennan, Jr., "The Constitution of the United States: Contemporary Ratification," in *Interpreting Law and Literature: A Hermeneutic Reader*, Sanford Levinson and Steven Mailloux eds. (Evanston, Ill.: Northwestern University Press, 1988), p. 14.

21. *Missouri, Kansas & Texas Railway Co.* v. *May*, 194 U.S. 267, 270 (1904).

22. *Baker* v. *Carr*, 369 U.S. 186 (1962).

23. Brennan, "The Constitution of the United States," p. 14. Brennan here was echoing Justice Robert Jackson's concurrence in *Brown* v. *Allen*, 344 U.S. 443, 540 (1953).

24. Neuborne, "The Brennan Legacy," p. 53.

25. Brennan, "The Constitution of the United States," p. 14.

26. Norman Dorsen, "A Tribute to Justice William J. Brennan," 104 *Harvard Law Review* 15, 22 (1990).

27. Woodward and Armstrong, *The Brethren*, p. 263.

28. See William J. Brennan, "Justice Thurgood Marshall: Advocate for Human Need in American Jurisprudence," 40 *Maryland Law Review* 390, 391 (1981).

29. *Lyng* v. *Northwest Indian Cemetery Protective Assn.*, 485 U.S. 439 (1988).

30. *Aguilar* v. *Felton*, 473 U.S. 402 (1985).

31. Ibid., p. 431.

32. David O. Stewart, "Justice William J. Brennan, Jr.: A Life on the Court," *American Bar Association Journal*, February 1991, p. 62. But cf. Woodward and Armstrong, *The Brethren*, pp. 238–39, recounting how Brennan changed his mind after initially voting to uphold certain laws regulating obscenity.

33. J. Skelley Wright, letter to Professor Edward Rabin, in Edward Rabin, "The Revolution in Landlord-Tenant Law: Causes and Consequences," 69 *Cornell Law Review* 517, 549 (1984).

34. *Federalist* No. 17 (Alexander Hamilton).

35. Philip Hager, " 'Judicial Activism,' " p. 1.

36. John Adams, *Massachusetts Declaration of Rights*, Massachusetts General Laws Annotated: *Constitution*, Part I, Art. 29.

37. Judicial Oath, Judiciary Act of 1789, 28 U.S. Code s. 453 (1992).

38. *Buck* v. *Bell*, 274 U.S. 200, 207 (1927).

39. See Judge John T. Noonan, Jr.'s analysis of *Palsgraf* v. *Long Island Rail Road* in *Persons and Masks of the Law: Cardozo, Holmes, Jefferson, and Wythe as Makers of the Masks* (New York: Farrar, Straus and Giroux, 1976), pp. 111–51.

40. Ronald Dworkin, "Dissent on Douglas," *New York Review of Books*, February 19, 1981, p. 3.

41. Paul D. Carrington, "The Theme of Early American Law Teaching: The Political Ethics of Francis Lieber," 42 *Journal of Legal Education* 339, 349–50 (1992).

42. Patrick M. McFadden, *Electing Justice: The Law and Ethics of Judicial Election Campaigns* (Chicago: American Judicature Society, 1990), pp. xiii–xiv.

43. Debra Moss, "Hawking Judges," *American Bar Association Journal*, December 1990, p. 26.

44. Mark Hansen, "The High Cost of Judging," *American Bar Association Journal*, September 1991, p. 44.

45. "What Brennan Wrought," *The New Republic*, August 13, 1990, p. 7. Cry foul they did, nevertheless. See the attack on Justice Scalia by Jeffrey Rosen, "The Leader of the Opposition," *The New Republic*, January 18, 1993, p. 20.

46. Paul D. Carrington, "Ceremony and Realism: Demise of Appellate Procedure," *American Bar Association Journal*, July 1980, pp. 860, 862.

47. Alexis de Tocqueville, *Democracy in America*, George Lawrence trans., J. P. Mayer ed. (New York: Doubleday Anchor, 1969), p. 240.

48. The advantages to the country as a whole of leaving states free to experiment within constitutional limits were well understood by Holmes and Brandeis. See *New State Ice Co.* v. *Liebmann*, 285 U.S. 262, 311 (1932) (Brandeis, J., dissenting). (One of the "happy incidents of the federal system [is] that a single courageous State may, if its citizens choose, serve as a laboratory.")

49. Abraham Lincoln, *Selected Speeches, Messages, and Letters*, T. Harry Williams ed. (New York: Holt, Rinehart, 1957), pp. 138, 145.

50. Carrington, "Ceremony and Realism," p. 860.

51. *Federalist* No. 78 (Alexander Hamilton).

52. Rosen, "The View from the Bench," p. S-17.

53. Milo Geyelin, "Bush Judges Take a Conservative Path," *Wall Street Journal*, May 17, 1993, p. B8.

54. Jeffrey Rosen, "The Next Justice: How Not to Replace Byron White," *The New Republic*, April 12, 1993, p. 21.

55. Letter to the Editor by Allen Ides, *The New Republic*, May 10, 1993, p. 4.

56. Kenneth Jost, "The White Legacy," *American Bar Association Journal*, October 1993, pp. 63–70.

57. Ruth Bader Ginsburg, "Speaking in a Judicial Voice," 67 *New York University Law Review* 1185, 1209 (1992). The quoted words were from Gerald Gunther's remarks at Justice Ginsburg's 1980 investiture.

58. Robert H. Bork, *The Tempting of America: The Political Seduction of the Law* (New York: Free Press, 1990), p. 351.

59. Richard A. Posner, *The Federal Courts: Crisis and Reform* (Cambridge: Harvard University Press, 1985), p. 220.

CHAPTER 9

1. "The Use of Law Schools," in *The Occasional Speeches of Justice Oliver Wendell Holmes*, Mark DeWolfe Howe ed. (Cambridge: Belknap Press, 1962), pp. 34, 36.

2. Karl N. Llewellyn, "A Come-All-Ye for Lawyers," in *The Common Law Tradition: Deciding Appeals* (Boston: Little, Brown, 1960), pp. 399–400.

3. Alasdair MacIntyre, *After Virtue: A Study in Moral Theory* (Notre Dame: University of Notre Dame Press, 1981), p. 207.

4. Frederic W. Maitland, "Origins of Legal Institutions," in *The Life of the Law*, John Honnold ed. (Glencoe: Free Press, 1964), p. 6.

5. Llewellyn, *The Common Law Tradition*, p. 36.

6. Ibid., p. 191.

7. Edward Coke, *The First Part of the Institutes of the Laws of England*, p. 97b, s. 138.

8. Ibid.

9. Daniel Webster, *Remarks at the Meeting of the Suffolk Bar on Moving the Resolutions Occasioned by the Death of the Hon. Mr. Justice Story* (Boston: James Munroe & Co., 1845), pp. 9–10.

10. See MacIntyre, *After Virtue*, p. 206.

11. See, generally, Robert B. Stevens, *Law School: Legal Education in America from the 1850s to the 1980s* (Chapel Hill: University of North Carolina Press, 1983).

12. Christopher Columbus Langdell, *A Selection of Cases on the Law of Contracts* (Boston: Little, Brown, 1870), pp. vi–vii.

13. See, generally, Stevens, *Law School*, pp. xiv, 123.

14. Jerold S. Auerbach, *Unequal Justice: Lawyers and Social Change in Modern America* (London: Oxford University Press, 1976), p. 94.

15. See the discussion of "institutionalist" legal writing in John H. Langbein, "Chancellor Kent and the History of Legal Literature," 93 *Columbia Law Review* 547, 585–93.

16. Ernst Freund, *Administrative Powers over Person and Property* (Chicago: University of Chicago Press, 1928); *Legislative Regulation* (New York: Commonwealth Fund, 1932).

17. "Book Notice," 14 *American Law Review* 233 (1880); see, generally, Mark

DeWolfe Howe, *Justice Oliver Wendell Holmes: The Proving Years* (Cambridge: Belknap Press, 1963), pp. 155–59.

18. Sallust, *The Jugurthine War / The Conspiracy of Catiline* (London: Penguin, 1963), p. 176.

19. "The Profession of the Law," *Occasional Speeches*, pp. 28, 29.

20. Mark DeWolfe Howe, *Justice Holmes: The Shaping Years: 1841–1870* (Cambridge: Belknap Press, 1957), p. 277.

21. Alexis de Tocqueville, *Democracy in America*, George Lawrence trans., J. P. Mayer ed. (New York: Doubleday Anchor, 1969), p. 301.

22. Howe, *The Shaping Years*, p. 282.

23. Oliver Wendell Holmes, *The Common Law* (Boston: Little, Brown, 1881), p. 1.

24. "The Profession of the Law," *Occasional Speeches*, p. 31.

25. In the *Oxford Dictionary of Legal Quotations*, 255 selections are from Holmes's writings, more than twice the number drawn from any other judge or lawyer. David Margolick, "At the Bar," *New York Times*, March 26, 1993, p. B6.

26. Oliver Wendell Holmes, "The Path of the Law," 10 *Harvard Law Review* 457, 469 (1897).

27. Ibid.

28. Holmes, *The Common Law*, p. 1.

29. Holmes, "The Path of the Law," p. 465.

30. Jabez Fox, "Law and Morals," *The Boston Law School Magazine*, March 1897, pp. 1, 6. American legal formalism could be caricatured as an infatuation with logic, but logic was not its hallmark. See, on American formalism, Richard Posner, *The Problems of Jurisprudence* (Cambridge: Harvard University Press, 1990), pp. 14–15; and Llewellyn, *The Common Law Tradition*, pp. 38–41.

31. Max Rheinstein, "Introduction," in *Max Weber on Law and Economy in Society*, Edward Shils and Max Rheinstein trans., Max Rheinstein ed. (Cambridge: Harvard University Press, 1954), p. li.

32. See, generally, Mary Ann Glendon, Michael W. Gordon, and Christopher Osakwe, *Comparative Legal Traditions*, 2nd ed. (St. Paul: West, 1994), pp. 56–57.

33. Peter Stein, "Logic and Experience in Roman and Common Law," 59 *Boston University Law Review* 433, 437 (1979). See also Howe, *The Proving Years*, pp. 152, 155.

34. Holmes, *The Common Law*, p. 1.

35. Holmes, "The Path of the Law," p. 460.

36. Ibid., p. 457.

37. Ibid., p. 459.

38. Ibid., p. 462.

39. Ibid., p. 464.

40. Ibid., pp. 468, 474.

41. Ibid., p. 469.

42. "The Law," *Occasional Speeches*, pp. 21–22.

43. Holmes, "The Path of the Law," p. 459.
44. Ibid., p. 473.
45. Hilton Kramer, *The Age of the Avant-Garde: An Art Chronicle of 1956–1972* (New York: Farrar, Straus and Giroux, 1973), p. 7.
46. For biographical data about Llewellyn, I have relied mainly on the excellent book by William Twining, *Karl Llewellyn and the Realist Movement* (London: Weidenfeld and Nicolson, 1973), and to some extent on conversations over the years with his widow, the late Soia Mentschikoff.
47. Karl N. Llewellyn, "A Realistic Jurisprudence—the Next Step," 30 *Columbia Law Review* 431 (1930).
48. Jerome Frank, *Law and the Modern Mind* (New York: Brentano's, 1930); *Courts on Trial* (Princeton: Princeton University Press, 1949).
49. *The Cheyenne Way: Conflict and Case Law in Primitive Jurisprudence* (Norman: University of Oklahoma Press, 1941).
50. *The Bramble Bush*, first published for student use in 1930, did not appear in a permanent edition until 1951 (New York: Oceana).
51. Twining relates the story in *Karl Llewellyn and the Realist Movement*, p. 422. See also the discussion of the Cardozo bust in Frederick S. Voss, *Portraits of the American Law* (Seattle: University of Washington Press, 1989), pp. 152–54.
52. Llewellyn, *The Common Law Tradition*, pp. 509–10.
53. Twining, *Karl Llewellyn and the Realist Movement*, p. 387.
54. Learned Hand, "Foreword to Williston's 'Life and Law'" in *The Spirit of Liberty: Papers and Addresses of Learned Hand*, Irving Dilliard ed. (New York: Knopf, 1953), pp. 140, 142.

CHAPTER 10

1. George L. Priest, "Social Science Theory and Legal Education: The Law School as University," 33 *Journal of Legal Education* 437, 439 (1983).
2. Joseph P. Bauer, "A Judicial Clerkship 24 Years After Graduation: Or, How I Spent My Spring Sabbatical," 42 *Journal of Legal Education* 427 (1992).
3. Patrick Griffin, "The Catcher in the Drain," *Reader*, May 28, 1992, p. 1.
4. See, generally, Anthony D'Amato, "The Decline and Fall of Law Teaching in the Age of Student Consumerism," 37 *Journal of Legal Education* 461 (1987).
5. Law School Admission Council/Law School Admission Services, *The Law School Admission Test: Sources, Contents, Uses* (September 1991), pp. 1, 2, 5.
6. Richard A. Posner, "The Decline of Law as an Autonomous Discipline: 1962–1987," 100 *Harvard Law Review* 761, 778 (1987).
7. That generous spirit toward younger colleagues and curricular innovation is well exemplified by the reflections of Clark Byse (reputed to have been one of the models for Professor Kingsfield in *The Paper Chase*) in "Fifty Years of Legal Education," 71 *Iowa Law Review* 1063 (1986).

8. Charles Rothfeld, "A Lament: Too Few Interesting Law Review Articles," *New York Times*, November 23, 1990, p. B23.

9. George L. Priest, "Social Science Theory and Legal Education: The Law School and the University," 33 *Journal of Legal Education* 437, 441 (1983).

10. Paul Brest, "Plus Ça Change," 91 *Michigan Law Review* 1945, 1949 (1993), maintains, however, that the proportion of "fatuous" articles remains about the same as it always was.

11. Stephen Labaton, "Profile: Louis Loss," *New York Times*, September 26, 1993, Section 3, p. 8.

12. On the culture of clinicians, see Don J. DeBenedictis "Learning by Doing: The Clinical Skills Movement Comes of Age," *American Bar Association Journal*, September 1990, pp. 54, 55.

13. William Blackstone, *Commentaries on the Laws of England*, Vol. I, p. 32.

14. Letter from Charles E. Wyzanski, Jr., to Lloyd N. Cutler, May 21, 1986 (Wyzanski Papers, Harvard Law Library).

15. William O. Douglas, "Law Reviews and Full Disclosure," 40 *Washington Law Review* 227, 229 (1965).

16. Learned Hand, "On Receiving an Honorary Degree," *The Spirit of Liberty: Papers and Addresses of Learned Hand*, Irving Dilliard ed. (New York: Knopf, 1953), pp. 134, 138.

17. Posner, "The Decline of Law as an Autonomous Discipline," pp. 761, 778.

18. Mark Tushnet, "Critical Legal Studies: A Political History," 100 *Yale Law Journal* 1515, 1516 (1991).

19. Roberto Unger, *The Critical Legal Studies Movement* (Cambridge: Harvard University Press, 1986), p. 8.

20. Ibid., p. 119.

21. Brian Timmons, "That's No Okie, That's My Torts Professor," *Wall Street Journal*, April 3, 1990, p. A20.

22. Roberto Mangabeira Unger, *False Necessity: Anti-Necessitarian Social Theory in the Service of Radical Democracy* (Part I of *Politics: A Work in Constructive Social Theory*) (Cambridge: Cambridge University Press, 1987), pp. 72, 208, 453.

23. Ibid., p. 588.

24. Ibid., pp. 406, 457, 530–35. See also Unger, *The Critical Legal Studies Movement*, pp. 39, 53.

25. Roberto Unger, *Passion: An Essay on Personality* (New York: Free Press, 1984), pp. 38, 46.

26. According to Robert Hughes, *The Shock of the New* (New York: Knopf, 1987), the decline of "graphic literacy" in the twentieth century was nowhere more evident than in the United States (p. 402).

27. *Justice Oliver Wendell Holmes: His Book Notices and Uncollected Letters and Papers*, Harry C. Shriver ed. (New York: Central Book Co., 1936), p. 139.

28. The anecdote is told by Nat Hentoff, "P.C. Law Schools," *Washington Post*, July 11, 1992, p. A19.

29. Paul D. Carrington to Robert W. Gordon," 35 *Journal of Legal Education* 9, 12 (1985).

30. Arlynn Leiber Presser, "The Politically Correct Law School," *American Bar Association Journal*, September 1991, pp. 52, 56.

31. David Margolick, "The Trouble with America's Lawyers," *The New York Times Magazine*, May 22, 1983, pp. 20, 39.

32. Julius Getman, *In the Company of Scholars: The Struggle for the Soul of Higher Education* (Austin: University of Texas Press, 1992), p. 14.

33. "Owen M. Fiss to Paul D. Carrington," 35 *Journal of Legal Education* 26 (1985).

34. Robert J. Borthwick and Jordan R. Schau, "Gatekeepers of the Profession: An Empirical Profile of the Nation's Law Professors," 25 *University of Michigan Journal of Law Reform* 191, 227 (Table 27).

35. See Chapter 12 ("One Vast Law School") below.

36. This point is made by Anthony Kronman, *The Lost Lawyer: Failing Ideals of the Legal Profession* (Cambridge: Harvard University Press, 1993), pp. 351–52.

37. Harry T. Edwards, "The Growing Disjunction Between Legal Education and the Legal Profession," 91 *Michigan Law Review* 34 (1992).

38. Ibid., p. 36.

39. Posner, "The Decline of Law as an Autonomous Discipline," p. 771.

40. Lee C. Bollinger, "The Mind in the Major American Law School," 91 *Michigan Law Review* 2167, 2175 (1993).

41. Guido Calabresi, "What Clarence Thomas Knows," *New York Times*, July 28, 1991, Section 4, p. 15.

42. Sanford Levinson, "Judge Edwards' Indictment of 'Impractical' Scholars: The Need for a Bill of Particulars," 91 *Michigan Law Review* 2010, 2011 (1993).

43. Robert Gordon, "Lawyers, Scholars, and the 'Middle Ground,'" 91 *Michigan Law Review* 2075, 2107 (1993).

44. Pierre Schlag, "Clerks in the Maze," 91 *Michigan Law Review* 2053, 2055 (1993).

45. The interview with Phillip Areeda was conducted by Professor Charles Nesson on November 2, 1993, in connection with Nesson's Harvard Law School teaching workshop.

46. Quoted in Harry T. Edwards, "The Growing Disjunction Between Legal Education and the Legal Profession: A Postscript," 91 *Michigan Law Review* 2191, 2198 (1993).

47. Derek Bok, "A Flawed System," *Harvard Magazine*, May–June 1983, p. 38.

48. "Beyond Litigation—an Interview with Robert Mnookin," *Stanford Lawyer*, Spring–Summer 1989, pp. 5, 45.

49. Remarks of José A. Cabranes, United States District Judge, District of Connecticut, Delivered at a Convocation of First-Year Students at the University of Connecticut Law School, August 25, 1980.

50. Harry T. Edwards, "A New Role for the Black Law Graduate—a Reality or an Illusion?" 69 *Michigan Law Review* 1407, 1417 (1971).

51. Edwards, "The Growing Disjunction," p. 40.

52. Margolick, "The Trouble with America's Lawyers," p. 39.

53. "Gannett House Looms Large as 1Ls Contemplate Law Review," *Harvard Law Record*, April 30, 1993, pp. 1, 14. The *Harvard Law Review*'s official affirmative action policy covers African Americans, Asian Americans, Latinos, Native Americans, and physically disabled individuals. Maria Politis, "Law Review: No Affirmative Action for Women," *Harvard Law Record*, April 23, 1993, p. 1.

54. Steven C. Bahls, "Political Correctness and the American Law School," 69 *Washington University Law Quarterly* 1041 (1992).

CHAPTER 11

1. Oliver Wendell Holmes, "The Law," in *The Occasional Speeches of Justice Oliver Wendell Holmes*, Mark DeWolfe Howe ed. (Cambridge: Belknap Press, 1962), pp. 20, 21–22. (Speech delivered at a Suffolk Bar Association dinner.)

2. Oliver Wendell Holmes, "The Path of the Law," 10 *Harvard Law Review* 457, 477 (1897).

3. Stephen Labaton, "Profile: Louis Loss," *New York Times*, September 26, 1993, p. 8.

4. Roger C. Cramton, "The Ordinary Religion of the Law School Classroom," 29 *Journal of Legal Education* 247, 262 (1978).

5. Roberto Unger, *The Critical Legal Studies Movement* (Cambridge: Harvard University Press, 1986), p. 8.

6. Carrie J. Menkel-Meadow, "Can a Law Teacher Avoid Teaching Legal Ethics?" 41 *Journal of Legal Education* 3, 7 (1991).

7. Lon Fuller, *The Law in Quest of Itself* (Chicago: Foundation Press, 1940).

8. Lon Fuller, *The Principles of Social Order*, Kenneth Winston ed. (Durham, N.C.: Duke University Press, 1981), p. 280.

9. Edward H. Levi, *Introduction to Legal Reasoning* (Chicago: University of Chicago Press, 1948).

10. Karl N. Llewellyn, *The Common Law Tradition: Deciding Appeals* (Boston: Little, Brown, 1960), p. 58.

11. Anthony Kronman, *The Lost Lawyer: Failing Ideals of the Legal Profession* (Cambridge: Harvard University Press, 1993), p. 211.

12. Llewellyn, *The Common Law Tradition*, p. 4.

13. Edgar Bodenheimer, "A Neglected Theory of Legal Reasoning," 21 *Journal of Legal Education* 373 (1969). Belgian legal philosopher Chaim Perelman independently developed a similar theory of legal reasoning; see *Justice, Law, and Argument* (Dordrecht: Reidel, 1980). See also Alain Lempereur, "Law: From Foundation to Argumentation," 24 *Communication and Cognition* 97 (1991). But it was Bodenheimer who recognized the common law as an especially illuminating case.

14. Aristotle, *Nicomachean Ethics*, Book I, Chapter 3.

15. As the philosopher Bernard Lonergan felicitously puts it in *Method in Theology* (New York: Seabury Press, 1979), p. 5.

16. Edgar Bodenheimer, *Jurisprudence: The Philosophy and Method of the Law* (Cambridge: Harvard University Press, 1974), pp. 392–97.

17. Unger, *The Critical Legal Studies Movement*, p. 11.
18. Richard A. Posner, *The Problems of Jurisprudence* (Cambridge: Harvard University Press, 1990), p. 459.
19. See, generally, *Der Einfluss deutscher Emigranten auf die Rechtsentwicklung in den USA und in Deutschland*, Marcus Lutter, Ernst Stiefel, and Michael Hoeflich eds. (Tübingen: Mohr, 1993), and in particular, the essay by W. Cole Durham, "Edgar Bodenheimer: Conservator of Civilized Legal Culture," p. 127.
20. "The Law," Occasional Speeches, p. 22.
21. James Boyd White, *Heracles' Bow: Essays on the Rhetoric and Poetics of Law* (Madison: University of Wisconsin Press, 1985); Kronman, *The Lost Lawyer*.
22. Oliver Wendell Holmes, "The Path of the Law," 10 *Harvard Law Review* 457, 459 (1897).
23. Llewellyn, *The Common Law Tradition*, pp. 19–61.
24. Kronman, *The Lost Lawyer*, pp. 66–74.
25. Ibid.
26. Ibid., pp. 140–41.
27. Ibid., pp. 142–43.
28. Ibid., p. 145.
29. Ibid., p. 269.
30. Cf. Fred Lawrence, "The Fragility of Consciousness: Lonergan and the Postmodern Concern for the Other," 54 *Theological Studies* 55, 60 (1993). ("Thus the bourgeois subject becomes the self-made man or woman who worships his or her maker.")
31. George L. Priest, "Social Science Theory and Legal Education: The Law School as University," 33 *Journal of Legal Education* 437, 441 (1983).
32. George L. Priest, "The Growth of Interdisciplinary Research and the Industrial Structure of the Production of Legal Ideas: A Reply to Judge Edwards," 91 *Michigan Law Review* 1929, 1930 (1993).
33. Ibid., p. 1939.
34. Donald A. Ritchie, *James M. Landis: Dean of the Regulators* (Cambridge: Harvard University Press, 1980), p. 138.
35. R. C. Lewontin, "Darwin's Revolution," *New York Review of Books*, June 16, 1983, p. 21.
36. Lisa Zornberg, "Elizabeth Warren Gets Tenure Offer," *Harvard Law Record*, February 12, 1993, p. 1.
37. Christopher Lasch, "The Baby Boomers: Here Today, Gone Tomorrow," *New Oxford Review*, September 1993, pp. 7, 8.
38. Roger Kimball recently reminded his readers of Hegel's remark that if, as is often said, no man is a hero to his valet, this may not be because the man is not a hero but because the valet is a valet." "Toward Truth and Greatness" (reviewing Gertrude Himmelfarb's *On Looking into the Abyss*), *Wall Street Journal*, February 15, 1994, p. 14.
39. "Tribute to Archibald Cox," *Harvard Law Bulletin*, February 1992, p. 17.
40. Ibid.

CHAPTER 12

1. Alexis de Tocqueville, *Democracy in America*, George Lawrence trans., J. P. Mayer ed. (New York: Doubleday Anchor, 1969), p. 270.

2. Les Ledbetter, "Jilted California Accountant Sues His Date for $38 in Expenses," *New York Times*, July 26, 1978, p. A10 and "Vain Hopes Remain Thus for Admirer Who Sued," *New York Times*, July 28, 1978, p. B1.

3. I borrow this figure from legal historian Lawrence Friedman, who has described life in modern societies generally as like a "vast, diffuse school of law." "Law, Lawyers, and Popular Culture," 98 *Yale Law Journal* 1579, 1598 (1989).

4. Lucinda Franks, "Little Big People," *The New York Times Magazine*, October 10, 1993, p. 28.

5. A striking proportion of the American revolutionaries were trained in law. See Robert A. Ferguson, *Law and Letters in American Culture* (Cambridge: Harvard University Press, 1984), p. 11.

6. Tocqueville, *Democracy in America*, p. 72.

7. Daniel J. Boorstin, *The Americans: The Colonial Experience* (New York: Vintage, 1964), p. 20.

8. See *Federalist* No. 25 (Alexander Hamilton) and *Federalist* No. 49 (James Madison). See also Abraham Lincoln's eloquent discussion of the importance of "reverence for the laws" in his "Address to the Young Men's Lyceum of Springfield," *Selected Speeches, Messages, and Letters*, T. Harry Williams ed. (New York: Rinehart, 1957), pp. 5–14.

9. Tocqueville, *Democracy in America*, Author's Preface to the 12th edition (1848), p. xiv.

10. Ibid., p. 274.

11. Ibid., p. 70.

12. Charles B. Rosenberg, "Inside L.A. Law," *American Bar Association Journal*, November 1, 1988, p. 56.

13. "Va. Judge Rejects Free Speech Claim," *Washington Post*, September 5, 1992, p. B5.

14. The "invitation to dinner" problem is discussed by Henry Hart and Albert Sacks in their influential teaching materials, *The Legal Process: Basic Problems in the Making and Application of Law* (Cambridge, Mass.: Tentative Edition, 1958), pp. 477–78.

15. Steven Lee Myers, "He's Not a Lawyer, but If Ruffled, He's Likely to Sue," *New York Times*, October 23, 1992, p. B1.

16. Judith Martin, "The World's Oldest Virtue," *First Things*, May 1993, pp. 22, 25.

17. Daniel Yankelovich, "How Changes in the Economy Are Reshaping American Values," in *Values and Public Policy*, Henry J. Aaron, Thomas E. Mann, and Timothy Taylor eds. (Washington, D.C.: Brookings, 1994), pp. 16, 20.

18. Martin, "The World's Oldest Virtue," p. 25.

19. Stewart Macaulay, "Non-Contractual Relations in Business: A Preliminary Study," 28 *American Sociological Review* 55 (1963).

20. Marc Galanter and Thomas Palay, *Tournament of Lawyers: The Transformation of the Big Law Firm* (Chicago: University of Chicago Press, 1991), pp. 43, 51.

21. Milo Gcyelin, "Suits by Firms Exceed Those by Individuals," *Wall Street Journal*, December 3, 1993, p. B1.

22. Robert J. Samuelson, "The Law as Pit Bull," *Boston Globe*, March 22, 1994, p. 40.

23. Mary Ann Glendon, *Rights Talk: The Impoverishment of Political Discourse* (New York: Free Press, 1991).

24. The organization and its activities are described in *Vision, Values, Action* (Austin, Texas: Texas IAF Network, 1990).

25. Gerald N. Rosenberg, *The Hollow Hope: Can the Courts Bring About Social Change?* (Chicago: University of Chicago Press, 1991).

26. Ibid., p. 52.

27. Ibid., p. 50 (Table 2.1).

28. Lawrence Friedman, *Total Justice* (New York: Russell Sage, 1985), p. 76.

29. Nearly three-quarters of all adults in the United States have consulted a lawyer at some point in their lives. Barbara A. Curran, "1989 Survey of the Public's Use of Legal Services," in ABA Consortium on Legal Services and the Public, *Two National Surveys: 1989 Pilot Assessments of the Unmet Legal Needs of the Poor and the Public Generally* (Chicago: American Bar Association, 1989), p. 57.

30. "All Things Considered," National Public Radio, April 9, 1993.

31. *Major League Baseball Properties Inc.* v. *Sed Non Olet Denarius,* 817 F. Supp. 1103, 1111 (S.D.N.Y. 1993). Judge Motley went on to hold that L.A.'s failure to use the Brooklyn Dodgers trademark in any significant way from 1958 to 1981 "constituted an abandonment of that mark and dramatically limits the protection to which that mark is entitled since its resumption" (p. 1134).

32. See Bella English, "The Tenant Who Won't Go Away," *Boston Globe*, February 15, 1993, p. 17.

33. Tocqueville, *Democracy in America*, p. 315.

34. Ibid., p. 287.

35. *The Spirit of Liberty: Papers and Addresses of Learned Hand*, Irving Dilliard ed. (New York: Knopf, 1953), pp. 189, 190.

36. Richard A. Posner, "The Decline of Law as an Autonomous Discipline: 1962–1987," 100 *Harvard Law Review* 761, 770–71 (1987).

37. See, generally, Mary Ann Glendon, *The Transformation of Family Law* (Chicago: University of Chicago Press, 1989), p. 235.

38. Plato, *The Republic*, Book IV, 420b, 421a, 432c.

CHAPTER 13

1. Wallace Stevens, "Sad Strains of a Gay Waltz," *The Collected Poems of Wallace Stevens* (New York: Knopf, 1973), pp. 121, 122.

2. Alexis de Tocqueville, *Democracy in America*, George Lawrence trans., J. P. Mayer ed. (New York: Doubleday Anchor, 1969), p. 268.

3. Ibid.

4. Ibid., p. 264.

5. Ibid., p. 699.

6. "Address to the Young Men's Lyceum of Springfield," in *Selected Speeches, Messages, and Letters*, T. Harry Williams ed. (New York: Rinehart, 1957), pp. 5, 6, 14.

7. Ibid., p. 264.

8. Ibid., p. 265.

9. See M. Mitchell Waldrop, *Complexity: The Emerging Science at the Edge of Order and Chaos* (New York: Simon & Schuster, 1992), p. 12. See also Roger Lewin, *Complexity: Science on the Edge of Chaos* (New York: Macmillan, 1992).

10. *Federalist* No. 1 (Alexander Hamilton).

11. See Thomas Kuhn, "The Essential Tension: Tradition and Innovation in Scientific Research," in *The Essential Tension: Selected Studies in Scientific Tradition and Change* (Chicago: University of Chicago Press, 1977); Arthur Koestler, *The Act of Creation: A Study of the Conscious and Unconscious Processes of Humor, Scientific Discovery, and Art* (New York: Macmillan, 1964); Mary Ann Glendon, "Knowledge Makes a Noisy Entrance: Tradition and Creativity in Law" (forthcoming).

12. Kuhn, "The Essential Tension," p. 234.

13. Ibid., pp. 227–28.

14. Wallace Stevens, "The Idea of Order at Key West," *The Collected Poems of Wallace Stevens* (New York: Knopf, 1973), pp. 128, 130; "Connoisseur of Chaos," ibid., p. 215.

15. Kuhn, "The Essential Tension," pp. 227–28.

16. *Max Weber on Law in Economy and Society*, Max Rheinstein ed. (Cambridge: Harvard University Press, 1954), pp. 298–99.

17. Christopher Lasch, "The Baby Boomers: Here Today, Gone Tomorrow," *New Oxford Review*, September 1993, pp. 7, 8, 10.

18. Louis D. Brandeis, "Opportunity in the Law," in *Business—a Profession* (Boston: Hale, Cushman & Flint, 1933), p. 329.

19. Cf. Bernard Lonergan, "Dimensions of Meaning," *Collection* (Toronto: University of Toronto Press, 1988), pp. 232, 245.

20. Oliver Wendell Holmes "The Law," in *The Occasional Speeches of Justice Oliver Wendell Holmes*, Mark DeWolfe Howe ed. (Cambridge: Belknap Press, 1962), pp. 21, 22.

21. Edward Gibbon, *The Decline and Fall of the Roman Empire*, D. M. Low ed. (New York: Harcourt, Brace, 1960), pp. 258–59.

22. Stevens, "The Idea of Order at Key West," *Collected Poems*, p. 128.

—

INDEX